FATAL FLAW

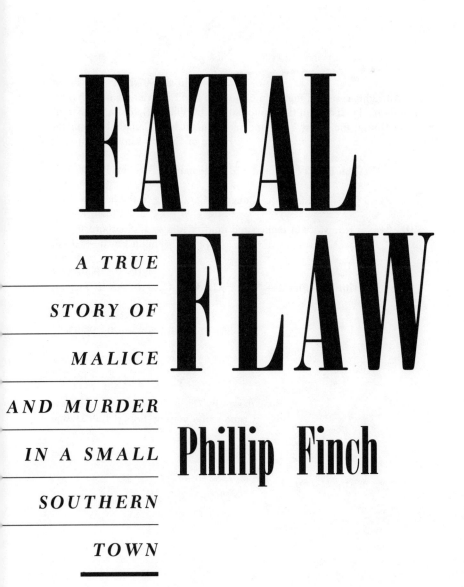

FATAL FLAW

A TRUE

STORY OF

MALICE

AND MURDER

IN A SMALL

SOUTHERN

TOWN

Phillip Finch

Villard Books ▪ New York ▪ 1992

Copyright © 1992 by Phillip Finch
All rights reserved under International and Pan-American Copyright
Conventions. Published in the United States by Villard Books, a division of
Random House, Inc., New York, and simultaneously in Canada by Random
House of Canada Limited, Toronto.

Villard Books is a registered trademark of Random House, Inc.

Library of Congress Cataloging-in-Publication Data
Finch, Phillip.
Fatal flaw: a true story of malice and murder in a small Southern town /
Phillip Finch.—1st ed.
p. cm.
ISBN 0-679-40861-4
1. Murder—Florida—Winter Garden—Case studies. 2. Ziegler,
Tommy. I. Title.
HV6533.F6F56 1992
364.1'523'0975924—dc20   92-53650

9 8 7 6 5 4 3 2
First Edition

Book design by Carla Weise/Levavi & Levavi
Crime scene map by Robert Bull Design

To the memory of my father,
FRANCIS D. FINCH

A loving man,
and just

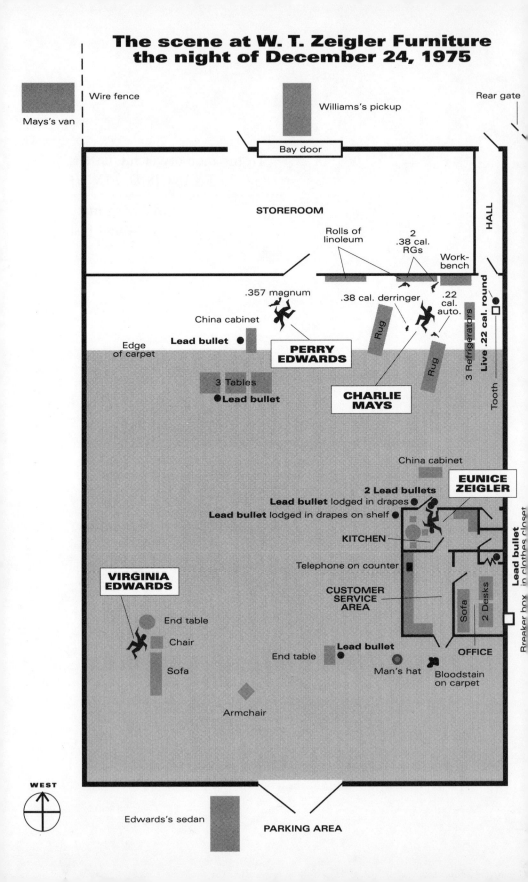

The scene at W. T. Zeigler Furniture the night of December 24, 1975

PROLOGUE

IT IS A MURDER MYSTERY. FIVE PEOPLE SHOT IN A DARK BUILDING ON Christmas Eve: four dead, one wounded in the abdomen, and a guilty man among them. A set piece fit for Poirot, but with the horror of real death and real bloodlust.

The killer was described as cunning. The proof of this was his convoluted murder plot, developed over half a year. He was also depraved: he beat his last victim so violently as to fracture the brain pan within his skull, spraying blood across ceiling and walls and furniture.

We are also told that a dogged police detective ferreted the truth out of the labyrinth of clues. This feat was said to be a triumph of inspired procedure.

I began to study the Winter Garden murders in early 1991, when the case was fifteen years old. I interviewed the principals in the investigation, the prosecution, and the defense, and Tommy Zeigler himself. But recollection can be faulty after so long a time. In important matters, memory tends to be conveniently (if innocently) self-serving. I decided that I could not in good faith rely on interviews to re-create the story; the events remain too controversial, and feelings still run too high. I accepted the word of others when they spoke of their impressions or their state of mind. On controversial matters, where I have used the memory of others, it is noted. But wherever I could, I took the story from what might be called the extended record: not only transcripts and briefs, but photographs in evidence, affidavits, correspondence, and investigators' work notes. Throughout my research I tried to resist conclusions. Although conclusions became inevitable, I based them solely on what the documentation showed. So it is in this work. I withhold my opinions until the end, and when they do appear they are founded almost exclusively in the formal public record.

That record consists of more than six thousand pages of sworn testimony and hundreds of supporting documents and photographs: an impressive artifact that time has not altered. It is perfectly accessible, a story waiting to be told. Amazingly, the case has remained almost unknown, while less spectacular murders—and less intriguing murderers—have become notorious.

To at least one of the lawyers who became involved, the case became nothing less than a reflection on American life and American justice. It touches matters of race and intolerance and judicial ethics. It raises essential questions about how crimes are investigated, how cases are prosecuted, how verdicts are obtained. It illuminates the vast gulf between what is legal and what is just.

The case is far from dormant. As this is written, in the spring of 1992, several legal issues still are unresolved. Moreover, the actual events of the crime remain uncertain. A trial verdict decided the legal issue of guilt, but did not end the debate about what actually happened in the W. T. Zeigler Furniture Store during two hours of Christmas Eve in 1975.

The record tells the story of the crime, to the extent that anyone except those who were actually involved knows it. It is the foundation of this story. But a paper trail has limits; I was certain that after fifteen years, after an investigation and a prosecution and a trial and a long series of appeals, the record contained nothing new. Surely every facet had been well examined and fully comprehended. If the truth was still being debated after so much time, I could not expect to come any closer to the ultimate solution of the mystery.

But I was wrong.

1

CRIME AND
PROSECUTION

ONE

THEY WERE SMALL-TOWN PEOPLE. THEY WERE A TEACHER AND A handyman, a retired minister and his wife, the foreman of a crew of fruit pickers. They were the mother and father and son who operated a family business. On Christmas Eve of 1975, they went about their ordinary lives in seemingly ordinary ways.

Charlie Mays and his wife, Mattie, took a day off from running a fruit-harvesting crew in the citrus orchards of Orange County, Florida. They went shopping.

Eunice Zeigler spent much of the day at home with her parents, Perry and Virginia Edwards, who were visiting for the holidays from Moultrie, Georgia.

Eunice's husband, William T. "Tommy" Zeigler, Jr., worked that day, as he usually did, at the retail furniture store that the Zeigler family owned at 1010 South Dillard Street in the town of Winter Garden, in the west end of Orange County.

Edward Williams, who did carpentry and construction around Orange County, moved into a new apartment in Winter Garden.

Beulah Zeigler and her husband, Tom, who had founded W. T. Zeigler Furniture in 1939, worked at the store with their son, Tommy, and with an employee, Curtis Dunaway.

As they went through the day, their paths crossed and intertwined. That is the way of small towns. But this day was different. These people would be bonded forever. Their movements, their routine conversations and actions, would be intensely examined and argued. What had seemed casual would become crucial; tragedy would elevate the mundane. In a few hours, all of these people would be drawn into a disaster. Four of them would be murdered.

TWO

CINDERELLA'S CASTLE, IN THE MAGIC KINGDOM OF THE DISNEY WORLD resort, stands nine miles due south of the scene of the crime, across a stretch of scrub and citrus groves. In geographic terms it is not a great distance—the drive back to the main gate of the resort is nearly as long—but Disney's charm and prosperity did not bridge the gap. Winter Garden's population, about six thousand, had hardly changed since the end of World War II. While the rest of Orange County rode a sustained boom, the several small communities at the west side of the county remained rural, agrarian, and stagnant.

The west side had always seemed a little different. It even had its own proper-name designation: to the *Orlando Sentinel Star* and to almost everyone else, it was West Orange, a scruffy place apart.

"Redneck City, Crackerville," is how one native of the county described West Orange to me in 1991, with a sort of smirk; then he added: "But don't use my name—those people would kill me."

This was not the East Coast Florida of palm trees and sweeping beaches, nor the sultry, laid-back Florida of the Gulf Coast. Winter Garden was almost a generic Southern town, with a one-crop economy that depended on cheap labor and good weather. Its public schools mixed the races by decree, but otherwise segregation was the rule, by practice if not by law. Most of Winter Garden's blacks—perhaps a third to half of its residents—lived in near-squalor in a section of town known as the Quarters, the boundaries of which were unmarked and without legal foundation, but unfailingly observed. In this way, too, Winter Garden and the rest of West Orange were typically Southern, closer in spirit to Selma than to Miami.

In the picking season, thousands of migrant workers, mostly black, filled the labor camps that were tucked away in groves surrounding the town. The most notorious of the camps was one known as Harlem Heights. At the outskirts of town, too, was an empty field known as the Stomping Grounds, where local Ku Klux Klansmen flogged their victims.

Stetson Kennedy, a Floridian who researched the Klan for more than forty years, has written that several klaverns thrived in West Orange at least into 1960. How long they survived after that is a matter of debate. In almost every other important way, though, the Winter Garden of '75 was the Winter Garden of '55.

In the meantime, much of Orange County was being transformed into the world's most popular playground. Twelve miles to the east, Orlando was a boomtown, and the *Sentinel Star* was one of its giddiest boosters. The afternoon of the murders, the top story on page one was the rush of tourists that forced Disney World to close its gates for only the second time in its three years of existence.

West Orange, though, was left out of the action. Most of the wild growth was in Orlando and south, along Interstate 4, where Disney World had its main entrance. Florida's Sunshine Parkway, built to funnel visitors into central Florida and the East Coast beaches, runs just below Winter Garden; almost anyone who drives to Disney World from the Midwest or the Deep South passes within half a mile of the furniture store.

But almost nobody stops in Winter Garden. The wall around the Magic Kingdom effectively seals West Orange from the magic and the money. On Christmas Eve of 1975, as today, Winter Garden, Florida, was an ordinary small town, maybe tougher than most, where ordinary people lived, and died.

Zeigler Furniture was one of the first stops for Charlie and Mattie Mays on Christmas Eve. They had traded there since they were married, fifteen years before. They were black, and in 1960 Zeigler Furniture was one of the few white-owned businesses in West Orange that routinely offered credit to black customers.

Today Mattie wanted new linoleum for the small rented house where she and her husband lived with their four young sons, in the rural community of Oakland, which adjoins Winter Garden. They parked their blue Ford van in the lot out front and went into the store, along with Brian Nedd, a sixteen-year-old fruit picker who worked with their crew.

Tommy Zeigler waited on them that morning. He brought them to the back of the showroom, where rolls of linoleum hung on racks that were bolted to the rear wall. Mattie Mays chose the patterns for three rooms.

What happened then would become a matter of controversy, as did much else that involved Tommy Zeigler over the coming hours, days, and months. According to the depositions of Brian Nedd and Mrs. Mays, Zeigler brought Charlie to the storage area behind the showroom. There Zeigler showed him a used console color TV, which the store was selling on consignment.

Brian Nedd testified that he overheard the conversation. He said that Tommy Zeigler offered to sell Charlie Mays the television on credit, at a price of $128. Mattie Mays supported Nedd's account, testifying that Charlie told her that it would be a surprise gift for her and the family. Charlie was supposed to pick up the TV at 7:30 that evening, after the store was closed.

But she learned all that later from Charlie, she said. That morning she was unaware of the arrangement; she only knew that when Tommy Zeigler and her husband came back from the storeroom, Zeigler told her: "You will have the surprise of your life."

Tommy Zeigler wrote out a sales contract, taking $50 in cash and adding the balance to the Mayses' account, which was already in arrears. The linoleum would have to be cut, and Zeigler said it would be ready in about an hour.

Tommy Zeigler was busy that day. Besides waiting on customers at the store, he made a round of deliveries in the morning and another in the afternoon.

This was not unusual. Tommy Zeigler had been working hard at his parents' business since he was a teenager, when he pedaled a bicycle through the neighborhoods of West Orange, making collections on store accounts.

To those who knew him casually, including most of the five thousand people in Winter Garden, Tommy Zeigler was a polite and earnest young man who was perhaps too sure of himself. He was twenty-nine years old, the only child of Beulah and W. T. "Tom" Zeigler, Sr. Young Tommy was a conservative Republican and a behind-the-scenes influence in local politics. Two years before, he had led a successful drive to unseat a longtime town mayor. Zeigler was tall and thin (six feet one, about 155 pounds) and severely astigmatic. He wore thick eyeglasses and kept his hair in an unfashionable brush cut. He was an active member of the First Baptist Church, the town's largest. He detested rock music. He drove pickup trucks and Oldsmobiles.

He was always in a hurry. Tommy and Eunice had married on his twenty-first birthday. He had urged his parents to move the store from its original location in downtown Winter Garden. He had chosen this new site away from the center of town, about half a block north of State Route 50, the main thoroughfare from the city of Orlando, about twelve miles away. Tommy had overseen the building's construction and the move of the business in 1973. At his urging, the family had bought several apartment buildings during the last few years. He managed the properties, besides working full-time at the store.

He kept at least five pistols in the store and in his truck, and carried another when he made his cash collections of rent and furniture payments. At the time, a gang of armed robbers known as the Ski Mask Bandits was active in Central Florida, robbing retail business and often shooting clerks. Zeigler would testify that his collections totaled thousands of dollars in cash, and that the store kept large sums on hand; the pistols were for protection.

The family's net worth was over $1 million, and growing. But it was a quiet fortune. Tommy and Eunice, and Beulah and Tom, lived in unpretentious ranch-style homes on adjoining lots at Temple Grove Drive, about a mile and a half from the store. Their clothes, their automobiles, their furnishings tended to be simple and solid.

Most of all, they worked as if they still needed the money. Eunice taught school through much of her marriage. Tommy immersed himself in the businesses. Beulah ran the store every day, usually from opening to closing. Tom senior had worked at the furniture store every day, often at the tasks of a minimum-wage laborer, until he suffered a stroke in July 1975. The Zeiglers did not avoid drudgery.

This morning Tommy Zeigler himself cut Mattie Mays's linoleum. He unwound it from the rolls on the wall, using a heavy metal crank that was kept in a box on the back wall. He sized the pieces and rolled them again, then placed them in the rear storage area.

Around midday of Christmas Eve, Edward Williams stopped at the store to see Tommy Zeigler.

Williams had known the family for nearly twenty years, as a customer and a part-time employee. He had helped to remodel the Zeiglers' apartments and had worked on the construction crew that had built the Dillard Street store. In the past week, he had worked around Tommy and Eunice's house and replaced a broken window in one of the apartment complexes.

Earlier in the week, Zeigler had asked Williams to help deliver several large gifts on Christmas Eve: a gas grill that he and Eunice had bought for Tom Zeigler, a La-Z-Boy recliner for Perry and Virginia Edwards, and a big potted plant that Winter Garden's chief of police, Don Ficke, had bought for his wife.

This morning Tommy Zeigler was cutting linoleum when Williams came into the store. Williams gave Zeigler the key to the apartment he had repaired.

Now (as Williams later testified) Zeigler reminded him that he needed help in the evening. According to Williams, Zeigler told him to be at 75 Temple Grove at 7:30, and they would drive to the store together.

Zeigler had done Williams many favors. In the past two days alone, he had loaned Williams $80 for a deposit on his new apartment and had called the local power company so that Williams—who still had a disputed bill from a previous address—could have electricity when he moved in.

Edward Williams, in turn, had done many favors for Tommy Zeigler.

"He'd say, Edward, I want you to do something for me," Williams testified later. "If I could get there, I do it. Edward, I want this thing done here. I say, okay, I try to make it possibly. I do that because the whole time I know Tommy, if I asked Tommy to do me a favor, he helped me."

Once again, Williams did not refuse Tommy Zeigler.

He would be there, he said: 7:30.

One of Eunice's errands this day was to bring a Persian cat named Silver to a veterinarian, for treatment of a slight abscess. Eunice and Tommy owned six Persians, which they bred and exhibited.

Tommy and Edward Williams had built a "cat room" in one bay of Tommy's two-car garage.

The cats also had the run of the house. When Eunice played the piano in the front room they would curl up on the furniture to listen to the music. Eunice and Tommy doted on the animals. Often the couple would leave a television playing during the day to entertain them.

After eight years of marriage, the couple were still childless. Eunice was under treatment by a fertility specialist in Orlando. She charted their intercourse on neat graphs that she kept beside their bed. The graphs would show that they had regular relations until about two weeks before Christmas, after which the notations ceased.

Eunice Edwards and Tommy Zeigler had met when she was a teacher at an elementary school in Winter Garden. He was coaching a youth football team. He barged into her office, demanding that she release one of his star players, whom she had kept after class. She adamantly refused.

From that day, he says, he never dated another. They were married less than a year later, at the red-brick First Baptist Church, which dominates the town center from a rise of ground at the corner of Dillard and Plant streets.

In a case that became a thicket of uncertainty and disagreement, everyone agrees about Eunice. Eunice was special.

She is remembered as kind, soft-spoken, genteel. She sang, played the piano beautifully, and was an organist at First Baptist. She is said to have detested gossip. When Winter Garden's public schools were forced to integrate, she volunteered to teach in a poor black neighborhood. After Tommy's father suffered a stroke in July 1975, Eunice often drove him to physical therapy. She would watch the exercises, then patiently work with him for hours at home.

"A lovely lady," her mother-in-law said of Eunice, years later. "A calm, quiet, refined lady."

"She never met anyone who didn't like her," Tommy Zeigler told an interviewer. "And she always believed that there was some good in everybody."

"The nicest person anybody could be around," Edward Williams testified.

On Christmas Eve of 1975, Eunice Zeigler brought the Persian back from the vet and later baked a cake with her mother, and she waited for her husband to come home.

After they left Zeigler Furniture for the first time, Charlie and Mattie Mays and Brian Nedd drove across Dillard Street to the Tri-City shopping center at the intersection of Route 50. They visited two stores, looking for Christmas gifts, and stopped to buy groceries at a Winn-Dixie supermarket.

From the supermarket they drove to a Zayre's department store near Orlando. At Zayre's they bought a ten-speed bike, and after a quick meal they returned to the furniture store for the linoleum.

Tommy Zeigler told them to go around to the back. Charlie Mays drove the blue van down a driveway that ran along the north side of the building, past a large electrical breaker box.

The store's front display windows faced east, toward Dillard Street. Directly behind the building was a paved area several times larger than the small lot out front. This asphalt had been added to comply with Winter Garden's zoning regulations. But it was rarely used by the public. It was surrounded by a six-foot chain-link fence that secured not only the parking lot but also the rear of the store. That fence separated the paved compound from the rear of the Winter Garden Inn motel, which was adjacent to the south side of the Zeigler property.

The store's rear compound was accessible only by a single swinging gate at the end of the driveway. The gate was open now. Charlie Mays drove through, and when he had parked, he and Tommy Zeigler and Brian Nedd loaded the three rolls of linoleum into the van.

Mattie Mays asked Zeigler about a cot she had ordered a couple of weeks before. Zeigler said that he might be able to deliver it later in the day.

Then, according to Brian Nedd, Zeigler mentioned the console television. He reminded Charlie that he should pick up the set between 7:00 and 7:30 that evening.

Charlie said that he would be there.

Curtis Dunaway was having car trouble that day. His 1972 Oldsmobile 98—a two-tone car with a beige roof and a brown body—was making strange noises. He planned to take it in for repairs on the 26th, but he was going to drive into Orlando on Christmas Day, and he worried that the car wouldn't hold up for the trip.

Dunaway had worked for Zeigler Furniture for more than four years. Tommy and Beulah managed the business; otherwise Curtis Dunaway did every job at the store. He sold and cleaned and swept, he clerked behind the counter, he helped Tommy with deliveries.

Dunaway was a quiet, diffident man in his forties, a lifelong bachelor who lived with his mother in a modest house less than a mile from the store. He knew nothing about automobiles. Dunaway asked Tommy to drive the Olds, to diagnose the problem. Zeigler knew cars, and until October he had owned a '68 Oldsmobile that was similar to Dunaway's.

Dunaway and Zeigler were friendly during working hours, but seldom socialized away from the store. Outside his family, Zeigler had seemingly hundreds of acquaintances, and a few very close friends with whom he felt completely comfortable. Most of those were married men with positions of influence in West Orange. Dunaway did not belong to that tight circle.

Around lunchtime, Zeigler tried the car. Afterward, as he had done several times before, he suggested that they switch cars so that Dunaway wouldn't risk a breakdown on the highway. Zeigler's new automobile was a white '75 Olds Toronado. This was the car that Eunice usually drove, and she used it that day to take the sick cat, Silver, to the vet. Tommy and Eunice had no travel plans for Christmas Day—they lived next door to Tom and Beulah. If Tommy did need transportation he could use Dunaway's car, or the green Ford sedan belonging to Perry and Virginia Edwards, or the store pickup truck, which he drove most of the time anyway.

It put Dunaway's mind at ease.

Dunaway finished lunch early and decided to take a short nap in the storeroom at the rear of the building. He lay down on a furniture pad and was dozing when Charlie Mays pulled up to load his linoleum. He recognized the sound of Mays's voice, but the words were indistinct. Later he was unable to recount any of the conversation.

Around four in the afternoon, a couple of hours before closing, Curtis Dunaway went with Zeigler on their second delivery trip of the day.

Near the end of the trip, Zeigler mentioned to Dunaway that he would be returning to the store that evening to pick up the gas grill for his father, the Edwardses' recliner, and Don Ficke's potted plant. Dunaway volunteered to help him, but Zeigler said he didn't want to interrupt Dunaway's family gathering; he would get Edward Williams to help him, he said.

The afternoon delivery was a large one. They separated it into two shipments, and when they dropped off the last piece their working day was almost ended. In four years, Curtis Dunaway and Tommy Zeigler had ridden through West Orange County hundreds of times on such errands.

This would be the last.

When they returned home in the afternoon, Charlie and Mattie Mays laid down their new linoleum with the help of Brian Nedd. Around this time, Mrs. Mays testified, Charlie told her about the color TV. He said that the down payment they had made that morning covered both the linoleum and the television. Tommy Zeigler was giving them a bargain price, $128 for a beautiful console set. They rearranged the living-room furniture to make a space for the console.

It was going to be a good Christmas. It got even better that afternoon, when someone from the First Presbyterian Church in Oakland dropped off a basket of food and about $40 that had been collected from the congregation. The church's pastor, Herman "Mickey" Fisher, had asked Oakland's police chief, Robert Thompson, to give it to a needy and deserving family. Thompson had chosen Charlie and Mattie Mays and their sons.

Thompson liked Charlie Mays. Charlie did not smoke or drink or cuss. He coached the local softball teams, he worked hard, and his children were well-behaved. You did not see the Mays boys on the streets after dark.

Sometime that afternoon, Tommy Zeigler arrived at the Mays home, making his late round of deliveries. He had brought the bed that Mattie Mays wanted. According to Mrs. Mays, Zeigler mentioned the TV again, and again her husband agreed to meet him at the store later that evening. Charlie Mays and Tommy Zeigler would meet one more time.

The afternoon wound down, dusk began to fall.

Sunset was at 5:35 P.M., full darkness about half an hour later. The moon would not rise until after midnight. The skies were clear. The night would be cool, about forty degrees.

Winter Garden was about to be shattered.

Nearly everyone had plans. Edward Williams later testified that he intended to spend the evening with friends in Orlando. Curtis Dunaway's two brothers and their families would be visiting him and his mother. Beulah Zeigler was going to attend the 7:30 candlelight service at First Baptist, then prepare food at home. The two police chiefs, Don Ficke and Robert Thompson, had been invited to attend an open-house party at the home of Ted and Mary Van Deventer, in Winter Garden. Ted Van Deventer was a local attorney and the municipal judge for the nearby communities of Oakland, Ocoee, and Windermere.

One of Van Deventer's friends and clients was Tommy Zeigler. Tommy and Eunice were expected at the party.

First, however, Eunice and her parents, Perry and Virginia Edwards, planned to attend the 7:30 service at First Baptist. On the way to the church they were going to stop by the furniture store and pick out the La-Z-Boy that they would be bringing home to Moultrie.

A little after six, Beulah Zeigler decided to close the store. Her husband had gone home earlier in the afternoon. Curtis Dunaway noted the time on the large electric clock that hung on the wall beside the service counter. Closing took about ten minutes. Dunaway put the day's cash receipts into an envelope, which he locked inside a combination safe.

Usually four overhead lights were kept burning at night, showcasing the merchandise in the front windows. But tonight Tommy Zeigler told Dunaway to turn off those lights. There would still be some illumination in the store, including two lamps on the floor and one near the service counter.

Curtis and Beulah went out the front door and locked it. Their cars were parked in the front lot. Tommy Zeigler went out the back of the building, where his gold-colored pickup truck was parked.

Beulah Zeigler stopped for groceries at a Thriftway store across the street from the Baptist church. By the time she was finished shopping, she knew that she wouldn't have time to go home and change clothes. She picked up a friend and went directly to the church.

Curtis Dunaway followed her north on Dillard, as far as the Thriftway. He continued on to Temple Grove Drive, pulled into Tommy Zeigler's driveway, and stopped along the right side of the drive.

Tommy drove up almost immediately and parked the pickup truck along the left side of the driveway, in front of the cat room in the garage. He went into the garage and backed out the new white Toronado.

Zeigler helped Dunaway transfer some gifts and boxes of baked goods from the '72 Olds to the Toronado. Zeigler invited Dunaway into the house. Eunice was there, with her mother, Virginia, and their cake was fresh out of the oven. Eunice cut a slice for Dunaway, and they chatted while Zeigler went into the family room to check the cat, Silver.

Dunaway stayed at the Zeiglers' house for about fifteen or twenty minutes. He left shortly before 7:00, when he went home in the Toronado, driving carefully. It was a beautiful new car, and he didn't have to worry that it would leave him walking beside the highway on Christmas Day.

Edward Williams, too, had car trouble on Christmas Eve. His Camaro sports coupe was already being repaired at a Texaco station on Route 50 east of Winter Garden, and his pickup truck had a balky carburetor: the engine wouldn't restart when it was warm.

Williams later testified that he spent several hours nailing up paneling in the home of Boyd Holt, a Winter Garden barber. Around four in the afternoon, he drove to Holt's shop, and Holt gave him $20. Williams stopped at the Thriftway, bought some soap, and went to his new apartment. He hadn't yet spent a night in the place. He had actually rented the apartment the day before, on Tuesday the 23rd, but the carpets were still damp from being cleaned.

Williams testified that he saw nobody and spoke to nobody while he was at the apartment in the late afternoon and evening of the 24th. He showered and—he swore—put on a black cardigan sweater and a pair of green pants and new dress boots, and then went out to meet Tommy Zeigler.

A few people got glimmerings of the tragedy as it erupted.

At about 7:20, a woman named Barbara Spencer heard three or four loud explosions, which she believed to be firecrackers. She was sitting by a back window in her parents' house, which was located about a block west of Dillard Street, near Route 50. She was watching the clock, waiting for her brother, whom she had been expecting to meet her at 7:00.

Fifteen or twenty minutes later she heard another series of reports, more than the first time, perhaps six or seven explosions. It was the same firecracker sound coming from the same direction.

The explosions were loud and distinct, and she was certain of the direction. They were from the east, across an open area. On the other side of that clearing, a couple of hundred yards distant, was the back of W. T. Zeigler Furniture.

At about 7:30, Kenneth and Linda Roach were driving south on Dillard, approaching Route 50. As they drove past the furniture store they heard a single loud pop, like a firecracker. It seemed to come from the direction of the store.

Linda Roach turned to ask her husband whether they had blown a tire—the sound was that loud and immediate.

A few seconds after the first report, they heard a series of explosions, ten or more shots; to Ken Roach it sounded like a string of firecrackers going off all at once.

They kept on driving.

Between 7:30 and 8:30 that evening, twenty-four-year-old Barbara Woodard was leaving the Tri-City shopping center. Most of the stores in the mall were still open, and she had just finished some late shopping with a friend. She was leaving the mall by the west entrance, which was on Dillard Street, beside a Kentucky Fried Chicken restaurant, directly across the road from Zeigler Furniture.

She looked over at the store and saw that it was completely dark. She thought that was odd. She noticed two cars parked in the narrow front lot of the store. One of the cars was green. Her identification of the second car was vague. Originally she told the police that it was dark-colored. At the trial she retracted that.

She also saw a man: a tall, thin white man with close-cut hair. He wore a dark blue or black jacket and was standing behind the glass doors of the store, as if he had just entered or was about to walk out. Barbara Woodard knew the owners of the furniture store. Though she couldn't see him well enough to be sure, Barbara Woodard believed that the man behind the glass doors was Tommy Zeigler.

Sometime between 7:00 and 8:30—accounts differ—Samuel Harrison, two of his teenage children, and two of their friends were shopping at the TG&Y variety store in the Tri-City mall when they met a fruit picker named Felton Thomas, whom they knew from Oakland and the citrus groves. Thomas was one of the hundreds of itinerant pickers who returned to Orange County every year for the harvest.

Thomas asked if they planned to return to Oakland. Samuel Harrison said yes, and Thomas asked him for a ride.

Thomas sat in the backseat and said little. But as they got into Oakland, Thomas mentioned that he had just left Charlie Mays. Something strange had happened to them, Thomas said. Something was wrong at Zeigler Furniture.

Edward Williams later told police that the garage door was open and the light was on when he pulled into the driveway at Tommy Zeigler's house. There were no cars. The only vehicle in the drive was Tommy's pickup truck.

Williams pulled in and blew his horn. When nobody came out, Williams went into the garage to knock on the door that led from the garage into the house. There, stuck in the crack of the door, was a note in Zeigler's handwriting. It read: "Edward Wait I'll be right back" and was signed "Z."

Williams noted the time: 7:28.

He got in his truck. He pulled in behind the pickup, on the left side of the driveway, to make room for the car when Zeigler drove in.

He sat and waited.

Beulah Zeigler returned home alone from the candlelight service. Eunice and her parents had not come to church after all.

Her maid, Mary, was gone by the time Mrs. Zeigler arrived home. Her husband, who was still showing the effects of his stroke the previous summer, was getting ready for bed.

Beulah Zeigler had work to do, preparing food for the Christmas meal. She did not go next door to her son's house. She did not hear or see anything unusual in the driveway. She was unaware.

Around 7:00, Don and Rita Ficke opened presents in their home with their children and Rita's parents, who were visiting from Jacksonville.

Earlier in the day, Eunice Zeigler and Rita had arranged for the two couples to drive together to the Van Deventer party. Don and Rita had moved to Winter Garden in late 1973 when Don became the town police chief, and the two men and their wives had become close.

Ficke understood that the party was to start at 7:00. He wasn't surprised that the Zeiglers hadn't shown up on time, however. Tommy and Eunice were inevitably late for any social occasion. Ficke wasn't especially anxious to attend the party: he had had disagreements with Judge Van Deventer. Ficke was not good friends with anyone who was going to be there except Tommy Zeigler.

A few minutes after 8:00, Don and Rita got in his unmarked police car and decided to find Tommy and Eunice. Ficke was not armed.

All of the Winter Garden locations that figure in the events of that night are found within a mile of the center of town. The longest reach is from the furniture store to the Zeiglers' home on Temple Grove Drive, a drive of five to ten minutes. So between 8:05 and approximately 8:45, the Fickes were able to drive past the Van Deventer house at least three different times, looking for the Zeiglers' car. They passed the Baptist church when the congregation was leaving after the end of the candlelight service. And three times they drove to the Zeiglers' house at 75 Temple Grove.

At one point they drove up Dillard Street to the furniture store. Rita Ficke pointed out the green Ford sedan of Perry and Virginia Edwards. It was parked out front, alone in the small lot between the store and the street. The Fickes saw nobody. The store was completely dark. Across the street, Don Ficke noticed a Winter Garden police car and another from the town of Oakland; they were parked at the Kentucky Fried Chicken restaurant in the Tri-City shopping center.

Finally the Fickes gave up on finding Tommy and Eunice. Around 8:45, they went alone to the Van Deventer home.

The Oakland chief, Robert Thompson, drove one of the two police cars that Don Ficke saw at the Kentucky Fried Chicken. The other belonged to Jimmy Yawn, a Winter Garden patrolman. Thompson had given his two officers the night off. He used his radio to log out of service at 8:30, and he met Yawn at the restaurant.

Thompson was an interesting figure. He was forty-two years old and had more than fifteen years of important experience in law enforcement with the Florida Highway Patrol and the U.S. Border Patrol. He had been in charge of the security force of Florida governor Claude Kirk. He had attended nearly two dozen special police courses or seminars. After an unsuccessful attempt at running a seafood business, he had become the police chief of Oakland in 1973. At the time he took over, the town's patrolmen kept no records or files and carried no guns. For the town to have filled so modest a position with someone of Thompson's background was remarkable.

At 8:50, Thompson logged in again, leaving the restaurant. As he drove onto Dillard Street he saw that the furniture store was dark. He noted the green Ford sedan with Georgia plates parked out front.

By his account, Thompson went back to Oakland to check out the local beer hall, some vacant houses, and the traffic in general. The town was quiet, and he decided to stop in at the Van Deventer party.

At 9:18 he checked out of service again, as he reached the Van Deventer home. The house had a large picture window that looked out on the street. As Thompson parked the patrol car, he could see Ted Van Deventer through the window, getting up out of a chair and walking to the back of the house. A few seconds later, Don Ficke followed Van Deventer to the back.

Thompson got out of the car and went up the walk. He was at the front door went Don Ficke came out, in a big hurry.

There was trouble, Ficke told Thompson. Trouble at Zeigler Furniture.

The Presbyterian minister Mickey Fisher was one of the guests at the Van Deventer home. He was at the buffet table when the phone rang and had a view of the front door when Thompson walked in. He could also hear Ted Van Deventer on the phone in the dining room.

"Tommy, what's the matter?" Van Deventer said.

On the other end of the line was Tommy Zeigler. Six months later—in hearsay testimony to which the defense did not object— Van Deventer recalled that Zeigler said, "Ted, I'm hurt," and asked to speak to Don Ficke.

Van Deventer was a good friend of Zeigler's and had known him to play practical jokes.

"Are you kidding me?" Van Deventer said.

"No, hurry," Zeigler said, and Van Deventer called for Ficke.

Ficke took the receiver.

"Don, I've been shot," Zeigler said.

Ficke asked him what had happened, and Zeigler repeated that he had been shot.

"Please hurry," Zeigler said.

Ficke ran into Robert Thompson and told him what he knew. In separate cars they rushed to the store with their emergency lights flashing.

The trip took less than a minute. On the way, Thompson radioed to the Winter Garden dispatcher that he was en route to the store on Ficke's authority, and that they should send other units. The dispatcher logged the call at 9:21.

Two other officers and their cruisers were within a quarter mile of the scene. Cindy Blalock was in the Tri-City parking lot, escorting TG&Y's manager as he carried out a bag of cash. Jimmy Yawn, who had been with Thompson less than an hour before, was at the Winter Garden Inn; Yawn cut through a service station on the corner of Route 50 and Dillard and drove up to the store.

Thompson, Ficke, and Yawn arrived almost simultaneously. Thompson and Ficke pulled up out front, so Yawn continued around toward the back, using the driveway along the north side of the building.

Thompson positioned his cruiser so that his headlights and spotlight illuminated the south side of the building, down to where the high fence joined the rear corner of the building.

He left his car. The front door of the store rattled. Thompson walked toward the door and pointed his flashlight beam through the glass.

He saw Tommy Zeigler trying to unlock the front door from inside. Blood was splattered on Zeigler's face. There was blood on his shirt, especially thick around his left underarm. He was calling, "Bobby, Bobby."

Thompson ran for the front door and reached it just as Zeigler got it unlocked. Thompson pulled the door open.

"I've been shot," Zeigler said.

In the corner of his eye Thompson could see Ficke standing at his left. He handed the flashlight to Ficke and grabbed the wounded man, who stumbled out of the store.

THREE

AT THE FRONT OF THE STORE, ROBERT THOMPSON PUT ZEIGLER OVER his shoulder, carried him to the Oakland patrol car, and laid him in the backseat. Zeigler was acquainted with most of the local cops in West Orange and often encountered Thompson while delivering furniture and making store collections in Oakland. But the two men were not especially friendly.

Thompson took a moment to look for wounds. He saw that Zeigler had been shot through the lower right abdomen. The entrance was at the front; Thompson saw a hole about the size of a quarter where the bullet had entered Zeigler's rust-colored shirt. The edges of the hole were blackened, and the blood around the wound was dry and dark. An exit hole, at Zeigler's back, showed no swelling or signs of fresh bleeding. From the blood around Zeigler's face, Thompson guessed that there might be a head wound, but he checked quickly and found none.

The local hospital was West Orange Memorial, about a mile up Dillard Street. Thompson told Ficke that he was taking Zeigler, and he accelerated north up Dillard.

"I'm dying," Zeigler said from the backseat as Thompson drove.

"No you're not, you're going to be all right," Thompson told him, and he radioed to the Winter Garden dispatcher that he was en route with a gunshot victim.

They reached the hospital at 9:23: three minutes had elapsed since Thompson sped away from the Van Deventer house.

Thompson got Zeigler to sit up. He took off Zeigler's gold-rimmed glasses and stuck them into one of the epaulets of his uniform shirt. He went in and got a gurney. With the help of a nurse's aide, Thompson lifted Zeigler onto the gurney and pushed him into the examining room.

Thompson returned to his car and got his notebook. He came back and leaned close to Zeigler.

"Who shot you?" Thompson asked.

According to Thompson's testimony, Zeigler answered, "Charlie Mays."

"Why?" Thompson said.

Zeigler didn't answer.

"Was he trying to rob you?" Thompson said.

"I think so," Zeigler answered.

"Where is Charlie now?"

"Back at the store."

"Did you shoot Charlie?" Thompson asked.

"Yes," Zeigler said.

"With what?"

"My gun," Zeigler said.

Then Zeigler began to babble. He talked about his parents' Christmas presents. He kept repeating, "Don's plant at the store." It made no sense to Thompson, and he asked no more questions.

After Thompson left with Zeigler, Don Ficke waited outside the store. He had no gun, and he wasn't going to enter the dark building without one. He asked Jimmy Yawn for a shotgun, but Yawn didn't have one in his patrol car. Cindy Blalock drove up, and Ficke asked her for a shotgun. She didn't have one, either. So Ficke sent Yawn to get weapons from their headquarters. Blalock went around to the back, outside the high fence—she must have passed Mays's van—to the southwest corner of the back lot, where she could watch the rear of the building. Out front, Ficke called for backup from the Orange County sheriff's office, and he waited.

Ted Van Deventer drove up with the Presbyterian minister, Mickey Fisher; they had followed Thompson and Ficke. Ficke asked them to go to Zeigler's house to notify Eunice that her husband had been shot; they left immediately. A former Winter Garden patrolman named Phil Cross drove up with a friend, Richard Sims. They had heard the call on a police scanner. Ficke deputized them both.

After about six minutes, Yawn returned with shotguns, and

Ficke passed them out to Sims and Cross. At about that time, Thompson came back from the hospital with the news that Charlie Mays might be wounded in the store.

Violence was not uncommon in West Orange, especially during harvest season, when the migrant camps were full. Yawn, Thompson, and Ficke all had known tense situations and had seen the effects of shootings, stabbings, and assaults. During the past year Ficke had even been involved in a hostage standoff, when a man in an apartment threatened to kill his wife; the apartment belonged to Tommy Zeigler, and Zeigler, who knew the man, had come to the scene and talked him out.

But this was something else: a large dark store, a wounded robber who was already supposed to have shot one person. And this on what was supposed to be the quietest night of the year.

Ficke may have felt the tension. Yawn reported later that the chief was unable to load his own shotgun. He fumbled with the shells, dropped them to the ground. Yawn loaded the weapon and gave it to Ficke.

"Let me go in first," Thompson said. "I know Mays, and he knows me."

Thompson and Yawn went in together, with Phil Cross behind Thompson and to his left. Ficke and Sims followed.

The store was dark and silent; the only sound was their own movement, as the five men made their way into the showroom, stepping around chairs and sofas and tables.

Yawn called Mays's name and got no response. Thompson veered off to the right, toward the front counter and the partitioned store offices.

The show room was 82 feet wide and 106 feet deep. About the first three-quarters of the floor area was covered with a dark orange carpet. But at the rear, past the counter and offices, the floor was white terrazzo. Yawn was approaching the end of the carpeted section when he spotted a body facedown near the back wall, in a pool of blood on the terrazzo. He had never seen so much blood from a body.

Yawn assumed that it was Charlie Mays, but some furniture blocked his view. When Yawn got closer he saw that it was a white man.

Yawn bent and checked his pulse at the neck. The man was dead. Yawn searched the rear pockets of the man's pants, looking for identification, but the pockets were empty.

Thompson, too, was calling for Mays, speaking into the darkness: "Charlie, it's Bobby Thompson. Let us know where you are. Give yourself up, Charlie." Thompson had approached the customer service area, about midway along the north side of the showroom. He saw that the telephone on the counter was covered in blood. The receiver was off the hook and hung down the front of the counter.

Thompson went behind the counter, to the cash register. To his right, as he faced west, was an office door on which the jamb was broken. It seemed to have been forced. Thompson used the tip of one finger to push that door open. Inside were two desks and a sofa. Everything appeared to be in order.

Directly in front of him, as he faced west, was a second door. It led to a small employee kitchen and lounge. Thompson swung that door open and found a white woman on the floor. She was motionless, face up and with her eyes open, in a pool of blood.

Thompson bent close to her, looking for some sign of life. She was quite pretty, and seemed very young—maybe a teenager, he thought. She was dead.

Thompson went back around the counter the way he had entered, and he started to the rear of the showroom. At about that moment, the beam of Yawn's flashlight fell across the body of a black man sprawled on the terrazzo, near the linoleum racks.

"That's him," Thompson said.

It was Charlie Mays. Thompson stooped near his head, checking his pulse. The man whom Thompson had recommended for Christmas charity was obviously dead. His face was disfigured by a savage beating. Gouts and sprays of blood radiated from his skull across the terrazzo, a ghastly corona. The store's black metal linoleum crank lay across Mays's right arm.

Yawn and Thompson—perhaps some of the others—had already flipped several wall switches, but the power was off. Yawn and Thompson began to look for a master switch. Three or four times Yawn passed near the body of Charlie Mays. He noticed two revolvers on the floor within a few feet of Mays's head, two more pistols near Mays's feet. A fifth pistol lay near the head of the white man, in front of a pair of metal doors in the back wall of the showroom.

Yawn went through these doors, followed by Thompson. They found themselves in the rear storage area. The big overhead doors at the loading dock were closed and locked. But at the back, a second swinging door was unlocked. Thompson and Yawn opened it and looked out into the fenced back parking area. They saw a pickup truck, no driver, parked at the loading dock.

They were in the store for several minutes. During that time Yawn went into the kitchen to look at the young woman. At first glance he thought she was a mannequin. She had no obvious wounds. Her left hand was in the pocket of her cloth coat; she seemed too straight, too composed, to have fallen where she lay.

Her feet were against a closed door that would open onto the rear of the showroom. Yawn noticed three bullet holes in the door.

Apparently Ficke did not go into the kitchen to see the body. Although his wife had pointed out the Edwardses' car less than an hour earlier, he failed to make the connection. None of the others on the scene knew Perry and Virginia Edwards. None knew Eunice.

Gerald Justice, a uniformed sergeant in the sheriff's office, was on road patrol when he got the call.

He found nobody when he parked out in front of the store. According to the message from the dispatcher, Don Ficke was supposed to be here.

The store was dark. Justice was walking around to the north side of the building when he heard shouting behind him.

He turned around and saw Ficke, Thompson, and the others leaving the store, through the front doors.

Ficke spotted Justice.

"God damn, Sarge, get me some help," Ficke shouted.

"What do you have in there?" Justice said.

"Multiple homicides," Ficke said. "I need assistance."

Justice made a radio call to Bruce Churchill, the sheriff's lieutenant who was in charge of the Criminal Investigation Division, and he told Churchill what Ficke had said.

Churchill asked: "Does he want us to take the case, or does he just want technical assistance?"

Justice relayed the question to Ficke.

"I want you to take it," Ficke said. "I want you to take the whole thing."

Justice told Churchill the answer. Then he stepped out of his car and addressed Ficke and the others. He ordered that nobody else enter the store; the crime scene now belonged to the OCSO— the Orange County sheriff's office.

———

Ted Van Deventer and Mickey Fisher drove together to 75 Temple Grove Drive, the home of Tommy Zeigler. They got no answer at the front door. The garage was closed, with a light on inside.

They went next door to the house of Tom and Beulah Zeigler. Tom was already asleep for the night; Beulah had just been called by a cousin of Tommy's who had been listening to a radio scanner.

She left for the hospital with Van Deventer and Mickey Fisher, without disturbing her husband. At the hospital they met Dr. Albert Gleason, the Zeiglers' family physician. Gleason allowed Mrs. Zeigler to see Tommy for a few minutes while he was being prepped for surgery.

Ted Van Deventer and Mickey Fisher were worried about Eunice. They wanted to be able to enter the Zeigler home, so they persuaded a nurse to bring them Tommy's pants, from which they took a key case. One of the keys in the case looked as if it might belong to a front door.

Meanwhile, Beulah Zeigler tried to speak to her son just before he was taken away. His voice was weak and his breathing was shallow. She asked him where Eunice was.

He squinted to look at her—he had no glasses.

"Isn't she with you?" he said.

By now people were gathering around the front of the store, and more Winter Garden patrolmen had arrived. Ficke sent Thompson and a Winter Garden patrolman named Revels to check on Curtis Dunaway. The sheriff's crime scene unit was en route from Orlando.

Mickey Fisher and Ted Van Deventer returned from the hospital and told Ficke that they hadn't found Eunice or her parents. Yawn described the young woman in the store, but nobody seemed to associate her with Eunice. Apparently Don Ficke did not make the connection.

Someone suggested that Eunice and the Edwardses might be hostages inside her home, and the idea seemed to make sense. Ficke ordered Yawn to Tommy Zeigler's house, with orders to enter the home if necessary. Yawn got in a car with Fisher, Van Deventer, Phil Cross, and a local photographer named George McClellan. They headed out to Temple Grove Drive, looking for Eunice Zeigler.

Soon a uniformed sheriff's deputy named James Pearson arrived at the store, followed shortly by Frank Hair, the sheriff's lieutenant in charge of the patrol shift.

Ficke, Hair, and Justice went back into the store. They went to each of the three bodies. This time, according to Hair, Ficke looked at the dead woman on the kitchen floor. But the light was poor, and he did not identify her.

Winter Garden firemen were roping off the parking lot and pushing back the onlookers when Hair and the others came out of the building. Hair decided to check the back of the building. He brought James Pearson with him, and they walked up the north drive, to the fenced rear compound.

Pearson saw that the gate was locked, and he climbed up on it. At about that moment, Hair turned around to look toward Dillard Street, and when he turned back, Pearson had jumped down on the other side of the fence and was looking around the back lot.

Hair walked up to the gate and found it ajar, open five or six inches. The prong-type latch was still padlocked, but one of the latch's prongs was bent, which allowed the gate to swing back into the compound.

Hair came up behind Pearson and surprised him.

"How the hell did you get in?" Pearson said.

Hair looked around. On the far side of the fence, in the Winter Garden Inn parking lot, was a shabby blue van. That was the van of Charlie Mays. Hair also noticed the pickup truck parked at the loading dock, inside the compound. The registration of that truck would show that it belonged to Edward Williams.

Jimmy Yawn knocked on the front door at 75 Temple Grove, looking for Eunice Zeigler. He got no answer. He could see lights inside, but no movement. Yawn walked around to the back; everything seemed quiet. He noticed a small tear in the back screen door, just above the latch.

Yawn got on the radio to request backup. Ficke sent Revels and Robert Thompson, who had returned after finding Curtis Dunaway at home with his family and bringing him to the store.

Yawn covered the front door while Ted Van Deventer tried the keys. None of them worked. Thompson used his flashlight to break a pane of glass in the French doors around back, and Yawn and Thompson entered.

They found two women's purses open on a settee in the living room. The dining room was clean and in perfect order. Cats lounged quietly on the countertops.

Yawn went into the garage and found Curtis Dunaway's 1972 Oldsmobile. He looked into the car and found a .38 caliber revolver on the floor behind the driver's seat. The gun's six chambers were loaded with live rounds.

Yawn put the gun in a paper bag. They continued the search, in every room and up in the attic. They found no hostages, no disturbance.

Eunice Zeigler's whereabouts were still unknown.

At the furniture store, the full extent of the carnage was about to be revealed.

Sheriff's officers were arriving in force. The chief of detectives, Morris "Gene" Blankenship, drove up at 10:00 with Jack Bachman, a former county chief of detectives who now was a state attorney's investigator. Bruce Churchill arrived at about this time. So did Wayne Bird, the staff duty officer.

Sheriff's detectives would investigate the crime. The sheriff's Technical Services specialists would collect the physical evidence. That night the detectives and technicians did not arrive immediately; most had been called at their homes.

The building now was secure; Winter Garden firemen had roped off the front of the store, pushing back the curious crowd that was growing by the minute. The victims inside were beyond medical assistance.

It is an axiom of criminal investigation that the scene should remain pristine until it has been photographed and the evidence preserved. Anyone intruding on a crime scene, however carefully, may inadvertently disturb the setting or leave some scrap—hair, fingerprints, clothing fibers, dirt—that could later be confused with true evidence.

Blankenship, Bird, and Churchill, all ranking officers, decided to enter the showroom. They began to tour the darkened store, going from one body to the next. This was the third party to enter the crime scene, a total of ten different men, using flashlights to navigate through the darkness.

They picked their way around the guns and the blood on the terrazzo floor. "There was such an amount of it, you couldn't go through it," Blankenship recalled later. "Blood all over the floor, splattered up on the wall and chairs and furniture around there. . . ."

Blankenship, Bird, and Churchill did not walk directly toward the front door when they decided to leave. Instead they made their way along the south side of the showroom, the wall opposite the offices and counter. That was how they found the fourth body, in a heap amid a display of living-room furniture. She was a middle-aged white woman, with a gunshot wound in the side of her head.

Some of the evidence technicians had appeared by the time Blankenship, Bird, and Churchill left the store. Blankenship walked around the north side of the building, down the driveway that led to the fenced parking area in the rear.

He found the electrical junction box on the outside wall. The lever of the master switch was down. Blankenship told one of the technicians to photograph it. Then he used his flashlight to push the lever up.

The lights came on inside.

Robert Thompson showed up twice at Curtis Dunaway's family gathering. The first time, Thompson only checked to be sure that Dunaway was safe. He told Dunaway that Tommy Zeigler had been shot, and asked why Dunaway had turned off the power at the junction box when he left the store that evening.

Dunaway told him that he had not turned off the master switch.

Thompson showed up again less than an hour later, to bring Dunaway to the store. A sheriff's detective brought Dunaway into the building, with instructions to keep his head down, not to look right or left but to follow the detective's path, step for step.

He was led to the body of Mays and asked to identify it.

Yes, Dunaway said, that was Charlie. Then he was marched out again with the same instructions.

Dunaway stood outside beside Rita Ficke until shortly after midnight, when he was brought into the store again. Dr. Guillermo Ruiz, a medical examiner, was on the scene. Dunaway followed Ruiz to each of the three unidentified bodies. He knew them all.

The white man was Perry Edwards, Eunice's father.

The older woman was Virginia Edwards.

The pretty young woman in the kitchen, straight and composed, was Eunice Zeigler.

Dr. Ruiz would perform autopsies on the bodies throughout most of Christmas Day. That night at the store, he made preliminary examinations where they were found.

He began with Virginia Edwards. She had been shot twice. One bullet had passed through an arm, penetrated her chest, and nearly exited the other side—Ruiz could feel it under the skin. The other bullet had entered her brain.

Charlie Mays had been shot twice in the abdomen, once from the front and once from the back, and had been badly beaten around the face and skull.

Perry Edwards, who lay about fifteen yards south of Mays on the terrazzo floor, also had been beaten about the head, and had multiple gunshot wounds. He had been killed—probably as he lay wounded on the floor—by two shots to the head.

Eunice Zeigler had been shot once in the back of the head. She had died at once.

Judging postmortem lividity,[1] Dr. Ruiz placed the time of death of all four corpses within an hour either way of 8:00 P.M.

Tommy Zeigler at that moment was in the intensive care unit at West Orange Memorial, recovering from surgery.

The entrance wound of the gunshot was about three-eighths of an inch wide—not a small caliber—and was about navel-high, a little less than five inches to the right of the center line of the body. The exit wound was slightly upward and very slightly to the left.

Gleason feared damage to the internal organs. In that region the greatest danger was to the ascending colon. Gleason performed a surgical procedure known as a laparotomy, to trace the path of the bullet. He found that it had grazed the peritoneum, the lining of the abdomen that holds the colon, but had not punctured it. It had passed within an inch of the liver. None of the vital organs had been affected.

---

1. Postmortem lividity is the color that results from the settling of blood within a human body. It is one means of placing time of death, if a body has not been disturbed.

Dr. Gleason cleaned and sutured the wounds. At 11:50 Tommy Zeigler was out of the operating room, resting under sedation in ICU.

He was about to become a suspect.

FOUR

DONALD FRYE'S BEEPER SOUNDED WHEN HE WAS AT THE MOVIES. HE telephoned the sheriff's dispatcher and was told that there had been a shooting and a robbery attempt at Zeigler Furniture in Winter Garden. He got to the store just after Blankenship, Bird, and Churchill discovered the body of Virginia Edwards.

Frye was twenty-nine years old and had nearly five years of police experience, all with the Orange County sheriff's office. He had been an OCSO detective since mid-1973, assigned to the Crimes Against Persons Section. Detectives in that unit usually worked in pairs and were assigned cases by rotation. In December 1975, Frye was teamed with Detective James Jenkins, and on Christmas Eve their names were at the top of the call list.

Frye took charge almost immediately. Jenkins was already busy with another case, to which he would be assigned full-time in the next day or two. From Christmas Eve on, Frye had day-to-day responsibility for the investigation.

No Orange County detective had ever investigated a quadruple homicide. Few had ever confronted a murder scene so large or complex; the building measured 10,600 square feet, and potential evidence could be found throughout, although the greatest violence seemed to have occurred near the back of the showroom, especially in the northwest corner where Mays's body was found. The signs there were obvious: furniture in a jumble, bullet holes in walls and ceiling, and dried sprays of blood.

That night and early Christmas morning the crime scene technicians collected and impounded items that included:

• A pair of glasses and a set of keys on a ring, near the northwest corner of the showroom, not far from Charlie Mays's body; both were later identified as belonging to Tommy Zeigler.

• A tooth found in that same general area, against the north wall.

• Receipt slips totaling about $415, and $405 in cash, stuffed in one of Charlie Mays's trouser pockets.

• A footstool with blood smeared on the legs, found at the back of the showroom where much of the carnage had occurred.

• A shoulder holster, found between Mays and the west wall of the showroom.

• What appeared to be the fingertip from a surgical rubber glove, just west of the kitchen door.

• Two bloody .38 caliber cartridges from the top drawer of Tommy Zeigler's desk in the office area behind the counter. Though the cartridges appeared to be live rounds, the primer caps showed the impression of a firing pin; apparently they were misfires.

There were no obvious fingerprints, but Frye and the technicians saw bloody shoe prints in several locations. One, very distinct, was at the edge of the blood pool around Perry Edwards. Another was on the office door with the broken jamb, as if someone had kicked the door open. Others were found in the kitchen, around Eunice Zeigler's blood. Several faint shoe prints ran down a narrow hallway that led from the northwest corner of the showroom to the rear parking lot. All seemed to be of a similar rippled-sole pattern.

Five pistols were collected.

The revolver near the head of Perry Edwards was a Colt .357 magnum, with six empty .38 Special cartridge cases in the cylinder. (A .357 revolver will fire .38 Special ammunition.) It had a broken grip and showed traces of what appeared to be blood.

The two near the head of Charlie Mays were nearly identical snub-nose .38s manufactured by RG Industries, cheap five-shot guns; one had a bent trigger guard. The damaged gun, RG #051827, contained two spent cartridges and three live rounds. The firing mechanism had been damaged. RG #051829 contained five empty cartridges and was in working order.

One of the pistols near Mays's feet was a two-shot Burgo

derringer, with a live .38 Special round in the bottom chamber and an expended case in the top.

The other gun near Mays's feet was a .22 Smith & Wesson automatic with a round jammed in the chamber; nearby was an empty .22 case and two live .22 cartridges.

The blood evidence was of special interest to Frye. In 1974, he had attended a one-week seminar conducted by Herbert Mac-Donell, a consulting criminalist in Corning, New York, who was expert in the flight characteristics of human blood—that is, various splatters from dripping wounds, from beatings, and from gunshot impacts. Frye had learned to use the size and shape of blood splatters to analyze crime scenes.

Blood from Charlie Mays's beating—splashes from the impact itself, and droplets cast off from the weapon as it was swung up and down—showed that he had been beaten to death where he was found. Most likely, the killer had sat astride his chest, and would have been speckled by the splashing blood.

Mays's trousers, oddly, were down around his thighs, and the fly was unzipped. His undershorts were smeared with blood. The bottoms of the trousers were blood-soaked, and blood was smeared along the tops of his tennis shoes and caked in the soles.

Smears and droplets of blood formed a trail past the west door of the kitchen, along the north wall of the store to the corner of the showroom. The trail continued as a series of faint blood swipes on the terrazzo, ending at the body of Perry Edwards. Frye surmised that this trail marked a fierce battle between Perry Edwards and his attacker. He decided that the swipe marks on the terrazzo had been transferred from bloody clothing during a struggle that ended when Edwards was shot through the head. Some of the blood droplets from Mays's beating had splashed on top of these swipes, and when Frye examined them closely he saw that the swipes had already been dry when the droplets fell.

This was startling. It meant that at least fifteen minutes—the minimum time required for the swipes to dry—had elapsed between the murders of Perry Edwards and Mays.

There was more. The shoulder holster was spotless, although it was found within the scatter of blood from Mays's beating. When Frye lifted the holster he found blood on the floor beneath it. However, none of that blood had spotted the bottom of the holster. So the holster had been placed there, on dry blood, sometime after Mays was killed.

And more. The kitchen door at Eunice Zeigler's feet was closed. Yet when Frye opened the door he found, along the door-frame, the minute blood spray that can only be produced by a high-velocity impact. It was located almost exactly at the height of the wound behind Eunice's left ear, the single shot to the brain that killed her. Frye, noting that her left hand was still in her pocket, believed that she had been surprised while standing in the open doorway. The door must have been closed later.

Frye realized that what had happened in the store had not been a single, frenetic event. Rather, Charlie Mays had been shot and beaten a quarter hour or more after the first three murders. Someone, presumably the killer, had walked around the scene after the murders: the bloody shoe prints and the holster on top of dry blood seemed to demonstrate that. To Frye, all of this cast doubt on Tommy Zeigler's statement that he had shot Mays in a robbery attempt.

Yet Tommy Zeigler was in West Orange Memorial with a gunshot wound in the abdomen.

A few feet east of the service counter, seventy or eighty feet from the carnage at the back of the showroom, was a large patch of blood that had soaked into the carpet. Some tiny pieces of glass lay in the blood. Frye assumed that they came from the broken lens of a flashlight nearby. A few feet from that pool of blood, on the facing of the counter, Frye could make out the high-velocity splatter from a gunshot wound. A bloody trail of drips and smears led from this spot to the front door.

Frye theorized that someone had been shot in the area east of the counter and then had made his way to the door. He believed that the bloody trail belonged to Tommy Zeigler.

Frye remained at the store all night. Before dawn he formed his working hypothesis: that Tommy Zeigler had committed all four murders, first his wife, then her parents, finally Charlie Mays at least a quarter of an hour later. And then had shot himself to divert suspicion.

In the earliest hours of Christmas Day, two witnesses came forth independently with support for Frye's theory. Their accounts, coupled with the evidence in the store, portrayed Tommy Zeigler not as a victim but as a calculating killer.

FIVE

EDWARD WILLIAMS FIRST TRIED TO TELL HIS STORY AT THE 33RD STREET sheriff's substation in south Orlando. The desk officer there, apparently unaware that the crime was now a county matter, told Williams that he should go to the Winter Garden police headquarters.

Williams left. The sheriff's officers at the store were dismayed to learn by radio that their first potential witness had been sent off into the night.

An OCSO detective, H. D. "Denny" Martin, was waiting for Williams when he arrived at the Winter Garden headquarters around midnight. Williams was driving his gray Camaro. He was accompanied by a woman named Mary Ellen Stewart, whom he described as a friend from Orlando, and Mrs. Stewart's son-in-law.

Edward Williams was a black man, a forty-seven-year-old native of the Bahamas who had come to the United States in 1953 with a harvesting crew and had become a citizen ten years later. He still spoke with a soft Bahamian accent.

This is the story he told:

At 7:28 that evening he arrived in his pickup truck at Zeigler's house. On Monday, Zeigler had asked Williams to meet him at 7:30, to help deliver some large gifts. Zeigler had reminded him of the appointment on Christmas Eve. Nobody was at home when Williams arrived at Temple Grove Drive; Williams found a note from Zeigler saying that he would be back in a few minutes.

Williams waited in his pickup. After about ten to fifteen minutes, Zeigler drove up in his car, accompanied by two people, one up front beside him and one in the backseat.

Zeigler went into his house while the passengers stayed in the car. When he came out, two or three minutes later, he walked up to Williams in the truck. He told Williams to wait another ten minutes, and he drove off with the two passengers.

Williams waited. After ten to twelve minutes another car came up the driveway, a white man and a woman; they backed out and left. The time now would have been about 8:00 to 8:10, based on Williams's estimates. After about twenty minutes Zeigler drove up again. This time he was alone. He parked the car in the garage and jumped out holding a small bag.

Zeigler went to a sink in the garage. He wet a towel or cloth and appeared to wipe around the car. He put the towel in the sink, came out, and closed the garage door with a remote control in his pickup truck.

He climbed into Williams's truck, and Williams noticed something strange.

From the transcript of his tape-recorded interview: "He [Zeigler] sat down, I wasn't paying no attention. In fact, I must speak what I, what my eyes see . . . when he faced me, when he coming from putting the rag back and coming towards the, the front of the garage to come out, the light shine, I saw under the light shine I saw a, like a patch of blood, or some stain was on his pants. But now I, not thinking anything [inaudible] because I know the man, I, now I wouldn't know he could do any evil or anything."

Williams started to drive to the store.

"Damn, I'm tired," Zeigler said.

Williams asked him which route he wanted to take to the store, and Zeigler gave him directions to a residential street that bypassed Dillard, out onto Route 50. Then they turned off the highway and drove the last half block up Dillard to the store. Zeigler told Williams to let him out at the front of the store and meet him around back. Williams noticed a car parked in front of the store with "foreign tags."

Williams did not know the time. But based on his estimates, it would have been about 8:40.

Williams did as he was told. He went up the driveway, stopped at the locked gate, and waited. About five minutes later, Zeigler came out, opened the gate, and motioned Williams in. Zeigler closed the gate behind them. He told Williams to back up to the doorway at the northwest corner of the building, and Williams did.

Zeigler went inside the store. But Williams wanted to urinate, so he stopped to relieve himself beside the truck.

Zeigler called to Williams: "Come on in, Edward."

"Mr. Tommy, I'm coming," Williams said.

Williams started up the short hallway that opened onto the terrazzo area of the showroom. The hallway was dark, and he had to feel his way along.

"Edward," Zeigler said.

Williams told him again that he was coming.

Williams stepped into the doorway. Zeigler stood four or five feet away, facing him, holding what Williams believed to be a gun. Zeigler pulled the trigger three times, and three times it dry-fired: no gunshot.

Again, in Williams's words:

"I heard the sound pop, pop, pop. Snapped three time. And I hollered, for God's sake, Mr. Tommy, don't kill me, don't kill me, Mr. Tommy. And I ran back out. And when I got out of the building he came behind me. He said, Edward, I didn't know that was you. I said, Mr. Tommy, don't tell me you didn't know that was me, why you tried to kill me, what I done, you know, I ain't do you nothing."

Zeigler still had the gun. He insisted that he meant Williams no harm. Williams asked Zeigler to unlock the gate so he could leave, and Zeigler asked Williams to follow him inside so he could get the key.

Williams refused. He was sure that Zeigler meant to kill him.

Zeigler told Williams to calm down and be quiet. He gave Williams the pistol, and he put an arm around Williams, trying to hold him. Williams noticed spots of blood on Zeigler's face and clothes, and he pushed Zeigler off.

Zeigler pleaded for Williams to come into the store with him: "Edward, if you don't go, you're gonna frame me."

Williams decided to lie his way to safety. He told Zeigler that he would follow him into the store if Zeigler would first open the gate.

Zeigler agreed. Instead, though, he got in Williams's truck. Williams ran in the opposite direction, to the southwest corner of the compound. He climbed the fence and jumped down into the back lot of the Winter Garden Inn.

Williams put the pistol in his pocket, went across Dillard Street to the Kentucky Fried Chicken, and asked to use the telephone. He also asked the number of the police.

A clerk gave him a telephone number and showed him to a phone in the office. Williams tried the number he had been given, and had a confused conversation with someone who told him,

"There ain't no police here." Frustrated, he left the restaurant. Outside he met two girls whom he knew; he asked them for a ride.

"They said they was on their way to Orlando. I said could you drop me in Orlando. She said yeah. I said will you hurry because it's urgent. I'm, I'm, I'm, I'm in a bad fix."

Williams was in their car when he remembered that his Camaro was supposed to have been repaired that day. He found it outside the service station where he had brought it, with the key inside. He drove to Orlando, to the home of Mary Stewart, whom he had known for years. He told her what had happened; she called her attorney, and on his advice they went to the sheriff's substation.

Williams concluded his statement: "This is Edward Williams speaking, concerning what happened to him on Christmas Eve. . . . [T]he only thing I was wondering was, what worries me why, it worries me wondering why Mr. Tommy being so nice to me, why he would try to take my life."

One of the crime scene technicians removed a chrome-plated Securities Industries .38 snub-nose revolver from between the front seats of the Camaro. All six cylinders were empty. According to Williams, this was the pistol that Zeigler gave him when he tried to coax him back into the store.

At 2:20 A.M., Denny Martin accompanied Williams to his apartment. Williams surrendered the clothes he was wearing, including a black cardigan sweater, dark slacks, and black ankle-length boots. Martin gave him a receipt for the clothes, then drove Williams to Mary Stewart's home in Orlando.

Frye's partner, James Jenkins, had sat in on Williams's interview. Jenkins went back to the store and reported it to Frye.

Williams's story was a stunning accusation. Though he had heard no shots and had seen no bodies, Williams contradicted any theory of innocence for Tommy Zeigler.

The account did pose one huge question: who were the two passengers in the car with Zeigler the first time Williams saw him?

Don Frye did not have to wait long for an answer.

Table One

TIME SEQUENCE: EDWARD WILLIAMS

Based on Williams's original statement and his subsequent testimony. Williams apparently looked at his watch only once on Christmas Eve, when he arrived at 75 Temple Grove Drive. All other times are approximate, based on his estimates and the known driving time between the house and the furniture store. Where Williams estimated a range of time—between fifteen and twenty minutes, for example—the greater figure is used.

7:28 P.M.   At Tommy Zeigler's house, Williams finds a note from Tommy Zeigler, checks watch.

7:40   Zeigler arrives in a car with two passengers, goes into his house, comes out, and asks Williams to wait about ten more minutes; then drives away.

8:00   A white man and a woman pull into the drive, then leave.

8:25   Zeigler drives up alone, parks the car, and wipes it down. Williams notices dark stain on Zeigler's pants. Zeigler gets into Williams's truck, and they drive to the furniture store.

8:35   Williams and Zeigler arrive at the store. Zeigler enters the front door and Williams waits at the back gate.

8:40   Zeigler brings Williams into the store, tries to kill him; chases him into rear compound, pleads with him to come into the store again; Williams refuses and climbs the fence.

8:45   Williams attempts to call police from Kentucky Fried Chicken.

SIX

AT ABOUT THE SAME TIME THAT DENNY MARTIN RETURNED FROM
bringing Williams to Orlando, the itinerant fruit picker Felton
Thomas[1] approached an OCSO patrolman in a coffee shop on
Route 50, between Winter Garden and Orlando. Thomas said that
he had information about what had happened at the store.

Denny Martin picked up Thomas. Frye and Jenkins brought
him into the store and interviewed him. Thomas was a twenty-
seven-year-old black man from Georgia who had been picking fruit
since he was fourteen, when he had quit the seventh grade. He
spoke softly, with an occasional stammer.

Thomas told the detectives that he was standing around a
bonfire in Oakland when Charlie Mays drove up in his van on the
evening of the 24th. Mays asked Thomas to come along for a ride.
Thomas got in the van.

Mays drove into Winter Garden and up Dillard Street to
Zeigler Furniture. He told Thomas that he was going to pick up a
color TV. Mays stopped in front of the store. Nobody was there,
and the store was dark, so Mays pulled around to the back corner
of the building. He parked in the rear lot of the Winter Garden Inn,
against the chain-link fence that separated the two properties.

Mays and Thomas passed time with a conversation about
betting jai alai; Mays told Thomas that he had won $400 the night
before.

1. That night he signed his statement to the police "Thomas Felton." For at least ten weeks,
both prosecution and defense, as well as the local media, referred to him as "Thomas
Felton" or "Buddy Felton."

Then a man whom Thomas did not know drove up in a Cadillac and told Mays, "Ain't nobody here yet, Charlie. Come ride with me."

Mays and Thomas left the van and got in the Cadillac. They drove out onto Route 50 and made a right turn onto an extension of Dillard Street that headed south away from town. The pavement ended, and they were in an area of orange groves. The man said he had bought three guns, and he wanted Mays and Thomas to try them.

From the interview:

Q (*JENKINS*): Okay, let me stop you and clear up a few things. Now this man in the Cadillac, was he a white man or a black man?
A (*THOMAS*): He, he was a white man.
Q: Okay, did Charlie introduce you to him?
A: He introduced me to him.
Q: Okay, did he tell you the man's name or tell you who the man was or what he did or anything like that to identify him?
A: He, he said it was Zeiglers, he said the man what name Zeiglers, he owned the place.
Q: Okay, the man named Zeigler who owned the furniture store that you were at, right?
A: Right.

Near Thomas's feet on the floor of the Cadillac was a supermarket paper bag containing three pistols. The white man whom Mays called Zeigler lowered the electric windows. Mays took one pistol and fired three or four shots outside, without leaving his seat. Thomas took a gun, but Zeigler told him to put it down, try another, and Thomas did. He fired a single shot.

Q: Okay, let me, let me clear a few things up about the weapons, now and when you were firing them. Did, whose idea was it for you to fire the guns?
A: It, it was his idea.
Q: Okay, you're talking about Mr. Zeigler?
A: Mr. Zeigler's, it was his idea.
Q: Okay, what did he say to you to get you to fire them?
A: He said he wanted our opinion about seeing whether they good guns, accurate guns, you know.
Q: So in other words he, he just wanted to, wanted you—

A: Just wanted us to fire the guns seemed like.

Q: Okay, just wanted you to fire the guns to see if they were good guns—

A: Right.

Q: —in your opinion.

A: Right.

Q: Okay, and after you had fired the weapons . . . you fired the one weapon and Charlie Mays fired the other one, is that right?

A: Right.

Q: Okay, now, did Mr. Zeigler ever fire any of the weapons?

A: No sir, he, he, he never touched the weapons. He just, just, just looked at the one I had in my hand and said try the other one.

Q: Okay, so he never touched the weapons as, as far as you saw, right?

A: As far as I saw, he never touched them.

After they had fired the pistols, Zeigler drove them back up Dillard Street to the furniture store. He put Thomas out of the car and told him to pull the switch at the electrical box along the north side of the store.

Mays and Zeigler left Thomas there and drove back to where the van was parked, at the high fence behind the motel. Thomas pulled the switch and went around to join them there.

And then Zeigler did a curious thing. He said, "What the hell, I'll just crack a window," and climbed the fence and jumped down into the rear parking lot of the furniture store.

Q: Okay, now you said Mr. Zeigler owned the place, right?

A: Right.

Q: Okay, but he wanted to hop the fence and break, break a window to get in.

A: Yes sir.

Q: Did he tell you why he wanted to do it that way?

A: He said because the, the, the, the guy was in Apopka[2] and said cause Charlie wanted his TV tonight for, for his wife because tomorrow was Christmas.

Zeigler urged Mays and Thomas to follow him over the fence. Mays did, reluctantly. Thomas stayed beside the van, on the motel

2. An Orange County town about fifteen miles north of Winter Garden.

side of the fence. Zeigler picked up a piece of pipe and swung it against a back window of the store.

This frightened Mays, who climbed back over the fence.

"I ain't going for no shit like that," Mays said. "I don't need it like that."

"Well, hell," Zeigler said, "I'll just go to the house, I think I got an extra key."

They drove to Zeigler's house and up a driveway.[3] Thomas saw a pickup truck and a car parked in front of the garage.

Zeigler went into the garage and came back with a key and a box of bullets. He gave the bullets to Mays and told him to reload the gun. Mays did.

They left and drove back to the furniture store, where they parked out front.

The store was dark, and Mays was nervous. Mays said that he would walk around and bring the truck out front. But Zeigler said no, first they would go in and bring the television to the front door.

Zeigler and Mays got out of the car. They were about to enter the front door when Zeigler turned and said, "Come on, Tom, we need your help. Come on, Tom."

But Thomas was frightened. He didn't like the dark store. He told Zeigler: "You cut on some light, I'll go in there."

"If you're not coming in," Zeigler said, "just sit back in the car."

But Felton Thomas had seen enough. He watched Mays and Zeigler walk into the dark store, then he got out of the Cadillac and crossed Dillard Street to the shopping center. There he met his friends leaving the TG&Y store, and they gave him a ride to Oakland. Around midnight he heard about the murders in the store, heard that Charlie Mays had been killed.

Q: Did you see what happened after they [went] in the door?
A: No sir, it, it was, it was too dark for anybody to see, see them after they stepped in the building.
Q: So the only thing you can say is that you saw Charlie Mays and, and Mr. Zeigler come in the building together and all the lights were off.

---

3. In the interview, Thomas described a roundabout route from the store to the city limits of Oakland and then to Temple Grove Drive.

A: Yes sir.

Q: Okay. Mr. Thomas, would you say that Mr. Zeigler was acting peculiar or was acting suspicious while entering the, entering the building?

A: Well, well well I didn't know the man['s] ways, but he had some peculiar ways about him. The, the, the way he seemed to be acting, you know, it, it, it wasn't right you know . . .

Q: Was there anything else about the way he was conducting himself or the way he was acting that made you feel suspicious that he was possibly doing something wrong, anything like that?

A: Well, well I said in, in my mind . . . Af, af, after what happened, you know, it all seemed like, like he, he was, you know, just trying to use somebody or something.

By now Robert Thompson had identified Charlie Mays's van across the fence, where Felton Thomas had said it was parked. The dirt road south of Route 50 and the grove were as Thomas described them. Above all, Thomas's story meshed with that of Edward Williams on a crucial point: apparently they had noticed each other when Zeigler drove to the house with Mays and Thomas. Williams had seen two passengers with Zeigler; Felton Thomas had seen a vehicle behind Zeigler's pickup in the driveway, exactly where Williams had claimed he was parked.

Thomas had identified that vehicle as a car, not a truck, and the Dunaway Oldsmobile was certainly not a Cadillac.[4] But the discrepancies seemed unimportant to Frye. He believed that Felton Thomas was telling the truth, that in watching Charlie Mays enter the store with Zeigler, Thomas had witnessed the last few moments of Mays's life. Frye believed that Zeigler had murdered Mays, shooting him and then beating him to death, within seconds after the front door closed behind them.

Frye had been at the scene less than ten hours, yet with the help of Williams and Thomas, and his own observations, he could already sketch the outline of what happened inside the store. Frye could even supply the reason for Mays's death.

"He was trying to use somebody or something," Felton Thomas had said of Zeigler near the end of the interview. Don Frye

---

4. The Zeiglers' new car was a white Oldsmobile Toronado, which did resemble a Cadillac.

agreed. He believed that Zeigler had brought Williams and Charlie Mays to the store—Williams on the pretext of an errand, Mays with the promise of a TV set—so that he could kill them and arrange a fake robbery, make it appear that the two black men had killed his wife and her parents. For this reason he had stuffed cash and receipt slips into Mays's pants. The purpose of the bizarre trip to the orange grove was to get gunshot residue on the hands of Mays and Thomas and to put their fingerprints on the guns. He had phoned the Van Deventer home and had asked specifically for his friend Don Ficke, on the assumption that Ficke would be inclined to accept his explanation.

But why should Zeigler kill at all?

Proof of motive is not legally necessary for a murder conviction. As a practical matter, though, jurors in a difficult case often want an explanation of motive before they will convict. That would be especially true in any trial of Tommy Zeigler, who had so much to lose. Why would he jeopardize his wealth and position?

Frye didn't know the answer yet. But he knew who did.

Table Two

TIME SEQUENCE: FELTON THOMAS

Thomas gave no specific times or intervals. Don Frye reconstructed a time line, on the premise that Thomas and Charlie Mays arrived at the furniture store around 7:30 P.M.

7:30 P.M.	Mays and Thomas are at store. Store is dark, Zeigler is gone. Edwardses' car is parked out front.
7:35	Zeigler drives up and parks beside Mays's van. Mays and Thomas leave with Zeigler in his car. Mays and Thomas fire pistols in the orange grove.
7:40	Back to the furniture store. Thomas pulls electrical switch, Zeigler attempts to break into the store, Mays objects. They drive to Zeigler's house.
7:50	The three arrive at Zeigler's house. Zeigler comes out of garage with a box of ammunition, tells Mays to reload. They return to store.

8:00   Mays and Zeigler enter furniture store. Thomas refuses, runs away, finds a ride back to Oakland.

2:30 A.M.   Thomas turns himself in to OCSO patrolman near Orlando.

SEVEN

AROUND 7:00 ON CHRISTMAS MORNING, FRYE AND JAMES JENKINS LEFT the store and met Don Ficke at West Orange Memorial. The three of them went up to the nurse's station of the intensive care unit on the second floor.

They wanted to interview Tommy Zeigler. Kathleen Clark, the head ICU nurse, told them that Zeigler could have no visitors. She had just come on duty and wasn't sure that he was in condition to be interviewed. And she didn't know whether Zeigler had been told of the four deaths; she didn't think he ought to hear it from the police.

Ficke wrote out a consent—in essence, a waiver of Zeigler's Fourth Amendment rights—on a piece of paper. Ficke later testified that Frye dictated it; Frye said that it was a mutual effort. The document read:

> December 25, 1975
> I Thomas Zeigler of Temple Grove Winter Garden Florida due [*sic*] knowingly and willingly give Donald G. Ficke and Det Frye permission to search my home in an attempt to aid there [*sic*] investigation into the shooting that took place at 1010 Dillard St. Winter Garden Florida on December 24, 1975.

Frye gave the document to Kathleen Clark and asked her to take it to Zeigler: she was to read it to him, make sure that he was alert, and ask him to sign it.

Zeigler within the past hour and a half had been given a one-eighth-gram dose of morphine sulfate for pain; he was sleeping when Clark went in with Doris Thompson, another nurse. Clark woke him and told him that the police were outside. He asked her to send them in, and she refused.

She read the document to Zeigler and told him that the police wanted him to sign it.

Zeigler said that he would. Clark gave him a pen, and he scrawled his signature at the bottom, witnessed by the two nurses.

Sheriff's officers had already decided that they were entitled to search throughout the furniture store and to impound any evidence they wished. Zeigler, after all, had invited police to the store when he called for help, and in any case they were empowered to investigate a crime scene. Now Zeigler's signature on the consent form gave them unrestricted access to the suspect's home. Sheriff's investigators had access to all the business records, files, personal papers, and belongings in both the store and the Zeigler home, without ever applying for a search warrant.

Frye and Ficke went from the hospital to 75 Temple Grove. They were joined by Jenkins and two evidence technicians, and the party searched the house for two hours or more.

In the bath of the master bedroom they found a Holiday Inn towel with reddish stains, suspected to be blood.

In a nightstand drawer they found twenty-four live .38 cartridges, twelve each of Remington and Winchester.

In the garage they found a damp hand towel.

They spent considerable time examining the Dunaway Oldsmobile parked in the garage. Frye found reddish smears, suspected blood, on the front of the driver's headrest. He found bloodlike smears on the interior door handle, driver's side. Later the car was towed to the 33rd Street station, where it was examined again. Technicians found a tissue paper with a bloodlike stain crumpled under the driver's seat.

Detectives questioned Dunaway. He had not bled in his car, he said; he had no explanation for the stains. They had not been there on Christmas Eve, when he exchanged cars with Tommy Zeigler.

Dr. Guillermo Ruiz began to autopsy the bodies at 7:00 A.M. on Christmas Day.

The first body was that of Virginia Edwards. She was five feet nine, 147 pounds. Ruiz traced the path of the bullet that had passed through her right arm, then penetrated her chest, one lung, the liver, and stomach. He recovered the .38 caliber slug nearly intact from under the skin on the left side of her torso.

The second shot, the killing bullet to her head, was in three fragments in her brain. Dr. Ruiz noted powder tattooing around a bullet wound in a finger of her right hand, and surmised that she had been shot at close range while holding her hand to her head.

Eunice Zeigler, five feet six and 114 pounds, had died from the gunshot behind her left ear. Ruiz recovered the bullet in two pieces. He found no other injuries.

Perry Edwards, who apparently had struggled so bravely at the back of the store, was five feet ten, 150 pounds. He had been shot five times. There were through-and-through wounds—that is, from bullets that had exited the body—in his right ear, his right shoulder, and his left shoulder. Ruiz recovered two .38 caliber slugs from his brain, the close-range shots that had killed him.

Ruiz counted seventeen contusions, abrasions, and lacerations along the left side of his face and at the top of his head. But there were no underlying fractures—his wounds were mostly superficial.

The blunt trauma injuries of Charlie Mays, however, were deep and brutal. One blow to his left eye had fractured the orbit and pushed the bone into the cavity beneath it. The wound measured about two by three inches. The left side of his face was shattered from the upper jaw to the eye. Fractured bone lay beneath four distinct lacerations of his face, forehead, and scalp.

Dr. Ruiz removed Mays's brain and found that the fractures extended to the anterior fossae, the front of the brain pan in the cranium. The base of the skull was traumatized and broken.

Mays was five feet eight, 140 pounds. There were abrasions and swelling on his right hand, possibly from a blunt object. He had one empty socket in his jaw, the left top canine tooth.

Ruiz used metal probes to trace the paths of two through-and-through wounds in Mays's abdomen. Mays had been shot once in the back, once in the front abdomen. One wound was superficial. The other bullet had passed through his liver. But Ruiz found only about 200 cc of blood in the peritoneum. This meant that neither wound had been fatal. Charlie Mays had been beaten to death by someone swinging a blunt object, probably the linoleum crank that was found beside him.

Mays's gunshot wounds were about the same size and circumference as those on the other bodies; apparently everyone had been shot and killed by .38 caliber bullets.

Early Christmas morning, the OCSO took custody of the clothes that Tommy Zeigler had been wearing when he was taken to the hospital. A nurse had picked them up off the floor of the emergency room, put them in a plastic bag, and given the bag to Beulah Zeigler, who apparently gave it to one of Tommy's cousins, L. M. Zeigler, at the hospital. He brought them home and left them outside, in his van.

He was awakened that night by a call from the Winter Garden police, asking him to return the bag to the hospital. He did. The bag was placed at the second-floor nurse's station, and an OCSO technician, Harry Park, retrieved it there. Park found the clothes jumbled together in the bag, so he put each item into a separate paper bag, then took them to headquarters, where he laid them out to dry.

Don Frye inspected the clothing. He saw that the left underarm of Zeigler's long-sleeved shirt was deeply stained with blood. Frye believed that much of that blood was from Perry Edwards. Edwards had been shot through one ear, and ears bleed profusely. Frye speculated that Edwards had bled on Zeigler's shirt while Zeigler held the seventy-two-year-old man clenched in a headlock and battered his skull with the crank.

The soles of Zeigler's shoes were of a ripple pattern and showed traces of what appeared to be blood. The OCSO technicians had lifted an impression of one of the bloody prints in the rear hallway. Frye performed an "overlay." That is, he lightly placed one of Zeigler's shoes over the impression of the bloody print.

Frye was not a footprint expert, but he knew the evidence of his own eyes. It was a match.

One of Tommy Zeigler's close friends in Winter Garden was Richard Smith, chief physical therapist and director of security and safety at West Orange Memorial. In the early 1970s they had served together in an Army Reserve unit.

On Christmas morning, Smith visited ICU several times to see his friend. Smith knew that Zeigler had not yet been told about the deaths of Eunice and the others. After speaking with Zeigler's physician, Dr. Gleason, Smith decided that he must break the news.

His account of that moment is contained in his trial testimony, and in the sworn statement that he gave to police on January 12.

Smith said that at around 11:00 Christmas morning he went into the ICU room with Wayman "Lee" Jones, who was also close to Zeigler. Lee Jones was president of Orange Federal Savings and Loan in Winter Garden.

Smith stood by Zeigler's side.

"Do you know what's happened?" Smith said.

"I went down there with Edward," Zeigler said.

Smith asked him again if he knew what had happened. Zeigler said that he had gone into the store. He tried a light switch, but the light didn't come on. He moved toward another switch, and he was hit from behind. He felt a sharp, hot pain.

Now he seemed to doze off again. Smith shook him and blurted, "Tommy, Eunice is dead."

And at that, Smith testified, Zeigler closed his eyes and began to cry, and Smith took him in his arms.

Table Three

TIME SEQUENCE (ESTIMATED): DON FRYE

Don Frye compiled a time line of the events in the store and at 75 Temple Grove, interpreting the statements of Edward Williams and Felton Thomas and other evidence. Frye believed that Williams's time estimates were generally ten to fifteen minutes too early. The times are approximate.

6:20 P.M. Furniture store closes, all vacate.

6:30 Curtis Dunaway and Tommy Zeigler exchange cars at Zeigler's house.

6:45–50 Dunaway drives home in Zeigler's white Toronado.

7:00	Zeigler arranges for Perry and Virginia Edwards to follow him and Eunice to the store. Zeigler writes the note for Edward Williams. The Edwardses drive their green Ford sedan, while Tommy and Eunice are in Dunaway's two-tone Oldsmobile.
7:05–15	Tommy and Eunice arrive at the store; Tommy kills Eunice.
7:20–25	Mr. and Mrs. Edwards arrive at the store and are killed by Zeigler; shot stops wall clock at 7:24.
7:28	Edward Williams arrives at Zeigler's home, finds the note.
7:30	Zeigler departs the store for reasons unknown. Three persons inside are dead.
7:30	Charlie Mays and Felton Thomas, in the blue van, arrive at the furniture store. The Edwardses' Ford is parked out front, but Dunaway's Olds is gone. Mays parks around back of the store to wait.
7:35	Zeigler meets Mays and Thomas behind the store. Mays and Thomas leave the van and drive with Zeigler to the orange grove, in Dunaway's car. Mays and Thomas fire several shots from pistols that Zeigler gives them in a paper bag.
7:40	Zeigler, Mays, and Thomas return to the store. Thomas pulls the main electrical breaker. Mays objects when Zeigler attempts to break into the store. They drive to Zeigler's house for keys.
7:50	Zeigler, Mays, and Thomas arrive at Temple Grove Drive. Thomas sees Williams's truck. Williams sees Zeigler and two passengers in Dunaway's car. Zeigler gets a box of ammunition from the house and tells Williams to wait a few more minutes. Zeigler, Mays, and Thomas return to the store.
7:55–8:00	Zeigler parks at the front of the store and coaxes Mays inside. Thomas runs away. Zeigler kills Mays.

8:10   Don and Rita Ficke drive to 75 Temple Grove, look-
        ing for Tommy and Eunice. They see Williams in his
        truck, no car in the lighted garage.

8:20–30 Zeigler arrives home and parks the Dunaway car in
        the garage. He wipes down the front seat and the
        outside door handle. After closing the garage door,
        Zeigler gets into Williams's truck, carrying a paper
        bag.

8:35–40 Zeigler and Williams arrive at the store in Williams's
        truck. Williams parks his truck in the back lot as
        Zeigler instructs him. Zeigler locks the gate.

8:40   Don and Rita Ficke drive to Zeigler's home. Wil-
        liams's truck is gone. Dunaway's Olds is parked in-
        side the garage.

8:40–50 Zeigler attempts to shoot and kill Edward Williams
        with an empty revolver (Securities .38). Zeigler gives
        the gun to Williams.

9:20   Zeigler phones the Van Deventer home.

EIGHT

THE INVESTIGATION CONTINUED IN AND AROUND THE STORE. MUCH OF
it was tedious. Through December 27, technicians collected blood
samples, mostly with Q-Tip swabs or filter paper. They tried to
preserve latent fingerprints and the bloody shoe prints. They continued to photograph the scene.

They searched for bullets and bullet holes. Eventually investigators would estimate that twenty-eight shots had been fired
inside the store.

Several bullets had struck the north wall, both east and west of the counter. Five shots had been sprayed westward from inside the kitchen, three of them passing through the closed west door of the kitchen—the door that had been open when Eunice Zeigler was killed. Spent slugs were recovered on the showroom floor, inside a china cabinet, and in the roofing insulation. One was found in the office closet, where it had come to rest after passing through at least two interior walls. Another was discovered in the back of an electric clock that hung above the east door of the kitchen. The slug had dislodged a gear, and the clock was now inoperable. It had stopped at 7:24.[1]

The same desk that yielded the two bloody misfires also contained a .22 Beretta semiautomatic pistol. Although it had not been fired, it would be the last of eight handguns introduced as evidence at the trial.

Technicians found no fingerprints in Williams's truck. Frye speculated that Zeigler had wiped off all the prints after moving it from the hallway door to the bay door where it was found.

Two dramatic discoveries broke the tedium.

On January 2, investigators opened a cabinet beside the overhead garage-type door in the rear storage area. Inside they found live and expended .38 Special rounds, three brown grocery bags (one of them apparently bloody), two empty boxes for revolvers, one empty box marked for .38 Special cartridges, and a blue towel. The evidence perfectly fit the stories of Felton Thomas and Edward Williams. Here, Frye believed, was the box of bullets that Zeigler had carried out of the garage and from which Charlie Mays had reloaded one of the pistols. Thomas identified one of the grocery bags as the one in which Zeigler carried the three guns that he took to the orange grove. And could this be the same towel with which Zeigler had concealed his pistol when he tried to shoot Edward Williams?

On December 26, Frye began to study the financial paperwork in Zeigler's office desk. In a locked drawer of the desk[2] Frye found three term life insurance policies. All had been applied for in

---

1. Curtis Dunaway testified that the clock was running normally just before closing time on Christmas Eve. Whether the clock was running when the bullet struck it—that is, whether the power was on in the store—could not be determined.

2. Investigators forced it open with a screwdriver.

September 1975. One was issued in October 1975, the others in November, less than two months before the murders.

One of the policies, in the amount of $250,000, was on Tommy Zeigler. Two others, each for $250,000, were on Eunice. Both of these had been applied for by Tommy. Counting smaller policies, Tommy Zeigler and the family corporation of which he was part owner stood to gain more than half a million dollars from the death of his wife. The policies not only provided a classic motive for murder, but suggested that Zeigler had contemplated the killings for many weeks. Other evidence implied that Zeigler had planned in thoughtful detail.

Mattie Mays told investigators about the promised TV, and the 7:30 appointment at the store.

Curtis Dunaway said the blue towel came from his car: he used it to cover up holes in the upholstery. Dunaway told how he and Zeigler had exchanged cars on Christmas Eve. Zeigler, not Dunaway, had initiated the swap. The new white Toronado would have been obvious as Zeigler drove around the streets of his home-town. But he would be much less conspicuous in Dunaway's drab four-year-old model. When he drove with Felton Thomas and, later, Edward Williams that night, Zeigler followed routes that bypassed busy Dillard Street. He literally went out of his way to escape recognition.

Don and Rita Ficke told Frye about their three trips to Temple Grove Drive when they were looking for Tommy and Eunice. On their second visit, around 8:10, they saw Edward Williams in his pickup truck, waiting in the driveway. There was no car. This corroborated Williams's account. On their third trip, the pickup truck was gone, and Dunaway's Oldsmobile was parked in the garage. This, too, was consistent with Williams's story.

Robert Thompson, the Oakland chief of police, told Frye that Zeigler had come to Oakland on December 23, specifically to invite him to the Van Deventers' party. At Zeigler's request, Ficke had posted a bulletin at Winter Garden police headquarters, inviting all officers to attend the gathering. Frye felt that Zeigler had contrived to have all the local police at the party and off the streets by 7:10, when he would be bringing Eunice to the store to kill her. Her parents would arrive a few minutes later, and Charlie Mays's appointment was less than a quarter of an hour after that. At the same time, Edward Williams would be finding the note in the garage at Temple Grove Street. Frye was convinced that Tommy Zeigler had planned four murders almost to the minute.

NINE

ON THE 26TH, FRYE WENT TO ORANGE MEMORIAL HOPING TO INTER-view the suspect. He met Ralph "Terry" Hadley III, a young local attorney whom Zeigler and his family had hired earlier that day. Hadley was becoming known as a skilled criminal lawyer; before going into private practice he had worked under the Orange-Osceola state attorney, Robert Eagan, who would prosecute the case.

Frye asked Hadley for permission to interview Zeigler. Hadley refused. But a day or two later Hadley did report Zeigler's version of the incident.

This is the story that Hadley related in part to Frye that day, and that Zeigler has maintained to this day:

Zeigler said that Eunice and her parents went to the store without him, in the Edwardses' Ford. Zeigler stayed at home, waiting for Edward Williams. According to Zeigler, the appointment with Williams was for 7:00, not 7:30, and Williams was late. Zeigler said he left a note for Williams and went to buy bourbon for the party, driving Dunaway's car. But he changed his mind before he got to the liquor store. He turned around and came home.

Zeigler said that Williams was waiting for him when he returned, and they drove to the store in Williams's truck. The store was dark when they arrived. Zeigler walked in ahead of Williams, entering the northwest hallway, and was assaulted by at least two men as he entered the showroom. He lost his glasses and was unable to see in the darkness. He may have fired one shot from the .22 automatic at his side, but the pistol jammed, and he threw it at his assailants. He was knocked back into the hallway, and he reached into a drawer where he had recently put the .357 Colt. He may have fired that gun—he didn't know how many shots—and then he himself was shot and knocked to the floor, and he lost consciousness.

According to Hadley, Zeigler said that the assailants were gone when he regained consciousness at the back of the store. He crawled along the floor near the back of the showroom, went into his office, found his spare pair of glasses, and phoned Don Ficke, who he knew would be at the Van Deventer home. The keys with which he opened the door, when Ficke and Thompson arrived, were the set that he had given to Eunice before she left with her parents. He had found them there in the lock.

Hadley suggested to Frye that retribution against Zeigler, not robbery, might have been the prime reason for the killings. He said that Zeigler had been compiling information on organized loan sharking in West Orange's migrant labor camps, and had made enemies.

Zeigler's story did not address the beating death of Charlie Mays, or the fact that Zeigler's shoulder holster was found on top of Mays's dry blood splatters. It did not explain why Edward Williams and Felton Thomas, two black men apparently unknown to each other, each had come forth with damning stories against a man whom they had no reason to dislike, much less to hate.

TEN

ON THE 26TH OR 27TH, SHERIFF'S OFFICERS AND THE STATE ATTORNEY'S staff made two crucial decisions.

Because Don Frye was not legally qualified to testify on blood spatter evidence, the state retained Herbert MacDonell, the professor and criminalist from New York, to examine the crime scene and make a report. MacDonell was not available until after the New Year, but the sheriff would hold the crime scene until Mac-Donell could fly to Orlando.

They also decided that the FBI Laboratory in Washington, D.C., would analyze and test the forensic evidence.

On the 28th, two OCSO technicians flew to Washington with nearly one hundred pieces of evidence that had been collected in the store, at Zeigler's home, and from the Dunaway car. It was the first of what would be several submissions to the FBI Lab. The specimens included pistols and bullets, blood and hair from the victims, swabs and filter paper, the store clock, and the stained car door latch. The transmittal letter requested ballistics matching, blood typing, chemical analysis, and hair and fiber analysis.

Ordinarily that would have been the work of the Sanford Regional Crime Laboratory, which operated under the Florida Department of Law Enforcement. But this was not an ordinary case.

Then, as now, the FBI Lab was considered the finest in the country, one of the best in the world. Its experts were often the final word on matters of serology, ballistics and toolmarks, fingerprints and shoe prints, hairs and fibers, explosives, handwriting identification, and other branches of the forensic sciences. The lab's services were, and are, available free to state and local police in criminal investigations.

The FBI Lab was not without drawbacks. Its experts were generally inaccessible: when they were not busy in the laboratory they were often out of town, appearing at trials around the country. They had to be scheduled well in advance for consultations, depositions, or trial testimony. But their reputation was impressive.

"We want results to be as fast and accurate as possible," OCSO Chief Deputy Leigh McEachern told reporters on December 28, explaining the decision to send evidence to Washington.[1]

McEachern said that he expected the two officers, Alton Evans and James Shannon, to have preliminary reports when they returned in two or three days. That estimate proved to be absurdly optimistic. Over the next weeks and months, Orange County's police and prosecutors learned that the term "fast" could in no sense be applied to the FBI Lab.

Speed was not the only consideration. Some of the results, when they were finally released, became instantly controversial. Before the trial was finished, both prosecution and defense would have reason to question the work of the nation's finest crime laboratory.

The murders and the investigation dominated local news.

Central Florida's most important print outlet was the *Orlando Sentinel Star*. On Christmas Day, because of deadlines, the newspaper reported the killings at the top of its Metro pages. The crime was described as a "robbery attempt," and by press time the four dead had not been identified. Sheriff's lieutenant Bruce Churchill was quoted as saying, "It will take us a long time to determine what happened."

Every day for the next week, the story was at the top of page one of the *Sentinel Star*. Much of the reporting relied on unnamed police sources, and the tone of the articles reflected a growing skepticism about Zeigler.

In the early editions of December 26, authorities were reported to be "totally baffled about how or why the shootings occurred—although not ruling out robbery." The afternoon edition, however, reported, "Exhausted investigators today predicted charges will be filed almost immediately. . . . While police first said

1. Most of the fingerprint lifts were sent to the Sanford Laboratory.

they thought robbery was the motive in the early evening gun battle, they now say 'there are other things to consider here.' "

The next day, the 27th, the headline was KILLINGS SURVIVOR REFUSES TO TALK. The lead paragraph read: "The lone survivor and only witness to a bloody Christmas Eve massacre . . . refused on the advice of his lawyer Friday to answer investigators' questions."

Sheriff Melvin G. Colman would not comment on whether Zeigler was a suspect. As for the robbery theory, Colman said, "We haven't ruled out anything in the case."

The article went on: "Some investigators said early Friday they believed they were ready to charge a suspect. But following an afternoon conference at the blood-spattered furniture store between Colman and Assistant State Atty. Lawson L. Lamar, it was decided to continue gathering evidence and await results of laboratory tests."

On Sunday, the 28th, the *Sentinel Star* reported the existence of an unnamed "mystery witness"—Edward Williams—who was described as having gone to the police "minutes after the shootings." Eunice Zeigler was said to have been found at the front of the showroom, her mother in the kitchen. By now the robbery story was relegated to the last paragraph: "Although detectives initially said they thought the killings were a result of an armed robbery, they could find nothing missing from the store."

The top story on the 29th was the decision to send evidence to the FBI. The chief deputy, McEachern, said that no charges would be filed "in the next day or two."

While that issue of the newspaper was on the streets, however, Frye was reviewing the evidence with his superiors and an assistant state attorney. On the afternoon of the 29th, Frye himself signed an arrest warrant. He and McEachern were among the official party that arrested Zeigler in his bed at West Orange Memorial and formally charged him with the four murders. He was no longer a suspect, but a defendant.

The next day, the photo at the top of page one was of Tommy Zeigler hiding his face behind a blanket as he was taken into custody.

Peter de Manio, a circuit court judge, read the charges against Zeigler at special proceedings held on the 30th in his hospital room. The *Sentinel Star* described him as "ashen-faced" when he listened to the accusations.

"Zeigler showed no emotion as the judge spoke," wrote reporter Paul Jenkins. "His eyes remained fixed on de Manio and he did not glance around the tiny hospital room crammed with newsmen, court clerks, and sheriff's deputies."

In the accompanying photograph Zeigler appeared impassive, stolid: perhaps stunned. De Manio asked him if he understood the charges against him, and Zeigler whispered, "Yes." De Manio explained that the penalty for each of the four counts was life imprisonment, or death.

On that day, the question of a death sentence was moot. Not since 1964 had the state executed anyone in its electric chair at Florida State Prison. In 1972, the U.S. Supreme Court had declared the state's death penalty to be unconstitutional.

But the state was preparing to argue otherwise. In the spring, Florida would ask the Supreme Court to uphold a sentence of death against Charles William Proffitt, a thirty-year-old warehouseman convicted of murdering a high school wrestling coach during a burglary. The decision, when it was announced in July, would have huge implications for the nearly seventy men who still remained on Death Row, and for Tommy Zeigler.

ELEVEN

THE PRELIMINARY HEARING IN *FLORIDA* V. *ZEIGLER* WAS SCHEDULED for January 16. Florida law required that a defendant either be indicted or be given a preliminary hearing within twenty-one days of arrest. The state attorney, Robert Eagan, chose a preliminary hearing. The deadline was January 18, a Sunday. So Friday, January 16, was the last practical day the hearing could be held. Otherwise Zeigler would have to be released, though he could be arrested again later.

The state attorney's office needed all the time it could get. So far the FBI Lab had not returned any results. In particular, there were no findings from the ballistics section. The prosecution hoped to show that Eunice and her parents had been killed by Tommy Zeigler's pistols. But until the FBI Lab came back with its report, none of the recovered bullets could be matched to any of the eight firearms. Professor MacDonell studied the crime scene on January 7, after which police reliquished the store to the defense. But MacDonell's report would not be ready in time for the hearing.

Frye and Denny Martin continued to work.

Thomas Hale, an acquaintance of the Zeiglers, told Frye that at around 7:15 P.M. on Christmas Eve he had seen Tommy and Eunice at Route 50 and Dillard. Hale said he was in the inner southbound lane of Dillard, waiting for the light to change, when Tommy made a left turn off Route 50. The two cars passed within three feet of each other, with Zeigler continuing north up Dillard, toward the store. Hale said that Eunice was beside Tommy in the front seat.

This was a breakthrough. Hale was the first witness to place Tommy and Eunice together near the furniture store at the time of the murders. The testimony contradicted Zeigler's assertion that he had stayed at home while Eunice drove to the store with her parents.

By inference, Hale's story supported the accounts of Felton Thomas and Edward Williams. The left turn that Hale noticed, from Route 50 onto Dillard, suggested the same indirect route to the store that both Williams and Thomas described.

Frye interviewed Rogenia Thomas,[1] one of the two young women who had met Williams outside the Kentucky Fried Chicken. She basically corroborated Williams's story, although later there was some disagreement about whether he had actually mentioned Zeigler's name to her.

Frye and Denny Martin tested a key point in Williams's story. Williams had said that he had entered the building from the back parking compound, walked up the northwest hallway, and stepped out into the dark showroom. There, according to Williams, Zeigler pulled the trigger on a gun three times in an attempt to kill him. Frye wanted to test Williams's claim that he could identify Zeigler and a pistol in the darkness.

One evening after nightfall, Frye and Martin turned off all the

---

1. Apparently no relation to Felton Thomas.

store lights. First Martin stood holding a pistol where Zeigler would have been standing, a few feet inside the showroom. Frye came up the hall, as Williams said he had done. Then the two detectives switched roles, and Martin walked up the hall while Frye held the gun in the showroom.

The results satisfied Frye. He was able to testify at least four times—at a deposition, the preliminary hearing, the grand jury hearing, and the trial—that he recognized Martin and the pistol in the darkness.

Frye was intrigued by Zeigler's account of a brawl in the back of the showroom. Did Zeigler have any injuries besides the gunshot? Frye and an assistant state attorney deposed Dr. Gleason, the only physician to have closely examined Zeigler between Christmas Eve and the 29th.

Frye wanted to know whether Zeigler had complained of head injuries or severe headaches. Gleason said that Zeigler did have a slight swelling and tender area at the lower right of his skull, but the skin was not broken. Gleason also said that Zeigler had complained of some soreness in his right index finger—his trigger finger. This interested Frye. He thought of the bent trigger guard on one of the RG revolvers. Frye believed that the RG had been damaged during the killings, probably when Perry Edwards swung the wooden footstool to defend himself; whoever had been holding the pistol could have sustained such an injury to his trigger finger.

Frye also learned that Zeigler's service in the Army Reserve had been with a Medical Corps unit. Here Zeigler would have been been exposed to the special knowledge of anatomy that would have allowed him to shoot himself in the abdomen without jeopardizing his life.

Edward Williams and Felton Thomas were now in protective custody. Thomas had disappeared from Christmas Day to December 30. When he was found at a friend's house in the town of Kissimmee, south of Orlando, Thomas asked police for protection. He told them that he had fled because he was in fear of his life. (WITNESS AT KILLINGS BEGS FOR JAIL was next day's headline in the *Sentinel Star*.) Now Thomas and Williams were under guard, living in motel rooms provided by the state attorney's office.

Zeigler, through Hadley, identified six of the eight pistols.

Zeigler said that the .357 Colt, which he admitted firing, normally was kept at his home. But he had hidden it in the hallway, supposedly as a defense against the Ski Mask Bandits, the gang of armed thieves who at the time were robbing businesses throughout central Florida. This was the pistol found near Perry Edwards.

The .22 Smith & Wesson Escort, which Zeigler said he had fired once before it jammed, was on loan to Zeigler from Don Ficke. Zeigler carried this little semiautomatic at his belt. It was one of the two guns found near Charlie Mays's feet.

The .38 Burgo derringer, also found near Mays's feet, was normally kept under the cash register at the counter. Zeigler could not explain how it ended up on the terrazzo floor with an expended shell in the top chamber.

The Securities Industries .38 also was used for Zeigler's personal protection. He said he usually kept the pistol and a shoulder holster in the custom metal writing desk built into the dashboard of his pickup truck, which he used for making collections on rent and furniture accounts. This was the gun that Edward Williams brought to the Winter Garden police after Zeigler apparently had tried to kill him. Zeigler did not explain how it had ended up in Williams's possession.[2]

The .38 Smith & Wesson belonged to Zeigler and normally was kept against a file cabinet in the store's customer service area. Zeigler did not explain how it had ended up in Curtis Dunaway's car, in Zeigler's garage, where Jimmy Yawn found it on the night of the 24th.

The .22 Beretta belonged to Zeigler, and had been found where he usually kept it, in his desk drawer.

According to Hadley, Zeigler had never seen and could not explain the two .38 RG revolvers found near the head of Charlie Mays.

Early in January, Thomas showed Frye and Martin the remote orange grove where he said Zeigler had driven them and they had shot the revolvers. Martin and a second deputy, James Lee Bryan, brought a crew of trusties from the Orange County Jail and began to dig for bullets in the earth. On January 12, after two days of sifting dirt and sand, Bryan reported that they had recovered a single .38 slug.

If that bullet could be matched to any of the guns from the store, it would lend great substance to Thomas's story. Without

---

2. The Securities Industries .38 was chrome-plated. The .357 Colt found near Perry Edwards was stainless-steel, and also bright. All the other handguns were black or dark blue.

ballistics testing, though, the slug meant next to nothing. The OCSO shipped it to Washington, where it was added to the earlier submissions. The chance was nil that it might be tested before the preliminary hearing.

As the date of the hearing approached, only one set of results came back. These were the test swabs for gunshot residue, taken from the hands of the four murder victims. The swabs had been submitted to the state's Sanford Laboratory rather than to the FBI.

The results did not advance the state's case. Chemical examination for the metals barium, antimony, and lead, which are used in the manufacture of cartridge primer caps, suggested that Charlie Mays, Perry Edwards, and Virginia Edwards all had recently handled or fired weapons. That information was not released to the defense until April.

The January 16 hearing would be the first public airing of the evidence against Tommy Zeigler. But the heart of that evidence, the possible physical proof that Zeigler had killed four people on Christmas Eve, was still in the FBI Lab, unexamined, when the two sides entered Courtroom E of the Orange County Courthouse.

TWELVE

AN ORANGE COUNTY JUDGE, FRANK KANEY, LISTENED TO NEARLY SIX hours of testimony in the preliminary hearing on January 16.

Zeigler had recovered from his wound and was brought by elevator from the county jail, in the courthouse building. A sheriff's deputy told reporters, "We've received some thirdhand, hearsay-type threats against Zeigler."

There was no jury. Preliminary hearings usually are less formal than a trial, and the rules of evidence are somewhat relaxed.

In the absence of physical evidence, the state pinned its case on Felton Thomas and Edward Williams. They were still in protective custody; each was escorted into the courtroom by a pair of sheriff's deputies.

Thomas again gave his name as Thomas Felton. Assistant State Attorney Lawson Lamar led him through virtually the same story he had told Frye and Jenkins in the early hours of Christmas Day. A crucial point came early in his direct testimony, when Thomas told of sitting with Charlie Mays in the blue van, parked behind the store:

Q (LAMAR): Did you say a guy drove up to your car?
A (THOMAS): Right.
Q: And did you all talk with him?
A: He told Charlie to come around and ride with him a minute.
Q: He told Charlie to come ride with him?
A: Yes.
Q: Who was this guy? Had you ever seen him before?
A: No, I haven't.
Q: Is that guy in this room today anywhere? Look around the room.
A: The guy right there.

He pointed out Tommy Zeigler, seated between his two attorneys.

The Zeiglers had retained Ed Kirkland, an experienced trial lawyer from Orlando, to assist Terry Hadley. Kirkland, like almost everyone else except the police and the prosecution, was hearing this account for the first time. Under Kirkland's cross-examination, Thomas admitted that he had drunk two or three beers in the late afternoon before he met Mays. But Kirkland did not shake him from his story.

Edward Williams followed Thomas to the stand. Williams, too, remained mostly consistent to his original account. He described again how Zeigler had leveled a gun at him as he entered the rear of the showroom: "[J]ust as I walk in, he turned around, and it snapped it three times, pop, like that."

Q (LAMAR): What did you see?
A (WILLIAMS): I saw, it looked like it was something like—he had this thing he was holding, and I saw the gun, and he had something holding it, and he was going pop, pop, pop three times.

Q: Was this a gun going off, or clicking?

A: Just the hammer hitting, the gun didn't go off.

Q: Did you see what color the gun was?

A: That night I didn't see what color it was.

Q: Was it dull, or was it shiny? Do you remember that?

A: No, I couldn't tell you whether it was shiny. I saw him pointing it on me. And then I holler, I say, "For God sake, Tommy, don't kill me." . . . And I run back out the hallway, back outside the door. When I got out the door, I went to open the gate, to get out the gate, and I found the gate was locked.

Q: The gate was locked?

A: So I turned there, and he came up, and he said, "Edward, I didn't know it was you."

Kirkland's cross-examination was aggressive. Lawson Lamar interrupted a series of questions to complain that Kirkland was badgering the witness. A few minutes later, Kirkland focused on the key moment in the store; according to Williams's account, the door where he entered the showroom was only a few feet from where Charlie Mays lay dead.

Kirkland's voice became louder, and his questions were rapid and insistent:

Q (KIRKLAND): Where was Mr. Tommy when you got in the building as far as you got in? Where was he standing?

A (WILLIAMS): When I got in, he was standing just straight ahead of me.

Q: Did you see a body on the floor just six or seven feet from him?

A: No, sir, I didn't see no body.

Q: Why didn't you see a body when it was within five or six feet of you?

A: I didn't see no body. When he called me, I was looking at him. He said, "Edward, come on, Edward." And I said, "I'm coming." And when I said, "I'm coming," I mean in the main building.

Q: Was it too dark to see a body in that building?

A: I wasn't looking for a body.

Q: Was it too dark to observe a body on the floor, if there had been one?

A: Maybe. If I was looking for one, I might have seen one, but I wasn't looking for no body.

Q: How dark was it in there?

A: It was clear enough for me to see the person ahead of me.

Q: What light was there available in that store?

A: It was a clear light from the outside of the store. I could see a clear light inside; I couldn't see nothing in the hall, but in the main store it was clear enough that I could see if anybody was there.

Q: In other words, you say right in this open hallway there's absolutely no visibility, that it's dark, but once you got even with this workbench, you could see?

A: When I got inside, it was clear enough that I could see Tommy, Mr. Tommy. And looking for a dead body, I wasn't looking for nothing; I didn't expect to see nothing.

Q: Just answer my questions.

A: Yes, sir, I just couldn't see—

Q: Just answer my questions.

Kirkland shifted to a new line of questions, implying that Williams was in need of money. Then he went back to the gun that Williams brought to the police.

Q: And you say you had a weapon then, a pistol?

A: No sir, I didn't have no pistol.

Q: He gave it to you, didn't he?

A: He gave me a pistol after he came out.

Q: So you had a weapon then. He came out of that building, and you say it was in Mr. Zeigler's hands?

A: He gave me the weapon, yes.

Q: So you were in the building that night, were you not?

LAWSON LAMAR: Your Honor, this is repetitious. •

JUDGE KANEY: I think he's entitled to ask him questions one at a time.

Q: What I'm saying is, you were broke, and you had an opportunity to kill these people, and you had a weapon in your hand that you turned in to the police, did you not, Mr. Williams?

A: No sir, I didn't kill nobody since I been born. I got the weapon from Mr. Tommy Zeigler.

Don Frye summed up the evidence against Zeigler. He testified to the bloody footprints, to the holster found on top of the blood spatters, to the cache of paper bags and ammunition and the blue towel found in the cabinet near the loading dock. He described the apparent bloodstains found in Curtis Dunaway's car.

Without lab results, Frye could not testify that the stains actually were blood. Without a ballistics report, he could not match any of the fatal shots to the guns found in the store. He testified about the insurance policies, but under cross-examination he admitted that in searching Zeigler's papers and records he had found no evidence that Zeigler or his family was in any financial difficulty.

Judge Kaney announced his decision after a short recess. He said that the defendant would be bound over for a grand jury. But he added that Zeigler was eligible for bond, which he set at $40,000. Considering the family's means, it was an outright release from custody.

Lawson Lamar protested. Kaney stood firm.

"The state didn't present a clear case against Zeigler," Kaney explained in an interview about a week later. "They showed me very little hard evidence—they didn't show me enough to deny bond."

Zeigler chose to remain in jail over the weekend, rather than pay the $4,000 bondsman's fee that would have bought his immediate release. On Monday morning his mother posted the full amount after cashing some certificates of deposit. Tommy Zeigler was a free man again.

THIRTEEN

ONE DAY AFTER TOMMY ZEIGLER'S RELEASE, POLICE INVESTIGATORS traced the ownership of the two .38 RG revolvers. They had been bought new the previous June from a pawnshop in Orlando. The purchaser was Frank Smith, a black twenty-seven-year-old cab driver who was a friend of Edward Williams.

Smith told Don Frye that he had bought the guns for Tommy Zeigler, whom he had never met. He said that in May he had spoken to Zeigler when Williams telephoned Zeigler from Smith's apartment. According to Smith, Zeigler wanted two revolvers that could not be traced. Smith said he bought the pistols two or three weeks later and immediately phoned Zeigler at the furniture store. The next day, according to Smith, Edward Williams gave him $159 from Zeigler and took a paper bag containing the two weapons.

Edward Williams corroborated Smith's story. According to Williams, Zeigler first approached him about buying "hot" guns in March or April 1975. Williams recommended Smith, on the assumption that a cab driver might know a source of stolen property. Williams confirmed that he delivered a sealed envelope—presumably containing money—from Zeigler to Smith in June, and that he had brought the paper bag from Smith's apartment to Zeigler's house. He said that Tommy was not home when he delivered the package, but that he gave it to Eunice. Later Zeigler told him that he had received the package.

This satisfied Frye. It seemed to prove that Zeigler actually had been planning the crime for more than half a year. All eight guns in the case—six from the store, one from Curtis Dunaway's Oldsmobile, and the one that Edward Williams turned in to police the night of the murders—now were tied to Tommy Zeigler.

Frye continued to work exclusively on the case. Since about the first of the year he had been interviewing the Zeiglers' friends and neighbors, acquaintances and enemies. Frye wanted to know more about the marriage of Tommy and Eunice: a happily married man does not plot for months to murder his wife.

Over several weeks, Frye compiled a portrait of a stifled, dissatisfied wife in an unequal marriage. He believed that Eunice had been unhappy, living next door to a meddling mother-in-law. He was told that Beulah Zeigler was an overbearing woman who dominated both Eunice and Tom senior. Eunice's beautician told Frye that Tommy berated her for running the air conditioner, and that there was friction between wife and mother.

Frye heard frightening stories about Tommy Zeigler as a youth. Unhappy that his parents had sold the family home, he returned there and vandalized the house after the new owners moved in. He had cut the leg off a dog, the family pet. One informant claimed that Zeigler had tried to drown his father in a lake while Beulah looked on from the shore.

Frye also heard rumors that Tommy Zeigler was a homosexual. This aspect of the case appears to have surfaced as early as the night of the murders. According to Don Ficke, Robert Thompson speculated to Frye and other officers that the crime might have been sexually motivated. The unusual position of Charlie Mays's pants, pulled down from his waist with the fly open, seemed to suggest some sexual component to the murders. And as he interviewed residents of Winter Garden, Frye kept encountering the rumor that Zeigler and some of his close friends were part of a homosexual ring involving prominent personalities in West Orange. He was told that Eunice had discovered her husband having sex with one of his male friends, and that she had decided to expose his secret and leave him, perhaps returning to Georgia with her parents after Christmas.

Tommy Zeigler's stature in the community was a powerful argument against his guilt. Even $500,000 in insurance benefits was not a completely compelling motive: Zeigler stood to forfeit much more than that, even in strictly financial terms, if he was convicted of murder. He had so much to lose.

But the weight of the argument shifted if Zeigler was a secret homosexual. If he practiced deceit every day of his life, the idea that he might shoot himself in the abdomen to cover up his crimes was not so farfetched. Moreover, all that Zeigler prized—his reputation, his businesses, his influence—rested in conservative Winter Garden. If he was revealed as a homosexual, he would become an instant pariah in his hometown. He would lose everything.

And Tommy Zeigler had so much to lose.

FOURTEEN

Ballistics examinations showed that the five bullets recovered from the bodies had been fired by two or three different pistols. The bullet in the brain of Eunice Zeigler was too badly deformed to be identified with a specific gun. However, its rifling twists and grooves were consistent with having been fired from either of the two RG revolvers. The two killing shots to the head of Perry Edwards had come from the Securities Industries .38, Tommy Zeigler's chrome-plated "truck gun," which Edward Williams gave to the police. The same pistol had also fired the killing shot into the head of Virginia Edwards. But the slug found in Mrs. Edwards's chest was from one of the two RGs.

The slug recovered from the orange grove could not be linked to any specific gun. However, it shared the unusual rifling characteristics of the Securities .38. This was also true of the .38 slug that had disabled the wall clock. Several other slugs recovered from around the store were generically identified with the two RG pistols.

Eight empty cartridges from the Securities .38 were identified from the bags in the cabinet at the rear of the store.[1]

Of the other weapons involved:

• The Colt .357 magnum found near the feet of Mr. Edwards seemed to have been fired six times without being reloaded.

---

1. In order to fire eight shots or more, this revolver must have been reloaded during the crime. The chambers were empty when Edward Williams brought it to the Winter Garden police headquarters. The killer must have dumped out the spent cartridges and then placed them in the bag where they were found. For some reason he failed to reload a second time, although live .38 cartridges were found in the bag along with the empty hulls.

• The .22 Smith & Wesson Escort automatic found at the feet of Charlie Mays apparently had been fired once before it jammed.

• The .38 Burgo derringer had fired one shot. The two bloody cartridges found in Zeigler's desk drawer probably had misfired in this weapon.

• Apparently neither the .22 automatic found in Zeigler's office desk nor the .38 Smith & Wesson from the Dunaway car had been fired.

The fact that Mrs. Edwards had been shot by two different guns suggested to Frye that she had run toward the front of the store after being shot through the chest. Frye believed that Zeigler, having fired all five shots from one of the RG pistols, used his truck gun to execute Perry Edwards, then stalked Mrs. Edwards and killed her with the same pistol. Mrs. Edwards fled to within a few feet of the large showroom windows at the front of the store. While her husband battled Tommy Zeigler at the back of the room, she might have escaped by breaking a window with any of the several lamps or chairs that were within her reach. But she did not. Frye believed that she was paralyzed with fear when Zeigler, having finished Perry Edwards, hunted her down in the darkness and killed her.

No usable fingerprints were found on any of the guns. All but one appeared to have been wiped clean. The exception was the Colt .357, which Frye believed Zeigler had flung to the back of the showroom after shooting himself. On that weapon the examiner developed two partial latent fingerprints, which were of no value for identification. However, Zeigler's palm print was identified on one of the grocery bags found in the cabinet at the rear of the store.[2]

The results of the blood tests were disappointing. Blood typing was inconclusive on many specimens, including Zeigler's shoes, the telephone, and the tip of the rubber glove. No blood was found on the door handle of the Dunaway Oldsmobile, and the amount on the headrest was too slight to be typed. No blood was found on the towel taken from the washing machine in the garage at 75 Temple

---

2. A latent print is one that is invisible until it is developed by chemical processes. Usable prints on pistols are said to be rare, since lifts are difficult to make from the film of oil on most weapons. But latent prints may be found on paper even after several years, since paper retains amino acids from the skin.

Grove Drive. Blood on the Holiday Inn towel, seized from the Zeigler's bathroom, could not be identified as human.

Perry Edwards, Charlie Mays, and Eunice Zeigler all had Type A blood, while both Tommy Zeigler and Virginia Edwards had Type O. Frye had assumed that Zeigler had left the blood trail from the end of the counter to the front door. But none of the specimens taken from that apparent trail were Type O. Of those that could be identified, every one was A.

A February 18 article in the *Sentinel Star* quoted Chief Deputy Leigh McEachern: "Their [the FBI's] findings are consistent with our hypothesis on what happened at the W. T. Zeigler furniture store."

Not all the results were disappointing. Significantly, no O blood was found at the back of the store, where Tommy Zeigler claimed to have been shot. Tests of Zeigler's shirt and trousers showed a preponderance of Type A.[3] The heavy blood around his left underarm was A, and A blood was speckled across the front of the shirt. In spite of his wound, Tommy Zeigler apparently had managed to collect mostly other people's blood on his own garments.

Herbert MacDonell's report on the crime scene, submitted on March 9, lent unqualified support to the state's case against Zeigler. The findings of the criminalist from New York State matched Don Frye's reconstruction and conclusions, almost point for point.

Professor MacDonell confirmed Frye's theory that Charlie Mays had been killed at least a quarter of an hour after Perry Edwards. ". . . Mr. Mays was not in the store at the time," MacDonell wrote. "The basis for this conclusion is the fact that when Mr. Mays was beaten his blood spatters did not mix with the already dried, swipe blood patterns that resulted from Mr. Edwards's movement throughout the rear of the store."

MacDonell also noted the holster that was found on top of dry blood. The absence of spatters on Mays's undershorts indicated that the killer had blocked this area, straddling Mays's waist as he beat him, or else that the pants were pulled down after the beating.

MacDonell was certain that Eunice Zeigler had been the first

3. One of the stains eventually found on Zeigler's trousers was a dark wood stain.

victim: "Had there been any activity of a shooting or beating nature, it is highly unlikely that Mrs. Zeigler would still have had her hand in her coat pocket. Also, being shot from behind further suggests surprise."

Perry Edwards, he said, was the second to die: "After the initial shots which killed Mrs. Zeigler, Mr. Edwards would have constituted the greatest challenge to the perpetrator."

Mrs. Edwards had died after her husband; she "was probably considered as the one who could most easily have been overpowered and, for this reason, held for last."

As for Charlie Mays: "Undoubtedly Mr. Mays entered the store after all three other victims were killed. To conclude otherwise would suggest that he was present while the other victims were being killed and did nothing to prevent their deaths. Had Mays been the perpetrator his bloody sneaker prints should have been detected after he had beaten Mr. Edwards so badly. Instead, Mays was both beaten and shot and another shoe print pattern in blood is evident over most of the uncarpeted area. Most likely this is a shoe print of the perpetrator."[4]

This last sentence referred to the clearest of the bloody footprints in the store: one in a thick swipe of blood near Perry Edwards. Don Frye was certain that this print had been made by Tommy Zeigler's right shoe.

MacDonell supported more of Frye's conclusions in a passage subheaded ADDITIONAL CONSIDERATIONS. It is quoted here in full, except for references to some numbered photographs. The emphasis in the second paragraph is his:

> Shoe prints made with blood are evident in several areas of the Zeigler Furniture Store. While some of these poorly defined markings could have been made by Mr. Edwards's shoes during his extensive struggle around the rear portion of the store, no bloody sneaker prints similar to Mr. Mays's sneakers were detected. The person who made the bloody shoe prints certainly was in several places throughout the store—after considerable bloodshed, not before!

---

4. Professor MacDonell uses this singular form—"the perpetrator"—four times in his five-page report, and all of his conclusions assume that the murders were the work of a single individual. He does not address the possibility that the crime may have been the work of more than one person.

Mr. William T. Zeigler left a rather well defined trail of blood from the general area of the telephone on the counter to the front of the store.[5] No similar such pattern was evident from the rear of the store where he was allegedly shot to the counter. The amount of blood on the telephone certainly suggests he was bleeding prior to using it. The absence of a blood trail *to* the telephone should be questioned.

The significance of Mr. Mays's trousers and underpants being pulled down should be considered. If this was the act of a homosexual, could such an opinion be helpful in understanding the kind of person who committed these crimes? A forensic psychiatrist may be worth consulting on this.

The suggestion that Zeigler was bleeding before he used the telephone contradicted Frye's belief that Zeigler had shot himself after calling the Van Deventer home, assured that help was on the way. Otherwise, MacDonell completely substantiated Frye's theories of the case, even on the issue of homosexuality. Frye and the rest of the prosecution had reason to feel confident two and a half weeks later, on March 25, when Robert Eagan himself presented the case to a grand jury at the Orange County Courthouse in Orlando.

Table Four

WEAPONS IN EVIDENCE

1. Colt .357 magnum six-shot revolver—found with broken handle grip near feet of Perry Edwards, six empty cartridges in chambers; two lead bullets recovered in store; bought by Zeigler, October 31, 1974, and kept in rear hallway desk.

2. .22 Smith & Wesson Escort automatic—found near Charlie Mays, one empty cartridge on floor, several live rounds in clip, one live round jammed in chamber; no bullets recovered; loaned or given to Zeigler by Ficke, carried by Zeigler.

---

5. In fact, none of Zeigler's Type O blood was found in the drops and smears that led to the front door. MacDonell admitted later that he had written his report without reference to the FBI test results and without examining most of the victims' clothing.

3. .38 Burgo derringer—found near Mays, one empty cartridge in top chamber, one live round in bottom; one lead bullet recovered, two misfired cartridges with bloodstains found in desk of Zeigler; owned by Zeigler, kept under cash register in store.

4. .38 RG five-shot revolver—found near Mays, five empty cartridges in chambers; lead bullet found in torso of Virginia Edwards; bought by Frank Smith, June 20, 1975.

5. .38 RG five-shot revolver—found near Mays with bent trigger guard, two empty cartridges, three live rounds in chamber; bought by Frank Smith, June 20, 1975.

6. .38 Securities Industries six-shot revolver—surrendered to police by Edward Williams, cocked, with all chambers empty; several lead bullets found in store, empty cartridges found in bag in storeroom cabinet, lead bullets found in Perry Edwards and Virginia Edwards; purchased by Zeigler, October 31, 1974, kept in "truck desk" of Zeigler's pickup.

7. .38 Smith & Wesson six-shot revolver—found in Curtis Dunaway's Oldsmobile, six live rounds in chamber; no bullets or empty cartridges recovered; bought by Zeigler, October 31, 1974, kept near file cabinet of store counter.

8. .22 Beretta automatic—found in Zeigler's desk drawer, no bullets or empty cartridges; owned by Zeigler and kept in desk.

Several wounds to Mr. Edwards and Charlie Mays were "through-and-through" shots and could not be traced to any one gun. Also, several bullets exited the exterior walls and were never recovered. The Securities revolver and the two RG revolvers apparently were the chief instruments of mayhem. The Securities .38 fired the close-range shots that killed Mr. and Mrs. Edwards. The shot that stopped the clock and the orange grove bullet were generically traced to this weapon, from which at least nine shots were fired. The shot that killed Eunice Zeigler probably was fired by one of the two RG revolvers. Five other lead bullets recovered around the store were traced to the RG pistols. There is no evidence that the Smith & Wesson .38 or the Beretta automatic was fired.

FIFTEEN

THROUGH MOST OF THE DAY ON MARCH 25 AND PART OF THE FOLLOW-
ing day, Eagan brought forth a series of witnesses, thirteen in all,
who laid out the state's evidence against Tommy Zeigler.

Many of these witnesses had appeared at the preliminary
hearing in January. In particular, Felton Thomas and Edward
Williams would be telling their stories under oath for the second
time. This day, though, they would face no hostile cross-
examination. Grand jury hearings are closed to all but the prosecutor, the witnesses, a court reporter, and the jurors themselves. The
atmosphere is usually informal. Jurors sometimes interject questions and observations, and there is no judge or defense attorney
to insist on rules of evidence.[1] In essence a grand jury hearing is a
sales pitch, and jurors are the prospective buyers. They may be
skeptical, but a good prosecutor, like a good salesman, knows how
to overcome resistance.

The privilege of prosecuting Orange County's most celebrated
murder case belonged to Robert Eagan by right as well as rank. He
was smart, tough, and compelling. He grasped the subtleties of
argument. He also possessed a certain physical presence: he was
tall and substantial, and he moved with a slightly shambling grace.
His deep voice had a gravelly timbre. He projected command and
authority. There would be no mutinies on any of Bob Eagan's
grand juries.

Eagan established the crime and the scene with his first witness. The associate medical examiner, Dr. Guillermo Ruiz, de-

---

1. However, defense attorneys may later seek to have grand jury testimony suppressed
from later hearings.

scribed the store layout and showed photo slides of the bodies from the store and at the morgue.

Russell Courtney, an agent of the Life and Casualty Company of Tennessee, testified that Tommy Zeigler had a four-year-old term policy on his own life, in the amount of $200,000. Courtney said that on September 9, 1975, Zeigler applied for $250,000 of term life insurance on his wife. Courtney said that he spoke to Eunice and that she was aware of the application. The policy cost about $600 a year, to be paid monthly through an automatic bank withdrawal, and Tommy Zeigler was the beneficiary.

George Henry, an agent of Gulf Life, told the jury that Eunice was present when Tommy applied for a $250,000 term policy on her life. The date was September 11, and Zeigler did not tell him of any other policy on Eunice. But Gulf Life did discover Life and Casualty's policy on Eunice, and issued its policy only after Tommy Zeigler agreed to bring his own insurance up to the level of his wife's. At that point, Henry said, Zeigler bought a $250,000 policy on his own life.

Don Ficke testified that he and his wife stopped by 75 Temple Grove Drive three times. The first time, a little after 8:05, they saw only one vehicle: Tommy Zeigler's pickup truck, parked near the garage in the left side of the driveway. On their second trip, a few minutes later, Ficke saw Edward Williams in his truck, parked behind Zeigler's. The third time, Williams's truck was gone. Zeigler's truck was still in the driveway, and Curtis Dunaway's Oldsmobile now was parked in the closed garage. He said that early in December he had loaned Zeigler the .22 automatic pistol that was found near Charlie Mays. He said that Zeigler admired the gun, but that that model was no longer being manufactured.

A juror wanted to know whether Zeigler had asked for Ficke's help since the incident. Ficke said that he had not, and that he himself avoided any contact with Zeigler. Apparently the crime had ended their friendship.

Robert Thompson testified about finding Zeigler at the store and bringing him to the hospital. He repeated his questioning of Zeigler in the emergency room, how Zeigler had told him of shooting Charlie Mays. He described finding the first three bodies in the store after he left Zeigler at the hospital.

JUROR: When you examined Tommy Zeigler at the hospital as to his wounds, was there any indication of any powder burns or anything on his clothes?

THOMPSON: Yes, sir. The point of entry of the projectile where it went through the front of his shirt, there is a large hole burned in the shirt just about that big [indicating]. It was black and burned around the edges. The entrance wound itself had no blood coming from it at all. It was also burned. The blood in the back was dried on his body. In fact, I had a white shirt on the night that I put him on my shoulder, and that white shirt had very little blood on the shoulder and just a little bit on my left cuff. It was not bleeding.

JUROR: You indicated that that shot came from a very close range.

THOMPSON: Yes, sir. It is my opinion that it was extremely close, yes, sir.

Thompson said that on the day before Christmas Eve, a Winter Garden police dispatcher told him over the police radio that Zeigler wanted to see him. A few minutes later, Zeigler arrived at Thompson's office with a small box of candy for Thompson's children. Then Zeigler invited him to the Van Deventers' party.

THOMPSON: I said, I don't know anything about it. I wasn't invited. He said, well, I want you to be there. I will have Mary, who is Mrs. Van Deventer, call you in the morning and invite you. So, I said, okay . . . I said if nothing was happening, I might try to get over for a few minutes. . . . The next morning, Mrs. Van Deventer did call and invite me there. I told her the same thing, that if circumstances allowed, then, I would try to ease in for a few minutes.

A juror wanted to know more about Zeigler and the party.

JUROR: Chief Thompson, I understand that this is a party that is given every year by Attorney Van Deventer for the police of West Orange County. Why was Mr. Zeigler so wrapped up in it? Was he a policeman?

THOMPSON: I don't know. I have no idea. . . . This is just hearsay, but they say he [Van Deventer] used to have a Christmas Eve open house. I have never been to one. . . .

JUROR: I still don't understand Mr. Zeigler's connection if he is not a policeman.

THOMPSON: I don't know.

Thomas Hale told of seeing Zeigler with Eunice just after 7:00
P.M. on Christmas Eve, making a left turn from Route 50 onto
Dillard Street. He said Zeigler was driving "a light-colored big
Oldsmobile."

Curtis Dunaway testified about seeing Zeigler together with
the Mays family, in the store the morning of the 24th. Dunaway did
not know what took place between Zeigler and Charlie Mays. He
related closing the store that evening, changing cars with Tommy
Zeigler, and later being summoned to the store to identify the
bodies. Bob Eagan's questioning was brisk and pointed:

Q (*EAGAN*): Mr. Dunaway, had you injured yourself in any way or
bled in the area of your neck or the back of your head?
A (*DUNAWAY*): No, sir.
Q: Do you have any account for the bloodstain that was found on
the headrest of your automobile by the law enforcement of-
ficers?
A: No, sir, I do not.
Q: The last you were in your automobile that day was when you
left it there at the Zeigler residence?
A: Yes, sir.
Q: Do you have any explanation, or can you give us any reason
why the law enforcement officers found blood on a tissue in
the backseat of your automobile?
A: No, sir, I cannot.

Felton Thomas repeated the story he had told at the preliminary hearing. Edward Williams followed him to the stand and was
mostly consistent with his first testimony, although this time, in
describing the scene in the back parking lot, he added that Zeigler
got down on his knees to beg him to come into the store.

WILLIAMS: . . . I was moving around the fence so maybe I could
jump the fence. I was scared, you know, he kept trying to pull
me and hug me so much. I keep pushing him off. In the
southwest corner of the fence, there is a big box there. So, I
made towards there. I thought maybe I could get over the
fence. When I got over to the boxcar, the lights were shining
bright from Winter Garden [Inn] there. He come over standing by the box, and he kneeled down on one knee, pleading for
me to go in. I saw the blood on his face, spots of blood.

Q: He got on his knees?

A: That is what he did. He say, Edward, for God's sake, come and go with me, please. I said I ain't going in there. You try to kill me, and I ain't going. . . .

Mattie Mays briefly told the jurors that her husband had agreed with Zeigler to buy a television on credit, at a price of $128, and that Zeigler had made a 7:30 appointment to meet Charlie at the store.

Near the end of her testimony, jurors asked a series of questions that referred to the money found in Mays's pockets.

Q (JUROR): Did Charlie go to the jai alai?

A (MRS. MAYS): Yes. He went the night before that.

Q: Did he win any money?

A: Yes, he did, because I was there with him.

Q: Did he win $400?

A: Yes, he won $420. That is how we did our Christmas shopping.

Q (EAGAN): Did Charlie own a gun?

A: He was scared of guns.

Q (JUROR): That night, did Charlie have any money in his pocket?

A: No, he didn't, because he didn't ask me for any.

With her testimony about the television, Mattie Mays provided the last important piece of the case against Zeigler. In a few hours Eagan had assembled it all: the insurance, the evidence of careful planning, and Zeigler's actions on the night of the murders as supplied by Felton Thomas and Edward Williams. But the mosaic could still be confusing. Eagan needed someone to correlate the different time lines and flesh out the case with details of the investigation.

Don Frye was Eagan's clinching witness. Eagan immediately asked him, "Can you wrap up these different time sequences for us and sort of show the events as they transpired?"

Frye answered with a long narrative that Eagan interrupted only briefly. It is still the most detailed explanation of the reasoning behind the prosecution of Tommy Zeigler.

Frye told the jurors that Tommy Zeigler had been planning the crime since the previous June: "So, this was thought out pretty well." He said that Zeigler talked his wife and her parents into going to the store on Christmas Eve. He used the Van Deventers' party to ensure that at 7:10 he "would have all the policemen isolated at one location, and nobody would be patrolling the streets of Winter Garden; that he could have free access from his house to the store without being observed by somebody that would recognize him later."

He led the jurors through his blood-spatter observations and his reconstruction of the crime. He correlated Felton Thomas's visit to Temple Grove Drive with Williams's observation of the two passengers in Zeigler's car. He described the fatal assault on Mays, Zeigler's arrival back at 75 Temple Grove after having killed his fourth victim, and the attempt to kill Edward Williams.

He displayed photographs as he told of comparing Zeigler's shoes to the bloody footprints:

"When I recovered Zeigler's clothing, I took the shoes myself and did an overlay of the print that we had lifted. It matched. They matched Tommy Zeigler's shoe prints. There are other shoe prints of Tommy leading away from the body of Mr. Edwards. . . . This is another shoe print of the area where Mr. Edwards was struggling. . . . This photograph shows the shoe impression again. This was caused by a dripping of blood from Edwards and Mr. Zeigler could not get his balance and continued the assault. He stepped in it again. This is another heel print. We found these throughout that floor area all over the floor."

Zeigler, Frye said, had shot himself after the phone call to the Van Deventer home. The proof of this is that when Ted Van Deventer spoke to him, Zeigler was "calm and not shaken."

Frye continued:

"Ficke got on the phone and he [Zeigler] said, I've been shot. Get to the store. I have been shot. Now he was real excited. Like I said, when he talked to Van Deventer, he was very cool, calm, and collected.

"After the phone call was made, he walks around here [east side of counter]. Again, our blood didn't pan out right. We couldn't type it. There is a high-velocity blood splatter on the counter. . . . A bullet went through the wall and lodged into the closet of the office. He was standing there and held the gun to his side like this, it went off, and the bullet passed through his body and lodged in the closet. . . .

"Tommy Zeigler used to be a medic in the Reserves. He has studied the anatomy. He knew the one place in the body where he could shoot and be relatively safe but it would be nothing more than just a superficial injury. . . .

"He shoots himself toward the front of the store and walks

toward the front of the store, back south toward the front doors. At this point right here there was a coffee table. There was a straight-down droplet where he stopped. . . .

"What he did, he stopped at this little coffee table and threw the gun back to the back of the store. With none around him, that would make the story more believable; that somebody else shot him, and he got to the front door and he called the Van Deventer house, and two minutes away, here comes the police to save him."

Frye said that only through an oversight had Zeigler picked up an empty gun to shoot Edward Williams.

So far, testimony had not been dramatically different from that of the preliminary hearing: evidence that had left Judge Kaney unimpressed. But now Frye shifted direction. Most of what he said in the next few minutes had not yet been spoken under oath, and never was heard at trial.

"You probably wonder how this wonderful man would do this," Frye said. "He was a prominent businessman in Winter Garden. He is wealthy. Well, not wealthy but he is well off. . . . He was a meager man. His wife and his mother hated each other. They moved into the house right next door to his mother. It was here that Mrs. Zeigler, Sr., picked out every item of furniture and drapes. She picked out everything for them. Eunice never had a say-so in the entire thing.

"Mrs. Zeigler is a very dominant and overbearing mother. The father was a passive guy. He was overpowered by the mother. . . . Tommy was a child brought up by a dominant mother. I have talked to people in Winter Garden, friends and confidential informants, I can't reveal the names. I have got one that is real close to the family. They said that Tommy Zeigler is highly capable of this.

"This is the type of pattern of a man who is brought up by a passive father and a dominant mother. There are rumors going around that Tommy Zeigler is a homosexual. I haven't been able to prove or disprove that. You will note that each of these men are beaten, but none of the women are. Why is this so?

"Schools that I have been to say that this act can be interpreted as that of a homosexual, a man trying to be bisexual. During the time he committed the beatings, all inside him, he's saying, I'm a man. You see, I'm a man. I've got power. This can also be considered as retaliation of the mother, trying to break from the mother.

"This all shows a consistent pattern with his upbringing, the way he was brought up. He was vicious as a boy. One time, he cut the leg off a dog to play a joke.

"People in Winter Garden like my informant did not want to be recognized because they were afraid of repercussions. But, of the people I have talked with, other than the three or four immediately around Tommy who are staying by his side, everybody seems to think that he is highly capable of committing these killings. . . .

"There is another point where you have a man of this caliber. As you people know, there are some who are sorry for what they did and admit to wrongdoing. When they get caught, they say, I'm sorry for it. You feel somewhat compassion for them. But, in Tommy Zeigler's case, he would not admit to it, and he probably never will. This is the kind of man that is a real threat to society, because he will do it again. He has no soul, no conscience and no remorse whatsoever. Neither does his mother. . . .

"There is one occasion when Tommy and his father were out in the lake, and Tommy was trying to drown him. The mother was standing on the shore looking. Some person came by and said what are you doing. Tommy said, we are playing, and they laughed it off. . . .

"Tommy was kind of a miser. He didn't allow Eunice to run the air conditioner in the summertime, as hot as it was in the house. He wanted to save the money. He drove an old 1968 Oldsmobile.

"Okay. Last year, Tommy goes out and buys an $8,000 vehicle. In November or December, he had a $13,000 swimming pool put in his yard. We find that he had credit-life insurance on himself and upon the death of his wife. These items are now paid off, and he doesn't owe a damn dime, not a dime."

Frye now discussed a loan for $866 which Edward Williams received by refinancing his vehicles. According to Frye, Zeigler took the check and cashed it, and never gave Williams the money. This launched the last important element of the state's case, the racial subtext that became a palpable part of the trial, though it was rarely explicit.

"Charlie Mays and Edward Williams were two nice guys," Frye said. "Charlie Mays was one of the leaders of the community in Oakland. He was the leader of a girls' softball team. He was a very likable person. Anytime anyone wanted to go somewhere, he would always take them.

"Edward Williams is the same way. Edward Williams and

Charlie Mays are what you might call a yes-man to Tommy Zeigler. They were black and he was white. He was dominant in their minds, apparently. Anything he said or he told them to do, they would do it.

"Why he tried to utilize these two men, he knew that they would be where he told them to be at a certain time. At 7:30, he had one at the store to kill, and back at the house was one to be killed. He knew Edward Williams would wait there for him."

Eagan had two more witnesses, both experts whom the defense had retained.

Dr. Theodore Mackler was a psychiatrist who had conducted a session with Zeigler on March 11. Mackler had administered a dose of the drug Brevital Sodium, a derivative of sodium pentothal, in an attempt to overcome his apparent amnesia about the events at the store.

Eagan allowed Mackler to show a videotape of the session, in which Zeigler, seemingly at the edge of consciousness, gave a halting account that was a slightly more detailed version of his sketchy original story.

Dr. John Feegel was the chief medical examiner of Hillsborough County, which included the city of Tampa. Feegel had examined Zeigler's gunshot wound.

FEEGEL: My opinion, it is very unlikely to be a self-inflicted deceptive wound. . . . As a clever dodge, to inflict a wound to look like you have been shot by someone else, it is a highly unlikely area that one chooses to shoot himself.
EAGAN: What do you base that opinion on, sir?
FEEGEL: First of all, on the basis of having seen other self-inflicted wounds, both suicidal and accidental, and the likelihood of using a weapon of this caliber in an abdominal shot with enough self-confidence, unfortunately, that nothing is going to go wrong with this angle of shot. Also your knowledge, working knowledge, of what is there. I can't think of a kidney surgeon that would dare shoot himself in that area. . . .

A juror questioned him on that point.

JUROR: Could a person with knowledge like I have take that gun against his body over his clothes and aim, knowing he is not going to hit any vital organs? Would he need just a little bit of knowledge?

FEEGEL: It would take very little knowledge, I would think. That is not the thing—I am not stupid enough to do it.

EAGAN: Or depraved enough to try it either.

Don Frye's testimony was the linchpin of what became a successful presentation. Around midday of the 26th, after listening to witnesses for a day and a half, the grand jury voted two indictments against Zeigler: for first-degree murder in the killings of Perry and Virginia Edwards, and for first-degree murder in the killings of Charlie Mays and Eunice. His bail was revoked, and he surrendered at the county jail that afternoon.

Supporters of the grand jury system see it as an essential safeguard of the rights of the accused, a valuable check on the power of the state. To its detractors, the grand jury is a near-pointless exercise, the prosecutor's rubber stamp of approval: not merely futile, but dangerous, too, because in the public mind an indictment, however obtained, often ends the presumption of innocence.

ZEIGLER ENTERS JAIL, INDICTED IN 4 MURDERS was the headline in the *Sentinel Star*, and the photo was of Tommy Zeigler at the jail's booking office, with his head bowed and his palms flat on the desk as he was being frisked.

SIXTEEN

CIRCUIT JUDGE MAURICE M. PAUL DENIED ZEIGLER'S REQUEST FOR BAIL. In the next several weeks he denied defense motions to suppress evidence taken from the store and 75 Temple Grove Drive. Paul ruled, in the first instance, that the police's right to a crime scene is a valid exception to Fourth Amendment protections. And he held that the permission that Zeigler signed on the morning of the 25th was a valid consent to search, in spite of the circumstances under which it was obtained.

With apparent great reluctance he granted the defense's motion for a change of venue. He denied a defense motion for a continuance. He denied two separate defense motions that he recuse himself—step down—from the case.

The trial was set to begin on Tuesday, June 6, at the Duval County Courthouse in Jacksonville.

Don Frye now was on temporary assignment to the office of the state attorney. During the weeks before the trial he spent at least part of his time attempting to corroborate the rumors he had heard in Winter Garden and had repeated before the grand jury.

On June 2, he tape-recorded an interview with a Winter Garden woman named Cheryl Clafler,[1] whom he described on the tape as "a close friend of the ex–Eunice Zeigler." The following is excerpted from the defense's transcription of the recording.

Q (*FRYE*): Is it okay if I call you Cheryl? You can call me Don. If you would, I know we talked briefly just a minute ago, but if you would just start all over with the tape. Just explain to me, you said you met her about a year ago.

A (*CLAFLER*): About a year ago we started talking and we met a couple of times like that and then we got, you know, friendly. And one day I walked in and she says, "Cheryl I've got to talk to you" and we got in the car and we went to Ronnie's, you know, Drive-In.

Q: That's in Winter Garden?

A: Yeah. On Dillard Street. She got to talking and well, I don't know, she was just tense and everything. She just let it all out. And that's when she told me that she had come in early one day and told me that she had found her husband in bed with a man and I'm not sure but I think it was [X][2] . . . And then she got to talking and she told me what all she had seen, you know. She—

Q: Let's go into—I know it's hard for you to recall but if you would, kind of go into detail with it. Everything that she told you.

A: Well, she said that they were in bed. Both of them was nude

1. A pseudonym.
2. A prominent local figure.

and they were all lovey-dovey and she got sick to her stomach. And she had to rush out and she run out of the house and she went back down to the store and a—she wanted to call me but I didn't give her my phone number so she couldn't call me because she didn't know where I lived. So she stayed in the store and in a few minutes he come on down. Then she left.

Q: Did she say whether or not he said anything to her when he first came in?

A: Yeah. He told her to keep her mouth shut or else. . . . She says, "Cheryl," she says, "he's in love with him." I says, "He's what?" You know, I've heard about it but I've never really known anybody that was that way. She was crying and I said, "Eunice," I said, "what are you going to do?" She said, "I don't know, he just threatened, he said, he told me, if I didn't keep my mouth shut that I knew what I was going to get." So I said, I said, "Have you told your mother?" She said, "I called Momma a few minutes ago," and she said, "they're supposed to come down." . . . So when he take the insurance out on her—she—about two weeks after—he had taken the insurance out on her she come—then she called me. And she says, "Cheryl I need somebody to talk to again." I said, "All right, I'll be there in a few minutes." So we met at Ronnie's again. And that's when she told me he had taken out all that insurance on her. . . .

So she says, "Now I am scared." She said, "But Momma said they'd be down Christmas Eve to pick me up—said then I'll have everything straightened out where I can leave." I said, "What you gonna straighten around?" She said, "Some things I got to take care of before I can leave," and the next thing I heard she was—she was killed.

Q: Okay. What about the a—you knew now for a fact that [X] and Tommy were homosexuals. What about [Y]?[3] Did she ever have anything other than just her own suspicions about him also?

A: All she had was just suspicions about him because, you know, he was buddy-buddy with them, too. And she said he acted like [X] did towards Tommy, but she had never caught [Y] with him like she did [X]. It just tore her up.

---

3. Another well-known Orange County man who was known to associate with Zeigler.

Q: I imagine it did.

A: She—she was a sweet girl.

Q: Yeah. The investigation we've done, of course, we've found out from everybody we've talked to that she was just an outstanding, really likable, lovable person.

A: She was a lovable person. . . .

Q: . . . Did she ever mention—I know they were going to adopt a baby one time.

A: No, she didn't mention that.

Q: Did she ever talk to you about wanting children?

A: Yes. She did. Very bad.

Q: Well, did she ever say anything about Tommy—as to why?

A: No, all she said was that every time she'd bring up the subject he'd pitch a fit so she said she just quit, quit even mentioning it.

Q: About having a baby or sex?

A: Well, she said that he'd have sex with her once in a while. But it weren't like it should be, you know. But, as far as having a baby, that was out of the question as far as Tommy was concerned.

Q: What about—I understand that—another rumor was that he wouldn't even allow her to run air conditioning in the summer and things like this. Did she ever talk to you about how tight he was with his money or anything like that?

A: He'd never give her no money at all. . . .

Q: . . . So all in all we have that she comes to you and she's concerned about—after she caught [X] and Tommy in bed together—

A: She was concerned about her life.

Q: . . . When—did she elaborate on when Tommy told her he was in love with [X]—what did she say exactly about that?

A: Well, she just, a—he never told her directly, you know, just on the phone. She answered the phone that afternoon and it was [X] and a—she heard Tom say, "Of course I love you, I don't give a damn who knows," you know. So that's how she found out it was an affair, you know—

Q: Makes you sick, doesn't it?

A: You better believe it makes you sick.

Q: So then she—after she finds this out and Tommy warns her, threatens her, and he starts taking out the insurance and then she calls her momma and arranges for them to take her back

Christmas—I asked you before—did she relate to you that Tommy knew her parents were going to take her back?

A: Yeah. She said that she was calling her mother. I guess it was a week before Christmas, you know, and she was writing down the dates and everything and this time of where to meet her mother and all that, and Tom come in and he overheard her talking on the phone and she, he made her give her the address and everything and the time that her mother was coming. . . . She was supposed to meet her uptown somewhere.

Q: So it was arranged where the parents weren't even going to come to the house?

A: Right, right. And she was—well, he tore the paper up. . . .

Q: . . . So apparently what she was doing was just biding her time until Christmas when she could leave him.

A: Yeah. That's all she was doing. Just making things rock on until she could get off.

Q: Did she ever come right out and tell you—I forgot what we were talking about before—about she had to get away before he kills her, or something like that?

A: Well, she made that statement, she said because—

Q: What did she say exactly—her exact words?

A: Well, she said a—that was the last time I saw her before I heard she got killed. She said that she had to get away because her life was in danger. I said, "Well why is your life in danger?" And she said, "Because," she said, "because he's already threatened to kill me." She said, "He's taken out the insurance on me," she said, "and that's proof that he does mean it." . . . She says, "Since I've found him," she says, "he's told me over and over and over if I said anything he would kill me. . . ."

II

THE
DEFENSE

SEVENTEEN

"I WAS A NINCOMPOOP," TOMMY ZEIGLER SAID IN JUNE 1991. HE WAS describing himself at age thirty. "Right's right, wrong's wrong, there's nothing in between. That's how I was raised. You never questioned authority. The people in authority were always right. They always played by the rules. The law was there to protect you."

And sixteen years later?

"I don't know which end is up anymore."

EIGHTEEN

TERRY HADLEY HEARD ABOUT THE CRIME FROM TED VAN DEVENTER, who called him at home on Christmas morning. Van Deventer stayed on the line while Hadley scanned the article in the *Sentinel Star*.

"Would you come out and talk to Tommy?" Van Deventer said. "The word is out that he's the prime suspect."

Hadley lived north of Orlando. His route to Orange Memorial took him past the furniture store, where the sheriff's vehicles out front gave some hint of the tragedy that had played out there the evening before.

Earlier that year, Hadley had become well acquainted with Zeigler. Hadley was defending a fifty-four-year-old black man named Andrew James against charges of selling marijuana to an undercover agent of the state Beverage Department. James was a friend of Zeigler's. He was also the only black man in West Orange to hold a full liquor license. Since the incident was alleged to have taken place at his bar in Winter Garden, James was in jeopardy of losing his license and a very profitable business.

He originally retained Ted Van Deventer, and pled guilty to the charge. But James apparently had misgivings. Zeigler referred James to Hadley, and Hadley withdrew the plea.

Zeigler remained actively involved with the case as Hadley prepared for trial. He told Hadley that James was getting a raw deal. Florida's liquor licenses were allotted on a strict quota system and usually were available only by private sale. Very rarely, though, the state Beverage Department resold licenses that it had revoked. Zeigler told Hadley that James had been set up for forfeiture because he had refused to sell his license to certain powerful white interests in West Orange.

According to Zeigler, that group included a local businessman whom Zeigler believed to be the operator of a large loan-sharking organization in West Orange's black communities and labor camps. Zeigler said that some elements of the local police in West Orange were connected with the operation, working as collectors and enforcers; he claimed that he had seen policemen assault debtors for having failed to make their payments.

Zeigler also said that the loan sharks were aware of his own interest in their operation. He said that a certain Winter Garden patrolman had threatened his life during a routine traffic stop.

Hadley found none of this difficult to believe. He knew West Orange, and he had heard of the loan sharks.

As Hadley understood the operation, migrant fruit pickers often wished to be paid at the end of every day they worked in the fields, and labor contractors paid only weekly. But a worker could receive daily wages through his crew boss, who paid him with cash supplied by the illegal lenders. On Friday afternoon, a worker would receive his paycheck from the crew boss outside small rural groceries—so-called "country stores"—owned by the loan sharks, who cashed the checks and retained the amount they were owed, plus 10 percent interest for the week. A crew boss would receive a portion of the interest that each of his workers paid. The scheme potentially involved many hundreds of migrant workers, each of whom might earn $40 to $50 a day, or more, at the peak of the season.

Zeigler said that the loan sharks coveted James's liquor license. Since the group already controlled most of the "country stores," which sold beer and wine, James's license would mean a virtual monopoly on sales of alcohol in the black areas of Winter Garden and Oakland.

Zeigler said that the same group had attempted to force James out of business in 1974 by enforcing codes against the ramshackle old structure where James owned the tavern known as Brown's Bar. Zeigler and his father had persuaded Winter Garden's pastors—in particular Fay De Sha, the influential minister of the First Baptist Church—to agree to a temporary relaxation of zoning laws so that James could rebuild.

Zeigler vouched for James's character and helped Hadley to organize a defense based on the theory that James was being framed. As Hadley recalled it in 1991, that defense would have been impossible without Zeigler.

What was in this for Zeigler? Nothing, as far as Hadley could tell. Zeigler seemed genuinely affronted that criminal methods were being used to deprive an honest man of his livelihood.

Zeigler said he knew that Andrew James was innocent, for he had visited James in the bar many times. Hadley thought this was remarkable: Brown's Bar was in a black neighborhood and had a black clientele. It was a place where few whites ever ventured without a compelling reason.

Hadley soon discovered that Zeigler moved through West Orange's black communities with ease and confidence, unlike any other white man Hadley had ever known. He did not seem to be an interloper. At one point, Hadley wanted to interview a black ex-convict who was wary of white authority. Andrew James could not persuade the man to speak to Hadley. But Tommy Zeigler did.

Hadley was also impressed by the friendship between James and Zeigler. James respected Zeigler, but did not automatically defer to him. Zeigler did not condescend to James. Tommy Zeigler's political ideas were reflexively conservative, but Hadley found him open and equal in his personal dealings with black people.

Andrew James's case went to trial. Hadley knew that if he was to have a chance of acquittal, he would have to attack the credibility of the beverage agent, a man named Herbert G. Baker. As Hadley remembered it in 1991, his impeachment of Baker's testimony forced the prosecution to call unscheduled rebuttal witnesses who would testify to Baker's integrity. One of those witnesses was a former attorney for the Beverage Department, who now was a circuit court judge and who had signed the original search warrant in Baker's investigation of Andrew James.

For a sitting judge to testify as a character witness was virtually unheard-of. Hadley found himself in a position few trial attorneys ever know, and none would envy: his responsibility to his client was forcing him to cross-examine a judge in whose court he had several active cases.

The judge was Maurice M. Paul, who in less than a year would preside at the murder trial of Tommy Zeigler.

James was found guilty and given probation, but the sentence was not adjudicated; technically, James was not convicted. Later Zeigler testified at a Beverage Department hearing that found that the evidence against James was insufficient to merit revocation.

The prosecution of James provoked anger in West Orange's black communities. Baker's house was burned, he became the subject of an inquiry by the NAACP, and he left his job.[1] Andrew James kept his license, and he probably had Tommy Zeigler to thank for it.

On Christmas morning, Hadley arrived at Orange Memorial around 11:00. Zeigler was groggy and somewhat disoriented. He had not yet been told that Eunice was dead. Twice he asked for her while Hadley spoke to him; he wanted to know why she hadn't been in to visit him.

Hadley, as he had been instructed, told Zeigler that he didn't know where Eunice was.

Zeigler was able to answer questions. In broken fashion, he told essentially the same story he would tell on the witness stand six months later: that he had last seen his wife when she went to

---

1. In 1984, Baker testified at a hearing that stemmed from one of Zeigler's appeal issues. He said he believed that Hadley had put him (Baker) on trial during those proceedings. "I think I was investigated by about every agency in central Florida over it. . . . [S]omebody brought the NAACP. . . . My house was set on fire once during this time. My kids were threatened in school. My wife wound up having to go to a psychologist over it." Baker also said that he believed that Zeigler had lied during the James trial.

the furniture store with her parents around 7:00 P.M. on Christmas Eve, that a few minutes later he had ridden to the store with Edward Williams to pick up some gifts, that he had been hit in the head and knocked down as he entered the dark showroom, that he had tried to shoot at one or more of the assailants and then had been shot.

The next day Hadley was in his office on Dillard Street when he took a call from the hospital. One of the sheriff's detectives was at ICU, asking to speak to Zeigler or to Zeigler's attorney.

Hadley went to the hospital and met Don Frye. Frye wanted permission to interview Zeigler. Frye told Hadley that he was sure that Zeigler had committed the murders. As Hadley remembers the conversation, Frye's words were: "Give me half an hour with him, I'll have a confession."

Hadley refused. He wondered whether Frye could actually be so naive: no attorney would allow his client to be questioned by a policeman bent on extracting a confession.

Later that day Hadley walked through the store with Frye and Lawson Lamar, the assistant state attorney. Hadley found the scene dreadful. *The blood,* he thought, *so much blood.*

Frye showed Hadley the evidence that he regarded as proof of Zeigler's guilt. Hadley thought the evidence was unconvincing, and he didn't believe that Zeigler was capable of such violence. He also remembered that Zeigler had told him, months before, of having been threatened because of his involvement with the West Orange loan sharks.

To Hadley, Frye seemed young and earnest and much too taken with his own deductions. He was like a crusader on a white horse, Hadley thought, going out to do battle with evil. And to Frye, Tommy Zeigler was evil.

Hadley didn't understand how Frye could be so certain. As yet the police had no test results. Many shots had been fired, but Frye could not yet know which guns had fired them. Much blood had been spilled, but Frye could not show whose blood had made any particular stain. No fingerprints had been studied. Even the footprints were of little value until experts analyzed them.

Frye did have the statements of Edward Williams and Felton Thomas. On the basis of their stories, Zeigler should be a suspect. But Hadley thought that Frye had gone much farther than that: Frye already seemed to have closed his mind to any possibility except Tommy Zeigler's guilt.

That afternoon Zeigler and his family formally asked Hadley

to represent him, and Hadley agreed. He knew that he had a fight ahead. The crime deserved a thoughtful, unprejudiced police investigation; but after listening to Frye, Hadley feared that a stampede to judgment was already under way.

NINETEEN

BETWEEN CHRISTMAS AND NEW YEAR'S DAY, HADLEY BEGAN TO ORGA-nize Zeigler's defense.[1] He hired private investigator Gene Annan, who had twelve years' experience as a special agent with the Air Force's Office of Special Investigations. William "Pete" Ragsdale, who had recently resigned as director of the Sanford Regional Crime Laboratories, hired on as the defense's forensics specialist.

Hadley also asked Vernon Davids, one of his two law partners, to join him on the case. Davids practiced mostly civil law, but he was a quick study and he had a mind for details. Davids began reading textbooks of forensic science. Later Hadley hired several other investigators. And his legal secretary, Leslie Gift, soon was working full-time on the defense team. It was a large, expensive effort. Zeigler's parents had the means to defend their son, which put him in a class beyond most defendants in important criminal cases.

At first the defense knew almost nothing about the case except what Hadley had seen at the store and had heard from Frye. Hadley offered Eagan an agreement for "mutual discovery" that would obligate both sides to reveal any relevant evidence. Under the disclosure agreement, Hadley would be legally and ethically bound to turn over any unfavorable information. In return, though,

---

1. Until he was arrested, Zeigler was technically considered a suspect. After December 29, he became officially identified as a defendant.

he would learn exactly what evidence the state had against his client.

Eagan refused the offer.

Zeigler, in a second interview with Hadley, supplied some details. He said that his home had been burglarized in 1974, and he had lost several guns. To replace them, he had bought three pistols: the Securities .38, the Smith & Wesson .38 (found in the Dunaway Olds), and the Colt .357. All three were purchased in October 1974 at Ray's Bait and Tackle, a local gun shop. The Colt and the Smith & Wesson were kept in the store, one in a desk in the rear hallway, the other near the front counter. He said that he had last seen the chrome-plated Securities Industries pistol and his shoulder holster in the truck desk, around December 11. The passenger door of the truck did not lock: anyone could have taken the gun.

Zeigler told Hadley what he remembered of the assault at the back of the showroom. He had struggled with at least two assailants, but in the darkness, and having lost his glasses at the beginning of the fight, he couldn't identify them. His memory of the fight was hazy. He had perhaps fired the .22 automatic that he carried with him; he could remember ejecting a jammed cartridge from the little pistol. After he was thrown into the hallway, he managed to pull the Colt revolver from the drawer there. He might have fired it, maybe several times, but he didn't know whether he had hit anyone.

After he was shot, and passed out, he woke up on the terrazzo floor. He crawled around in the darkness, trying to find his glasses. Eventually he got his spare pair from the desk in his office. He remembered Bobby Thompson bringing him to the hospital, but he could not recall Thompson questioning him in the examining room. He did not remember mentioning Mays's name to Thompson, and could not explain how Thompson learned that Mays was in the store.

Above all, except for having fired in self-defense, he knew nothing of the four deaths in the store.

Police obviously knew more. Before New Year's Day, the accounts given by Edward Williams and Felton Thomas began to surface, piecemeal, in rumors. Hadley assigned his investigators to learn everything they could about the crimes.

There were gaps in even the basic outline of what had happened in the store. The defense learned details of the wounds inflicted on Eunice and her parents only when Annan spoke to an attendant at the mortuary that had prepared the bodies. The funeral home where Charlie Mays had been taken was less helpful.

Defense investigators tried without success to locate Edward Williams and Felton Thomas, in hopes of interviewing them. They also searched for a "Robert Foster" whom Don Frye's original arrest report listed as a witness. An article in the *Sentinel Star* of December 31 prominently mentioned the name.

One report was that "Foster" had followed Charlie Mays into the store and had run away after seeing the body of a white woman inside. After many black residents of Oakland and Winter Garden denied knowing anyone by that name, Gene Annan finally found a witness who claimed to know Robert Foster.

Mary Wallace, manager of the apartment complex where Edward Williams moved on the 24th, said that her husband and Mays played on the same local baseball team; Robert Foster, she said, was an acquaintance of Mays's who umpired some of the games. She described him as "a big black man" about six feet two, weighing 250 pounds.

One eyewitness, an elderly man named Ed Nolan, testified that a man fitting that general description was with Mattie Mays outside the furniture store in the early hours of Christmas morning when a plainclothes sheriff's officer informed her that her husband was dead. Nolan, whose testimony would become significant in another regard, remembered that Mrs. Mays cried, "Lord have mercy," and collapsed in the officer's arms.

Nolan said that the plainclothes officer walked Mrs. Mays out from the police lines and spoke to a man whom Nolan described as "tall" and "stout-built." This man said that he was a friend of the family, and the officer advised him to take Mrs. Mays to the hospital. Nolan said that the man's name was "Robert somebody."

But Hadley's investigators found no other evidence that such a man actually existed. In April, Don Frye told Hadley that a clerk had inadvertently typed "Robert Foster" for "Thomas Felton" in preparing the arrest report, and that he had signed it without catching the mistake. It was, he said, "a typographical error."

The defense chased other mirages.

On Christmas Eve, the Winter Garden police dispatcher had received an anonymous tip: "If you want to know what happened at the furniture store, talk to Oday Jackson." Investigators identified a man by that name in Orlando but could never locate him.

And shortly after Tommy Zeigler was arrested at the hospital, his parents received a call from a man who claimed to have information about the crime. The Zeiglers put him in touch with the law office, and Vernon Davids met him at the Zeigler home.

His name was Nathaniel Brown. He was black and in his early twenties. He told Davids that a white man had planned the crime, and that Mays was one of three accomplices. The other two were black men, named Don and Jerry. Brown described them both and said that the white man had paid them $1,000 each. They had wiped the weapons clean before they left.

According to Nathaniel Brown, Jerry was shot during the crime, and was now hiding near Oakland with a bullet wound in his right shoulder.

Tommy Zeigler was innocent, Brown said, the victim of a setup; the victims were already dead when Zeigler entered the store.

Brown wanted a reward from the Zeiglers. Davids thought the story sounded like a con job, interesting but unsupported; the fact that all of the guns actually *had* been wiped clean would not be known for several weeks. Davids gave Brown's information to the state attorney's office. Later Frye reported to the defense that Brown's story was without substance, and that Brown was a petty criminal and a habitual liar.

Annan and Ragsdale continued trying to establish the facts of the case. Annan became convinced that he was being stonewalled by police and prosecutors. He felt that they deliberately misled him when he tried to find the citrus grove where Zeigler was said to have brought Mays and Thomas.

Still, most of the answers—or at least keys to the answers—were in the store itself, and the OCSO continued to control the crime scene. Pete Ragsdale warned Hadley that some of the distinguishing enzymes in human blood would not be detected in stains more than ten days old. A thorough sampling of the blood evidence in the store could provide a virtual diagram of who had bled, and where. It would show whether a sixth person had left blood at the scene. But any specimens would have to be collected and tested immediately if they were to be fully subgrouped.[2]

---

2. As late as 1960, only the tests for ABO blood grouping were considered reliable. By 1976, criminal labs using micro-methods could test for eight or more groups of enzymes, proteins,

Eventually the sheriff and prosecutor held the store for two weeks, and yielded it only after Professor MacDonell had completed his inspection. Sheriff's officers assured Hadley that the samples had been properly collected and would be subgrouped as far as possible.

On January 7, Gene Annan was allowed to follow MacDonell around the store while the professor examined the scene. Mac-Donell dictated notes into a tape recorder; Annan was struck by how closely MacDonell's observations paralleled Frye's theory of how the crimes had been committed.

After the sheriff relinquished the crime scene, Ragsdale and Vernon Davids immediately went to work, taking photographs and collecting evidence. By now, though, the dried blood had lost much of its value for identification. Some of the footprints were still visible, and the bullet holes still remained.[3] But the defense had to assume that most of the useful physical evidence was now in the custody of the sheriff or the FBI Lab.

After they were embalmed, the bodies of Perry and Virginia Edwards were shipped to Georgia. Beulah and Tom Zeigler attended their funerals on Sunday, December 28, at a Baptist church in the Edwardses' hometown of Moultrie.

Both Perry and Virginia, like their daughter, had been schoolteachers. They had touched many lives, and their friends and admirers filled the church.

Beulah thought the service was disappointing. In his eulogy, the minister didn't talk very much about what wonderful people the Edwardses had been or all that they had done. Instead, he kept condemning the murderer who had taken their lives.

---

and antigens in small samples of blood. The various combinations of these substances, varying from one sample to another, allowed investigators to differentiate among several persons who had bled at a crime scene, often even if their blood was mixed.

If a specimen was too small to allow testing of all these factors, forensic serologists still could subgroup the known blood (that is, the relatively copious specimens drawn from Zeigler and the four dead victims) to learn which two or three factors would differentiate the unknown specimens; then they could test the unknowns only for those critical factors. Assuming that the samples were properly collected and promptly tested, the odds of distinguishing among the five persons known to have bled in the furniture store amounted to a virtual certainty.

3. Several can still be seen in the store.

Some of the Edwardses' relatives, particularly their son, Perry junior, had been in contact with the Orange County authorities. At a reception following the service, one of Eunice's aunts told the Zeiglers that Tommy was about to be arrested.

On the 29th, Perry Edwards, Jr., and a deputy from Georgia came to Winter Garden and tried to claim Eunice's body from a funeral home. Tom and Beulah refused to relinquish the body. Eunice was Tommy's wife; he and his parents believed that she should be buried in the Zeigler family plot at a local cemetery.

That afternoon, Tommy Zeigler was arrested in his hospital bed at West Orange Memorial.

Eunice's funeral was on Wednesday, December 31, at the First Baptist Church in Winter Garden. Originally the family had planned a small, closed-casket service. But after Tommy's arrest, a closed casket seemed to imply shame or guilt. Beulah believed that they had nothing to be ashamed of, nothing to hide. And she was certain that Tommy was not guilty.

So the casket stayed open during the ceremony. Tommy Zeigler was not present. He was still hospitalized, in police custody.

The Zeiglers decided to postpone burial. On Wednesday, January 7—at the same time that Professor MacDonell examined the crime scene—sheriff's deputies escorted Tommy Zeigler to the funeral home to view the remains of the wife he was accused of killing.

She was buried the next day. Zeigler was not allowed to attend.

Months later, Beulah Zeigler realized that she had never properly mourned Eunice. It was not from neglect, she thought, and certainly not a lack of feeling. But so much else was happening. Every time she confronted the fact of Eunice's death, she also faced the reality that her son was accused as a murderer. It became a matter of priorities. Eunice was gone. Tommy was fighting for his life.

TWENTY

EVEN BEFORE HIS PRELIMINARY HEARING, ZEIGLER'S ATTORNEYS REAL-
ized that he had problems beyond the evidence.

One of these was the spate of rumors that spread throughout
West Orange after his arrest, small-town gossip gone amok. Terry
Hadley thought that some of it was predictable, even understand-
able. Nothing like this crime had ever happened in Winter Garden.
Moreover, Zeigler was not an ordinary citizen: he had money and
influence, and he had bruised some feelings with his political mach-
inations. He was a natural target for jealous chatter.

But one topic was especially obnoxious: the speculation that
Zeigler and several other important men in the county had formed
a secret homosexual ring. Maybe nobody hears a community's
whispers more clearly than its lawyers, but neither Hadley nor
Vernon Davids had ever encountered this rumor until after Zeigler
was arrested.

Davids was forty-one years old, at five feet ten a former all-
state high school basketball player: a tenacious, combative personality. He decided to trace the rumor by confronting someone who
he knew was spreading the information. As Davids recalled it later,
he said to the man: "It's my understanding that you think Tommy
Zeigler is a homosexual."

"Well, yes," the man said.

"Tell me," Davids asked, "how many blow jobs did you receive from him, and how many did you give?"

The man quickly said he had only *heard* that Zeigler was a
homosexual.

"Who told you?" Davids said, and when he got the name he
went to that person and followed the same routine. He pursued

this for several days, in nearly a dozen interviews. He found nobody who would admit to having direct knowledge of Zeigler's sexual preferences. He became convinced that the rumor got much of its momentum from sheriff's investigators who now were interviewing Zeigler's friends, acquaintances, and enemies. According to Davids, the usual line of questioning went like this: "How long have you known Tommy Zeigler? Did you know that he's a homosexual?"

Davids thought that if Don Frye was hearing rumors, it was probably the sound of his own voice coming back to him. Davids believed that the OCSO's original source of that information was Robert Thompson, the Oakland chief of police, who had mentioned it to Frye and others on the night of the murders.[1]

The chatter was not confined to Winter Garden and the OCSO. The defense attorneys began hearing it from friends and contacts within central Florida's legal community: that Zeigler mutilated dogs, that he had tried to kill his father, that he was a closet homosexual. These were the same unfounded rumors that eventually became the keystone of Don Frye's grand jury testimony. Hadley and Davids believed that sheriff's officers and members of the prosecution team were leaking the information. There would inevitably be intramural gossip about one of the biggest and most sensational criminal cases the state had ever seen, but this was especially direct and damaging. Even among those for whom the presumption of innocence is supposed to be a byword, Tommy Zeigler had been summarily convicted.

---

1. From Don Ficke's deposition of May 5, 1976:

Q (Hadley): Are you familiar with the rumors concerning the alleged homosexuality of Tommy Zeigler that have been circulating, both in the city of Winter Garden in general and in your department in particular?
A (Ficke): Yes sir, I am.
Q: Who started the rumors within the Winter Garden Police Department?
A: The night of the alleged motive of Mr. Thompson, we were discussing it and, I guess it was Officer Yawn was in the store; and I asked Thompson to get him out of there because if this was the motive, I didn't think it would be good to get it around. And I'm led to believe that Chief Thompson has told another officer in our department at our headquarters that night of alleged homosexuality. . . . Officer Barry Smith . . . He, in turn, told ten other people.
Q: Who else was present besides yourself and Don Frye when Chief Thompson related this possible motive?
A: I would say the entire investigative staff that was there. . . .

Even more troubling to Hadley and Davids was the outrage that the death of Charlie Mays provoked in local black neighborhoods. Defense investigators found themselves shut out when they tried to question blacks in Oakland and Winter Garden. One of Hadley's investigators got into a shoving match with Brian Nedd, the sixteen-year-old fruit picker who had gone shopping with Charlie and Mattie Mays on Christmas Eve.

Feelings ran hot. It wasn't just that a white man was accused of killing a black—that was no novelty. What set this incident apart was that Zeigler was said to have brought Mays to the store on the pretext of a kindness and killed him solely to cover up his own guilt.

This tapped a wellspring of racial mistrust and resentment. As most blacks saw it, Zeigler had not just slain one of their own, he had betrayed their trust and showed contempt for their judgment. Most troubling of all, they were ready to believe his guilt before a single piece of evidence had been introduced, before a single witness had testified: it simply rang true to what they knew about white attitudes. If even those who knew and liked him felt this strongly—and many did—then what would be the reaction of black jurors to whom W. Thomas Zeigler, Jr., was just another white man?

In addition to the criminal charges, Zeigler and his parents became involved in a series of civil actions stemming from the crimes.

On January 5, Mattie Mays sought an injunction to prevent the Zeiglers from spending any of the proceeds of the two insurance policies on Eunice. Shortly afterward, Mrs. Mays filed a $1 million wrongful-death suit against the Zeiglers. Attorney J. R. Hornsby, who represented Mrs. Mays and her children, said that the suit would stand regardless of the outcome of the murder charges: "We feel that Zeigler, as owner of the store, had a duty to protect his customers and we feel that the duty of care has been breached."

Tommy had already renounced the benefits from the two policies, in favor of his mother. The two insurance companies, Life and Casualty Company and Gulf Life, sued to void the policies. Beulah Zeigler later countersued the two companies.

The suits dragged on for years. Eventually, too, lenders foreclosed on the commercial real estate owned by the family corporation. Whoever committed the murders on Christmas Eve was responsible not only for four violent deaths, but for the slow strangulation of the financial structure that Tom and Beulah Zeigler, and their son and his wife, had worked so hard to build.

TWENTY-ONE

EVERY DAY FOR ALMOST TWO WEEKS, PETE RAGSDALE AND VERNON Davids examined the furniture store, floor to ceiling.

Gene Annan went looking for witnesses. According to the state's theory, as the defense came to understand it, more than an hour and a half had passed from the time Zeigler brought his wife to the store to the time he shot himself after Edward Williams's escape. During that time, Zeigler was supposed to have fired more than two dozen shots; left the store after the first three murders for some unknown reason, and then returned to meet Charlie Mays; attempted to break into the store; driven from the store to the orange grove and back; and made three trips between his house and the store.

Dillard was a major street. On Christmas Eve, the Tri-City shopping center was open until 9:00, and the Kentucky Fried Chicken restaurant served customers even later than that. Hundreds of people must have driven past the store while Zeigler was supposedly executing his plan.[1]

Moreover, the two-story back wing of the Winter Garden Inn directly overlooked the furniture store's rear compound, where Zeigler was supposed to have coaxed Mays over the fence and later begged Edward Williams to come back into the store.

---

1. Dillard Street is also a direct route to the First Baptist Church, which held its Christmas Eve service from about 7:30 to 8:30. Apparently neither prosecution nor defense ever canvassed the congregation to find out who had used Dillard to get to and from the church that night.

Besides Thomas Hale, the prosecution had statements from Barbara Spencer, who heard the shots while she sat in her parents' home nearby, and Barbara Woodard, who saw someone resembling Zeigler at the front of the store as she exited the shopping center on Christmas Eve. Surely dozens of others could contradict—or confirm—details of the state's theory and the statements by Williams and Felton Thomas.

In fact, four people close to Zeigler came forth with information.

Lee Jones had driven past the store at about 7:25, when Zeigler was supposed to have been killing Perry and Virginia Edwards inside. Jones was the bank executive who was in the hospital room on Christmas Day when Zeigler learned of Eunice's death. He said that the store was completely dark; he took notice, because the store was always lit at night.

Jones said that he saw two cars parked in front of the store. At this point, according to the state's theory, both the Edwardses' Ford and Curtis Dunaway's Oldsmobile should have been parked at the store. But Jones claimed that one of the two cars he saw was a dark automobile, a description that didn't fit the light green Ford or the two-tone Olds with its beige top.

Richard Smith, the physical therapist who had told Zeigler of Eunice's death, said that he and his wife, Patricia, had driven past the store at 7:57 on Christmas Eve. The Smiths were exact about the time, because they had been hurrying home to greet guests who were due at 8:00, and had glanced at a time-temperature display outside the First State Bank on Dillard.

Both Smiths said they noticed that all the lights were out in the store—they had never seen that before. Both noticed two cars parked side by side at the front of the store: a large sedan and a smaller car that was a very dark color, parked directly south of the larger one.

Richard Smith described the dark car as being about the size of a Camaro or Mustang, with a boxy design. His wife said that the smaller car was parked with its wheels up on the walkway in front of the store; she said it was black or deep blue, not as large as a full-sized sedan, with a squared-off rear window. This did not remotely describe either the Edwardses' Ford or the Dunaway Olds.

The Smiths took their information to Don Ficke on December

27.[2] Ficke sent them to Frye. On January 12, Frye and two assistant state attorneys questioned the Smiths under oath. Patricia Smith said that she knew Curtis Dunaway's Oldsmobile, and that it was not either of the cars that she saw in front of the store that night.

Frye pressed her:

Q *(FRYE):* But, the car you saw parked up on the curb, do you think it could have been Curtis Dunaway's car?
A *(PATRICIA SMITH):* No, sir.
Q: Think hard on it.
A: The car I saw was dark.
Q: I don't deny that. I'm not saying that.
A: It was not two-toned. It was a totally dark car.

The dark car popped up again. Edward Reeves, who lived across Temple Grove Street from the Zeiglers, said that he had left his house to buy some liquor at 8:00 on Christmas Eve. At that time, according to the state, Edward Williams should have been sitting in his truck, parked behind Tommy's pickup on the left side of the driveway. But Reeves told investigators that he did not see two trucks. He saw Tommy's pickup, with a dark automobile parked behind it. When he returned about forty minutes later the same car was still parked behind Zeigler's pickup.

Gene Annan visited most of the businesses around the intersection of Dillard and Route 50. He found a man named Donald Dugan, who on Christmas Eve had been at a service station on the corner of Dillard and Route 50. Dugan told Annan that at around 9:00 P.M., two black men drove up to put gas in a dark 1967 Mustang.

Both men seemed to be drunk. The driver was a young man, with a bushy Afro. The other was middle-aged, with short curly hair that was tinged with gray. This older man, speaking with what seemed to be a Caribbean accent, told Dugan: "You're in the wrong place, you should be at Zeigler's. They just had a killing, a shooting, and a robbery over there."

Apparently this occurred before the police arrived at the store.

---

2. Richard Smith had served in the same Reserve unit with Zeigler. He later told the defense that Zeigler had been only a clerk, and had received no specialized medical training.

Annan made several trips to the Kentucky Fried Chicken restaurant where Edward Williams had used the telephone on Christmas Eve. What Annan learned there suggested that Williams had come into the restaurant after 9:00 that night. Two waitresses and a seventeen-year-old employee named John Grimes had been on duty that night. Grimes was not exact about when Williams entered the restaurant, though he recalled that Williams was wearing a brown sweater. One of the waitresses believed that Williams appeared after 9:00 P.M. The second waitress, whose shift had ended at 9:00, said that she never saw Williams. Amy Crawford, a customer who had driven to the restaurant shortly before closing time, said that Williams had come in around 9:15 or 9:20.

On one of his visits to the restaurant, Annan met Ed Nolan, who lived in a trailer court across Route 50. Nolan was seventy-four years old and was dying of cancer. He visited the restaurant nearly every day, and on Christmas Eve he was in the store from 7:00 P.M. until after closing.

Nolan told Annan a startling story, which he repeated at a deposition in May. He said that after 9:00 P.M. on Christmas Eve, a black man came to the restaurant asking to use the telephone. Nolan got the impression that there had been an accident. The man was wearing a light brown sweater. He asked the telephone number of the police, and Nolan told him.

Then Nolan turned around and saw his brother, J.D., outside. J.D. and his wife, Madelyn, were driving south on Dillard when they were nearly broadsided by Jimmy Yawn as he rolled out onto Dillard from the Winter Garden Inn.

J. D. Nolan and his wife confirmed Ed Nolan's story. They told defense investigators that they were driving to her mother's house, headed south on Dillard, when they were nearly broadsided by a car peeling out of the service station at the corner of Dillard and Route 50. This was the unmarked Winter Garden police car driven by Jimmy Yawn, responding to Robert Thompson's original call at 9:21.

J. D. Nolan made a U-turn and parked near the furniture store to watch what was happening. After several minutes he noticed his brother, Ed, standing in the door of the restaurant. J.D. crossed Dillard Street, and the two brothers spoke. Then a middle-aged black man came up and asked to use the telephone inside the restaurant.

Madelyn Nolan corroborated the two brothers' account. She remembered seeing Thompson help Zeigler out of the store and into his patrol car. Minutes after that, she saw Williams at the restaurant.

Five witnesses now placed Edward Williams at the Kentucky Fried Chicken after 9:00 P.M. Three of those witnesses would swear that Williams appeared at the restaurant *after* the police arrived across the street, nearly as late as 9:30.

Gene Annan interviewed Thomas Hale, the young man who claimed to have seen Tommy and Eunice driving together near the furniture store around 7:10 on Christmas Eve.

As Annan described it later, he stood beside Hale at a counter where Hale worked, at the McCoy Jetport on the south side of Orlando. Annan carried a notebook with the photograph of an automobile clipped inside the front cover. They chatted for a few minutes, and Annan opened the notebook. This gave Hale a glimpse of the photograph.

Hale remarked at the photo: that was it, he said, that was the car Eunice and Tommy had been driving on Christmas Eve.

Annan asked him if he was sure. Hale said yes, he recognized the car from the style of the rear-wheel fender skirts. Annan suggested that Hale sign and date the back of the photograph, and Hale complied.

Hale was an acquaintance of the Zeiglers. The photo he signed was of the 1968 Oldsmobile that the Zeiglers had sold three months before the murders.[3]

3. Hale is the only witness who ever claimed to see Tommy and Eunice together immediately before the murders. His identification of the car was controversial, as was the method that Annan used to obtain it. Zeigler's 1968 Oldsmobile, which Hale identified in the photo, and Curtis Dunaway's 1972 Olds 98, which Zeigler was driving on Christmas Eve, shared the same basic body style. Hale said that the Zeiglers were riding in a "light car." Dunaway's two-door automobile was beige over a darker brown; Zeigler's four-door 1968 Olds was a special Holiday model with a brown vinyl top over a body of "Palomino gold." The style of its fender skirts was somewhat different from the '72 model. Annan testified that he did not bring Hale's attention to the photo, but that it was in view, and Hale pointed to it without prompting.

TWENTY-TWO

TOMMY ZEIGLER TELLS THIS STORY:

After his preliminary hearing, the afternoon of Friday, January 16, he was returned to his cell on the sixth floor of the Orange County Courthouse. He had just been granted bond of $40,000.

But Zeigler had already decided that he would stay in jail until Monday, when his parents could raise a cash bond. A bail bondsman could have him out in time for dinner. But the bail fee would be $4,000. That struck Zeigler as awfully expensive for a weekend of freedom.

The captain in charge of the jail had Zeigler's belongings in a box on a desk, ready to go. Zeigler told him to put the box away, that he would be staying for the weekend.

"What do you mean?" the captain said.

"I can wait," Zeigler said.

The captain turned to a guard.

"This son of a bitch is crazy," he said.

Zeigler was not crazy, and in a few months he would have a psychiatrist's testimony to prove it.[1]

But he was in many respects an unusual man, a personality of contradictions, not always easy to know or like. He could be brusque, he could be gracious. He was modest, he was full of himself. He was a rube, he was a canny businessman. He was the

---

1. In May 1976, Dr. Allen Zimmer conducted a four-day longitudinal psychiatric examination of Zeigler in the Orange County Jail, after which he found that Zeigler "is not a psychopath. My diagnosis was that he has no mental disorder."

embodiment of a nineteenth-century Southern cavalier and a pro-
totype of the 1980s want-it-all-want-it-now hyperachiever.

He was not inclined to self-doubt or deep reflection. He knew
his own way, and until Christmas Eve of 1975 he was that rare
lucky man who could afford to follow his own path generally without resistance or upset.

Now he was caught up in a system to which nobody dictated
terms. Criminal justice ground on regardless.

Between the preliminary hearing and the grand jury's indictment, he was free for nine weeks. It was an awkward period. He
lived with his parents: the house at 75 Temple Grove was empty
and too quiet. The store opened again after Beulah Zeigler and her
niece Connie Crawford scrubbed the blood from the floors and
rearranged the stock. But business was slow, and everyone agreed
that Tommy should not deal with customers.

The firm of Davids, Henson, and Hadley was located on Dillard Street, several blocks from the store. Zeigler was at the offices
often.

Ed Kirkland left the case after the preliminary hearing. Hadley, Davids, and the paralegal, Leslie Gift, were the full-time legal
team, and only Hadley knew Zeigler well.

Vernon Davids had little contact with Zeigler during this time.
Davids was busy, and he thought that Zeigler was primarily Hadley's client. From the little time they had together, Zeigler struck
Davids as very naive, with an almost childish faith in the legal
process. He seemed to believe that juries were imbued with a
supernatural sense of truth and falsehood. Any trial would be just
a formality: he was innocent, and therefore he certainly would be
perceived as innocent.

Davids thought that Zeigler had a lot to learn.

Gift had begun to compile ring binders of police reports, statements, and other evidence; by the time the trial began, the binders
would contain several thousand pages of cross-referenced material.
Her first strong impression of Zeigler was that he was a classic male
chauvinist. That was not all bad: according to his code, men were
at all times expected to show women consideration and kind regard. But women, for their part, were expected to defer at once to
the wishes of men.

Gift found this not so much infuriating as amusing. She was a
good-looking blonde in her early twenties. She was also bright and
capable. She had been through this before.

Zeigler knew that one of Gift's files contained reports of all the rumors about him that Davids, Annan, and others had heard. The attorneys had decided that Zeigler should not be privy to the details of the evidence against him. Among other considerations, they wanted his recollection to be untainted by knowledge of things that only the killer—or killers—could know. This itself was an act of faith. If Zeigler was guilty, it would be a risky strategy.

Zeigler had agreed to this. But he did want to know what was being said about him in his hometown. One day, instead of asking Hadley or Davids, he waited until he was alone with Gift. Then he demanded to see the rumors file.

Gift refused. He fixed her with a scowl that she had seen from him a few times before, glaring disapproval over the rims of his glasses.

It got no reaction from her.

"Don't you know what this look means?" Zeigler said.

"I don't know what it means to anybody else, but it doesn't mean a damn thing to me," she told him.

That was the end of his posturing with Gift. They became friends. During the weeks and months before the trial, he spent more time with her than with either of the attorneys. If Hadley and Davids were busy—and they usually were—she would listen to his questions or complaints. Zeigler didn't easily open up to anyone, but eventually he talked to her about Eunice and his marriage. Gift became convinced that he truly loved his wife, and that he hadn't yet fully grasped the fact of her death.

He could be a prickly client. As details of the state's case trickled in, Hadley would bring Zeigler into the office to confront him with the new evidence and ask him to explain it.

The first few times this happened, Zeigler would protest, as if he couldn't understand why anyone, especially his own attorneys, would doubt his version. But he always answered, and Gift noticed that his answers were always consistent with the statements he had been making since he awoke in the hospital on Christmas Day. If he was a liar, she thought, he was the most effective liar she had ever known.

He would bristle if Hadley's questions became personal. Hadley asked him about his sex life with Eunice; Zeigler told him that was none of his business. Hadley wanted to see the logs of their intercourse that Eunice had kept. Zeigler refused and stormed out of the office.

A day later he brought the logs to Gift. Some were torn and repaired with transparent tape. Zeigler said that he had started to destroy them to keep them out of the public record, but had changed his mind.

At one point Zeigler confronted his attorneys with their doubts. They were in Hadley's office: Zeigler, Hadley, Davids, and Gift. One by one, he asked them whether they believed in his innocence.

Yes, Gift said.

Yes, Hadley said.

It was Davids's turn. Davids didn't like it. He felt that he was being pressured into a sort of loyalty oath. Davids was a libertarian by temperament and philosophy, and didn't care to be pressured into anything.

He told Zeigler the truth: that as yet he hadn't made up his mind about the question of Zeigler's guilt, that he wanted to know more before he finally decided.

Zeigler was affronted. He didn't understand how any lawyer who didn't completely believe in his innocence could represent him.

Zeigler gradually accepted the doubts and the questions. He still thought it was more fuss than necessary, but he put up with it.

In March he accepted without much protest when Hadley wanted him to undergo a session at a clinic near Tampa. The arrangements were already made. Annan drove Zeigler to his appointment with the psychiatrist, Theodore Machler. Hadley kept the details deliberately vague, to give Zeigler as little chance as possible to prepare for what was about to happen.

Mackler specialized in the treatment of amnesia. In a procedure known as narcotherapy, he would probe the memory of his subjects while they were in a semiconscious state induced by the drug Sodium Brevital. He met Zeigler at his office in the clinic, told him about the therapy, and informed him, "If you're trying to hide something, and you think you can beat me, you'd better walk out now."

Zeigler stayed. His session is preserved on videotape.

Zeigler lay on a hospital gurney, with a microphone propped on his chest. After the first injection, Machler continued to add small doses. Zeigler appeared to be barely conscious, and at times he dozed off. Machler sometimes had to repeat questions two or three times before Zeigler would answer in a slurred, halting voice.

Hadley had briefed Dr. Machler on the case and had given the psychiatrist a list of areas that he would like to have explored. Mainly, he was interested in what had happened when Zeigler walked into the store.

Zeigler related his day at work and the switch of cars with Curtis Dunaway. Eunice left with her parents in the Edwardses' car, he said. He described starting for the liquor store, turning around on Bay Street, and finding Edward Williams parked in the driveway when he got back.

He put the car in the garage and rode in Williams's truck. The route he described to the store was the same one Williams claimed, up Park Avenue to Route 50, then east to Dillard.

But now Zeigler's account diverged from Williams's. Zeigler said that he did not get out in front, but rode around back with Williams and opened the gate.

"Start seeing things as though they're happening," Machler urged him.

Zeigler slipped in and out of the present tense. Several times he came close to entering the building and walking up the dark hallway, but he seemed to back away from the memory. More than once his breathing became so labored that the microphone slipped off his chest. His voice remained mostly colorless, though.

Finally, as Machler prodded him. Zeigler stepped into the store:

"I unlock the hall door. Edward is backing his truck up to the bay door. . . . I tried to turn the lights on, the store was dark. The exit lights were off, the store was dark."

"How do you feel?" Machler asked.

"I figured there was a power failure," Zeigler answered. "Edward was backing his truck. . . . I walked into the store, thinking Curtis [Dunaway] had turned off the back lights. I got hit over the head."

"Can you see who's hitting you?"

"No." Zeigler's voice now had a troubled tone. "I get up. I see two men."

"Describe the men."

"I can't. It's two blurs. I pulled Ficke's pistol, I tried to fire. But it jammed. I ejected a shell and tried to fire again."

"What do you feel?"

"I threw the pistol at 'em."

"Can you see any better?"

"No, sir. They grabbed me and threw me off the wall. I'm being bounced around . . . bounced around."

But Zeigler's tone was surprisingly flat.

"What are your feelings?"

"They threw me down the hallway. I have a .357 magnum hidden in a hallway desk. I got the magnum and I fired. They were on me, too close to fire again."

"Can you see them?"

"No, sir. Just a blur." Zeigler was still speaking slowly. "They grabbed me and threw me into the rug rack, I hit the floor. And another man shot me."

"Another man? Can you see him?"

"Just a blur."

"Is this a third man?"

"I think so. Just a blur. He was a big man."

"How did it feel when you were shot?"

"It was awful hot. Like somebody jamming a hot poker in me."

"Did they say anything?"

"No. When they shot me, he said, 'We've got to dispose of Mays, he's been hit, we can't take him with us.'"

"Those are the exact words?"

"Yeah. The third man said, 'Kill him, he's no good to us.'"

"What did his voice sound like?"

"He—I think he was a white man."

Zeigler described waking up on the floor, trying to put his hands on his glasses, but instead finding only Christmas bows.[2] He tried to locate the back telephone, but could see nothing.

"Did you see or hear Edward Williams?"

"No."

"How do you feel?"

"I was cold, I was burning up, I needed a drink of water," he said: the symptoms of shock.

"Did you see any bodies?" Dr. Machler said.

"No." But Zeigler sounded uncertain.

"Think about it."

"I crawled over one." Zeigler seemed almost close to a whimper.

"Whose body?"

"I don't know."

2. Dozens of Christmas bows were found on the terrazzo floor, apparently having been knocked off a wrapping table in the back of the store.

"A man or a woman?" Machler said.

"I don't know."

"What do you feel?"

"I was just trying to find my glasses . . . there was nothing but bows . . . these damn bows."

"Where is the body?"

"Near me . . . I tried to find my glasses."

"Did you at any time see any other bodies?"

"No."

"What did you do next?"

"I tried to go to the back phone [on the back wall of the showroom] but I couldn't find it." Zeigler's words were slurred now; the effects of the drug were obvious. "I went to the front office. I got my glasses on the desk. I was so cold and so thirsty—"

"Did you see any other bodies?"

"—I went into the kitchen, I think I got a drink of water." In the kitchen was Eunice's body, stretched out full-length in a room barely nine by fourteen feet. But Machler did not question him.

Zeigler continued: "I came out of the kitchen, I leaned up against a stool, I called Ted Van Deventer's home. . . . I asked to speak to Don Ficke. . . . I told Don Ficke, hurry, hurry, I've been shot. . . . I went to the front of the store and sat down in a yellow lawn chair to wait."

Machler had a series of questions from Hadley.

"Did you throw the breaker switch at any time?" he asked.

"No."

"Did you talk to Charlie Mays that day?"

"He came in the store. He wanted to buy some linoleum." Zeigler struggled to pronounce that word.

"Did you talk to him about a television?"

"He asked me about a television set. I carried him back to the back. Curtis Dunaway was snoozing in the stockroom as we went in.[3] I told [Mays] the television set would be $350 cash, 'cause it didn't belong to me."[4]

---

3. Dunaway was napping during Mays's second visit to the store that day.

4. The price of the TV was disputed. The state, based on Mattie Mays's testimony, claimed that Zeigler offered Mays the set at $128 in order to entice him to the store. Zeigler claimed that he quoted Mays a price of $350 cash.

"Did you sell him the TV set?"

"No. He said he'd be back for it."

"Did he say when?" Machler asked.

"No."

"Did you believe he'd be back that day or some other time?"

"I thought he'd be back that night or late that afternoon."

Near the end of the interview, Machler asked Zeigler when he had last seen Edward Williams.

"Edward was backing his truck up to the bay door," Zeigler said, and again he picked up his narrative of what happened in the store: "I opened the hall door. I tried the light switch but it didn't work. I tried the next light switch. . . . I walked into the store and I was hit on the side of my head. . . . I tried to fire Ficke's gun. . . . I fired [the magnum] but they were on me so close that I started swinging it . . . they threw me up against a rug rack. This third blur shot me."

"What did you see?"

"Just fire. It looked like a house on fire."

The session had lasted more than forty-five minutes. Machler ended it by telling Zeigler to sleep, and suggesting that when he awoke he would remember as much or as little of the session as he wished.

Machler believed that the interview was genuine. Zeigler's confusion, his indistinct speech, and his tendency to repeat minor details were all signs that the drug was having its effect. The fact that Zeigler reverted to the past tense was unsurprising. Only rare patients were able to recount events as if they were actually happening. And Zeigler's emotionless manner didn't bother him: Machler thought that was in character.

Next morning Machler and Zeigler watched the videotape together. Zeigler apparently had retained no memory of the interview; as the tape played he leaned forward in his chair and began nodding. He took off his glasses, and Machler thought that he was on the verge of tears.

"What are your feelings?" Machler asked.

"My God, that is it," Zeigler said. At the mention of leaning against a stool, he said, "And it fell with me," as if it were something he had just discovered.

The tape ended, but Zeigler went on talking to Machler. He seemed to need to keep talking. He described the trip to the hospital and how it had felt: the bumps in the road, the pain, the burning and the chill and his thirst.

"How do you feel physically?" Machler said, meaning now, at this moment.

Zeigler held his head up.

"It is going to be all right," he said.

The second day of the grand jury's hearing was a Friday. Hadley and the rest of the defense expected an indictment. Zeigler's nine weeks of freedom were at an end.

Hadley wanted to avoid having deputies arrest his client. Leslie Gift arranged for Zeigler to stay in the offices of another attorney while they waited for the formal announcement of the indictment. When it came, she took Zeigler to surrender at the courthouse in Orlando.

She drove into the basement sally port and walked with Zeigler to the ground-floor booking desk. Don Frye was waiting there, with Orange County sheriff Melvin Colman. Reporters and photographers crowded a few feet away.

As both Zeigler and Gift remember it, the booking officer suggested that they avoid the media by booking Zeigler upstairs, at the jail; there was an elevator nearby.

According to Zeigler and Gift, Colman declined the idea, saying: "That's all right. The press can have its pound of flesh."

Frye told Zeigler to assume the position, as cameras clicked and whirred.

The indictment allowed Hadley to move for discovery of the state's evidence against Zeigler. His motion invoked Florida's Mutual Criminal Discovery Agreement, obligating both prosecution and defense to disclose any relevant evidence. In theory, both sides would share the fruits of their investigations, favorable or otherwise. Without mutual discovery, the defense was entitled only to potentially exonerating evidence: so-called Brady material.[5]

This tactic was not without some risk for the defense. Hadley already had assigned Gene Annan to follow any lead that impli-

5. From the landmark U.S. Supreme Court case *Brady* v. *Maryland*.

cated Zeigler; if there was bad news, Hadley wanted to know about it. Now the defense was obliged to reveal any unfavorable facts that Annan or any of the other investigators happened to find.

Hadley was willing to take the chance. He had virtually no evidence that could damage Zeigler. The payoff was a close look at the state's case, and insurance against an ambush at trial. He got much more than he expected.

TWENTY-THREE

THE DEADLINE FOR THE FIRST MAJOR RELEASE OF STATE'S EVIDENCE was April 12. That afternoon, the last few hours of the last day when the state attorney's office could remain in compliance with the law, the prosecution turned over copies of police reports, witness statements, Professor MacDonell's report, partial results from the FBI Laboratory, and copies of crime scene photographs.

The defense team spent much of the next weekend reviewing the photocopied material. Terry Hadley was wary of a "bombshell": any indisputable fact or test result or statement that would conclusively show that Tommy Zeigler had murdered anyone in the furniture store on Christmas Eve.

The state's files contained no such evidence.

The blood-typing results were so sketchy as to be almost useless for either side. A transmittal letter from the sheriff's office to the FBI had asked that the FBI Lab "type and group [the blood specimens] as far as possible." But for some reason, none of the specimens had been subgrouped.

It was a curious lapse—almost an amateurish one. Not for the last time, some members of the defense speculated that the FBI and the prosecution had a verbal agreement that the FBI would not report any test results that tended to exculpate Zeigler.

On May 7, defense investigators also inspected physical evidence in the sheriff's lockers.

In all, the state's own evidence contained much to contradict the prosecution's theory of the crime. There *was* a bombshell, from the FBI Lab. But the only case it threatened was the state's prosecution of Tommy Zeigler.

What Hadley and the others found in the prosecution's files included:

The second tooth. One of the close-up photographs of Charlie Mays on the terrazzo showed what appeared to be a human tooth lying on the sleeve of Mays's dark sweatshirt. Mays had lost a single tooth when he was beaten, and one tooth was recovered against the north wall of the showroom. None of the other victims had lost a tooth. According to police property receipts, the tooth in the photograph was never recovered. Yet it clearly did exist, and the inference was that it had come from a sixth person in the store: a person who could not exist, according to the prosecution's theory.

Eunice's coat. Some light "transfer stains" of blood were found along the underside of the lapel at the front of Eunice's coat, as if it had been grasped by fingers that were damp with blood. Also, there were small blood drops on the inside lining of the coat. The drops could not have resulted from her wound; they suggested that the coat had been open while someone stood over her and dripped blood. This ran counter to the prosecution's theory that her body had not been disturbed after she was shot.

It was not a minor point. Eunice was found completely stretched out on the floor, with the coat buttoned up, her legs straight, her left hand still resting in a coat pocket. The Winter Garden patrolman, Jimmy Yawn, even took her for a mannequin at first glance. The position of her left hand was the sole basis for the prosecution's theory that she had been killed instantly by a single surprise shot while she stood in the kitchen doorway. Frye believed that Zeigler had deliberately sprayed the other bullet holes in and around the door after he had committed all the other murders.

Frye and MacDonell took this "surprise shot" as a given. Evidence that the body had been disturbed would discredit the theory, and with it the rest of the prosecution's hypothetical sequence of events in the store.

No one on the defense team accepted the idea of a "surprise shot." The absence of powder tattooing around the wound meant that the shot had been fired from more than two feet away; yet Zeigler should have been able to approach his wife within point-blank range. Gene Annan and others also thought that the position of Eunice's body was unnaturally straight: he felt that if she had been instantly killed, her body would have collapsed as it fell.

(Today, at least one member of the original defense team believes that Zeigler may have found his dead wife while stumbling around the store after regaining consciousness, and that he straightened her body and buttoned her coat in a numb gesture of care—he himself was freezing cold, as he recalled for Dr. Mackler. By this theory, the shock of seeing her dead, after having been attacked and shot, induced a post-traumatic stress amnesia.)

The broken eyeglasses. Gene Annan was examining the shirt and jacket of Perry Edwards when he discovered an eyeglass case, a broken pair of glasses, and a spent bullet, which police had overlooked. Apparently the case had stopped the bullet. Later, pieces of eyeglass lens were matched to shards of glass that had been found in the bloody patch east of the sales counter, suggesting that Mr. Edwards had been shot at that spot, and that he may have been down on the floor.

Professor MacDonell's report, while dwelling on splatters and fine sprays near the back of the store, did not attempt to explain this obvious concentration of blood. It did not fit the prosecution's hypothesis of the crime. Frye and MacDonell claimed that Perry Edwards was first assaulted near the back of the store, probably after coming to investigate the "surprise shot" that killed his daughter. But this new evidence showed that Mr. Edwards had been shot and knocked down near the front of the store.

(Frye now believes that Perry and Virginia Edwards left 75 Temple Grove several minutes behind Tommy and Eunice, and that Tommy had killed his wife by the time his in-laws arrived at the store. This would explain how Mr. Edwards came to be killed at the front of the store—he never heard the "surprise shot"; however, the contention is otherwise unsupported by any evidence.)

The missing slug. Property receipts showed that technicians had found a .22 Long Rifle cartridge hull in the back of the store. Of the eight pistols connected to the case, this shell could only have been fired from the .22 automatic that Zeigler carried at his side on Christmas Eve: the jammed gun which Zeigler said he had tried to defend himself with at the back of the showroom.

So the pistol had been fired once. Where was the slug?

In their two-week examination of the store, Vernon Davids and Gene Annan had found a .38 caliber slug and a .38 caliber exit hole in the north wall, which deputies had missed. They believed that this accounted for all of the .38 caliber shots that were fired in the store.

But there was no sign of the .22 slug. Neither Zeigler nor the four murder victims had been shot by a .22. If the slug did not exit through the walls, it could only have left the store one way: in one of the perpetrators, as he walked out or was carried out.

Vernon Davids thought of Nathaniel Brown, the informant who had approached the Zeiglers in January and told of weapons wiped clean, of a plot engineered by a white man, and of a wounded robber hiding out after being shot in the furniture store. In the weeks since then, the defense had learned that all but one of the weapons *had* been wiped clean. Zeigler in his narcotherapy session had remembered hearing a white man's voice in the back of the store. A .22 is a small slug. Still, the fact that it had not been found after nearly a month of close searching suggested that a sixth person had been shot in the store.

Davids and the investigators went looking for Nathaniel Brown. But Brown could not be found.[1]

Mays's bloody sneakers. Crime scene photographs showed some heavy smears of blood on the sneakers of Charlie Mays. But the quantity of blood on Mays's shoes and the bottoms of his pants was even greater than the photos suggested. The left cuff of his pants was caked with blood, as if it had been wicked up from a pool. Blood almost completely covered the bottoms of Mays's shoes, so thick in places that it nearly filled depressions in the sneaker soles. Frye had never mentioned these heavily stained shoes; neither did MacDonell's report note them.

Frye believed that Mays had been killed almost immediately after entering the store; as MacDonell put it, "To conclude otherwise would be to suggest that he was present while the other victims were being killed and did nothing to prevent it."

Blood in this quantity was inconsistent with any theory of

---

1. Defense investigators learned that he had left Orange County. Years later, Vernon Davids was told that Brown had been murdered in New York City.

Mays's innocence.[2] Only two deposits of blood were large enough to account for the stains around Mays's feet and cuffs. One of these was the pool that flowed from Eunice Zeigler, completely out of sight in the kitchen. The other was the pool around Perry Edwards, at the far rear of the showroom. If Mays were innocent, being coaxed into the store by Zeigler, he would have run away or begun to struggle long before he reached either of these locations.

Mays's shoe prints were nowhere in the store. Yet the blood on his soles had come from somewhere. The defense theorized that he had picked it up from the Perry Edwards pool, and that the trail of swipe marks that ran beside the showroom's rear wall—a pattern that Frye and MacDonell ascribed to a running battle between Edwards and Zeigler—actually showed where Mays's bloody tracks had been wiped up.

And, in fact, the regular spacing of those swipe marks, tracking straight along the edge of the terrazzo, was consistent with footsteps.

On Christmas Eve, Curtis Dunaway had left a London Fog raincoat in the office closet. When he returned to the store in January, the coat was missing. Some members of the defense speculated that the raincoat may have been used to wipe up bloody footprints, and perhaps to move one or more of the bodies.

The black cardigan and the boots. On Christmas morning, detective Denny Martin went to Williams's apartment, and Williams gave Martin the clothes he was wearing. According to Williams, he had last changed clothes at about 6:00 P.M. on Christmas Eve, before he drove to meet Zeigler. Those clothes, except for the trousers, were in the sheriff's evidence lockers. They included a black cardigan sweater. According to the prosecution, the pants were at the FBI Lab and were not available for inspection. But they were dark green.

Several witnesses claimed that Williams was wearing a brown jacket and light brown pants that evening.

Williams's black ankle-high boots were remarkable. Supposedly he had worn them throughout the evening and night of Christmas Eve, had climbed a chain-link fence in them, and had

2. One of the items found in Mays's pockets was a business card for an Orlando bail-bonding service.

run across the asphalt parking lot of the Winter Garden Inn when he escaped from Zeigler. Yet the boots were completely new. The soles showed no wear at all; a price tag was still stuck to the instep of one of the boots.

Signs of a robbery. Tommy Zeigler told Hadley that Eunice wore two diamond rings, but they were not listed among the physical evidence. Tom Zeigler, Sr., told investigators that he gave Eunice two $20 bills as she was leaving for the store with her parents. But no money was found on her. Her purse, and her mother's, had been left at 75 Temple Grove. Perry Edwards's empty wallet was found in his car, in front of the store.[3]

Eventually Hadley incorporated all of these issues into his defense. The state's own evidence, along with Zeigler's testimony, would provide the backbone of the defense.

And then there was the bombshell.

Among the April 12 disclosures the defense found a letter from the FBI Lab dated March 10, and received by the sheriff's office five days later, announcing the result of comparisons between Zeigler's shoes and photographs of the bloody footprints.

The letter read, in part (emphasis added):

> Due to the absence of sufficient detail in the photographed shoe print marked "A/S-A" for minute comparison purposes, it could not be determined definitely whether this shoe print was or was not made by either the Q52 shoe or the Q53 shoe. *It was determined that the remaining photographed shoe prints were not made by either of the submitted shoes.*

The implications of that single paragraph were enormous. The Q-52 and Q-53 specimens, as the FBI numbered them, were Zeigler's shoes. If the bloody footprints were not made by Zeigler, then they must have been made by a sixth person. The state's case did not have room to accommodate a second murderer.

Moreover, the "remaining photographed shoe prints" included one that Professor MacDonell had specifically mentioned in

---

3. After the police relinquished the store on January 7, Beulah Zeigler claimed that more than $800 in cash was missing from a file cabinet. She also said that an antique gold watch and several gold coins had disappeared from a large office safe after she opened it for sheriff's officers during their investigation of the store.

his report. "Most likely this is a shoe print of the perpetrator," MacDonell had written.

According to the nation's greatest crime lab, that print was not made by Tommy Zeigler.

TWENTY-FOUR

BY NOW TERRY HADLEY COULD ASSESS THE CASE AGAINST HIS CLIENT.

The cache that investigators seized from the storeroom cabinet on January 2—the ammunition and spent hulls, the blue towel from Curtis Dunaway's car, and a grocery bag with Zeigler's palm print—certainly suggested Zeigler's guilt, but did not prove it. The same was true of the evidence from the Dunaway Olds. The blood on the car's headrest, the tissue with his fingerprint, and the unfired Smith & Wesson revolver on the backseat all suggested his guilt, but did not prove it.

Zeigler's fingerprints, predictably, were found throughout his store. But none incriminated him.

Don Frye and the prosecution believed that Zeigler had worn rubber surgical gloves to commit the crimes, and had lost a glove tip in the struggle with Perry Edwards. But no fingerprints were recovered from the nipple of latex found near the northwest corner of the showroom. (Zeigler was prepared to testify that he had gotten some surgical rubber gloves while he was in the Army Reserve, and that he kept them in the store to use while polishing or retouching furniture.)

The insurance policies were suggestive, but Hadley believed that they could be explained at trial.

Only one witness, Thomas Hale, supported the state's claim that Zeigler had driven Eunice to the store on Christmas Eve. Hale's identification of the wrong automobile would compromise his testimony, and Hadley believed that he could impeach it even further. Felton Thomas's testimony was vague; Hadley thought that he was vulnerable to a strong cross-examination.

By far the most damning evidence against Zeigler was the testimony of Edward Williams. It was mostly uncorroborated, and Williams could hardly be called a disinterested witness: his truck was found at the murder scene, and he had ended up in possession of the principal murder weapon, the Securities .38. And the paper trail to the RG revolvers, one of which had killed Eunice Zeigler, led to Williams's friend Frank Smith. Yet Williams had been an effective, convincing witness at the preliminary hearing, and apparently once more before the grand jury.

Zeigler and Williams could not both be telling the truth; their versions of what happened when they arrived at the store together were irreconcilable. Unless unfinished tests from the FBI Lab produced some startling evidence, the trial verdict could swing on the conflicting testimonies of Tommy Zeigler and his former handyman.

If Zeigler was innocent, both Williams and Charlie Mays must be guilty. What would be their motive in the crime?

The defense believed that money was the answer for both men. The fact that the Zeiglers kept substantial amounts of cash at the store was no secret, and the defense found reason to believe that both Mays and Williams needed the money.

Mays was thought to be a heavy gambler. The past June, he had been arrested and convicted on charges of illegal betting. Defense investigators heard reports that during the past year he had bet and lost a large sum that did not belong to him: according to the reports, it was cash that belonged to loan sharks, intended to be the daily payouts to his fruit-picking crew.

Defense investigators learned that in the past year Williams had twice been laid off construction work, and that aside from his irregular work as a handyman he had worked full-time only five of the last twelve months. During much of that time he had drawn unemployment of $74 a week. In December 1975 a local bank was preparing to foreclose on a loan that he had cosigned for a friend.

Around mid-January, as Mrs. Zeigler prepared to open the store, Williams's truck was still parked behind the bay door, where it had sat since Christmas Eve. She asked Annan to move the truck; inside, Annan found documents showing that his telephone, electricity, and gas had been shut off because of nonpayment. (Williams later denied in a disposition that he had failed to pay his utility bills.)

A Florida statute known informally as the "speedy trial law" was intended to protect a criminal defendant from an endless unresolved prosecution. Speedy trial mandated that a criminal defendant be tried within 180 days of his arrest.

For Zeigler this would be no later than the last week in June. The trials on his two indictments were set for June 1 and June 15.

The defense was not ready. Discovery material from the state suggested dozens of leads that had to be pursued, and there was more to come. Witnesses from the state's list had to be interviewed, or else subpoenaed and deposed. Furthermore, the state seemed unable to locate some pieces of physical evidence, including Edward Williams's slacks, which the defense wanted to examine and test. Hadley, Davids, and the investigators were already working twelve- to fifteen-hour days, seven days a week, and the work was still piling up.

Hadley needed more time. He suggested that Zeigler waive his speedy-trial privileges and request a continuance.

Zeigler didn't see the point. Slacks, minor witnesses—how much could they mean? Since he had been denied bond, a continuance could mean an indefinite stay in jail.

The defense was not ready for trial, Hadley insisted.

But Zeigler was ready. He had been ready since he woke up in the hospital bed on Christmas Day. He would tell his story, and the jury would see that it was true, and this nightmare would be over.

No continuances, no delays. That was his decision, and he would not budge. Tommy Zeigler wanted to go to trial, the sooner the better. He wanted it finished; he was ready to get on with his life.

TWENTY-FIVE

FOR FIVE WEEKS, BEGINNING IN LATE APRIL, HADLEY AND VERNON Davids deposed all the major witnesses in the case, and most of the lesser ones.

Depositions are testimony given out of court, but under oath. They are a powerful tool in criminal proceedings, useful not only in fact-finding but for compiling a record that may later be used to impeach the witness's testimony at trial.

The most important depositions in the Zeigler defense were those Hadley took from Felton Thomas and Edward Williams. Hadley hoped to discredit the two men whose statements on December 25 had led to the arrest of Tommy Zeigler.

Hadley deposed both Thomas and Williams on April 26, in a conference room at the state attorney's office in Orlando. Robert Eagan himself appeared for the state at the Thomas deposition, in the morning.

Hadley began with the question of Thomas's true name.

Thomas answered: "Well, they call me Felton Thomas; but they don't never use my name as Buddy Felton or Thomas Felton. They always call me Buddy. If they call my real name, they call me Felton Thomas."

Thomas said that he was twenty-seven, born in Pelham, Georgia, and that he had been picking fruit for nearly half his life. He had harvested in Orange County several times since 1972. In November 1975, he and a friend had come down from New York for the harvest season.

On Christmas Eve he borrowed a friend's car and made several trips from Oakland to Winter Garden and Orlando. In the evening he joined some friends around a bonfire in Oakland:

"It began to get dark then, when I got back off my last trip. It began to get dark. And so, Charlie Mays come up in his truck, his panel truck."

Thomas said that he knew Mays, had worked for him the previous season, around January of 1975.

Q *(HADLEY):* What time was it that Charlie drove up?
A *(THOMAS):* Just like I say, it was starting to get dark, you know. He drove up and asked me to come ride with him. So I told him I ain't have nothing better to do.

Thomas said that Mays drove from Oakland into Winter Garden, then south down Dillard Street and into the furniture store's front parking lot. There he saw a car, which he believed to be a Buick. The store was completely dark, and Mays said that "the man wasn't there to open the store yet."

Then, according to Thomas, Mays pulled around to the back parking area of the Winter Garden Inn.

Q: Well, did he run right along beside the store to get to the hotel parking lot?
A: No, he went through—he went between these buildings. You couldn't go through the first part. He went through the buildings. He went between the two buildings, but it's three buildings down, so he went between the last two buildings.

Hadley asked Thomas to draw the store and the nearby buildings, and to trace the route that Mays followed into the back lot of the motel.

Immediately south of the store on Dillard Street, and directly across the street from the Kentucky Fried Chicken, were twin single-story office/commercial structures known as the Tucker Buildings, separated by a common parking area.

Felton Thomas drew a route straight from the front of the store to the Tucker Buildings, then between the twin buildings and into the rear of the Winter Garden Inn, then finally up to the high fence that enclosed the back compound of the furniture store.

Hadley asked Thomas to sign the diagram, and Thomas complied.

Thomas said that they had parked on the west side of a truck, which was between the van and Dillard Street. They waited there for about five or six minutes, until a car pulled in beside them and a man got out. There is no record that, until this moment, Thomas had ever been asked to describe the man who met him and Mays in the motel parking lot. According to the transcript of his Christmas-morning statement, Thomas had simply identified him as Zeigler—whom he had never before met—and the Orange County detectives had accepted that identification.

Now any description would potentially have lost some value: Thomas had already seen Zeigler at the preliminary hearing. But Hadley pursued it.

Q: Okay. Now, you tell me what this man looked like, Mr. Thomas. Just describe him.
A: Well, he was tall and wearing glasses; and his hair kind of thin.
Q: His hair was kind of thin?
A: Yeah.
Q: Was he going bald?
A: Nope. I don't think so. I wasn't paying that much attention.
Q: How about his clothes? Did you notice what kind of clothes he had on?
A: Not too good, but I know he had on kind of light clothes.
Q: Kind of light clothes?
A: Yeah.
Q: Did he have on a short-sleeved shirt, long-sleeved shirt? Do you remember, sir?
A: I don't remember what type of shirt he had on, but I believe it was long sleeves.
Q: Do you remember the color?
A: No, I don't.
Q: How about the pants? Do you remember what color pants he had on?
A: No. I don't.
Q: All you remember then—if this is a statement—that it was sort of light clothing?
A: Light-colored.
Q: Light-colored?
A: Right.

Once again Thomas told how he and Mays had gone for a ride with the man in his car. At the preliminary hearing he called the car a light-colored Cadillac, a description that did not fit Curtis

Dunaway's two-tone Olds. Now: "I say it was a Cadillac because it was a big car. That's what I say it was."

Thomas continued with the now-familiar story of shooting the pistols in an orange grove, returning to the store, and pulling the master switch as the tall man ordered; and of the white man jumping over the fence and trying to coax Mays and Thomas over, and then driving to a house and parking at the garage.

Q: He pulled up into the driveway?
A: Right. There was a car and a truck there.
Q: There was a car and a truck there?
A: Yeah.
Q: What order were they parked in? Was the car behind the truck, or the truck behind the car?
A: Well, the truck was behind the car.
Q: Did you happen to notice what kind of car it was?
A: No; I didn't.
Q: Was it a light- or dark-colored car?
A: Well, I ain't paying no attention.
Q: Did you park right beside the car? Or where did you park?
A: Up alongside of the car.

Thomas said that Zeigler "messed around at some shelves" in the garage, then came back to the car with a box, which he gave to Mays. As they backed out of the driveway he ordered Mays to reload the gun, and he drove to the store.

Now Thomas recounted the final scene at the store. He said that he stood beside the car as Zeigler unlocked the front door for Mays. Zeigler told Thomas to come in with them, but Thomas refused.

Q: How long did you sit in the car?
A: I ain't sitting in the car no time. As soon as they closed that door and got into the store, I just got right out of the car and went cross over there to TG&Y over there.
Q: Why did you do that?
A: Because he had been acting a little strange. I ain't paying too much attention because he was on the truck when everybody trying to get their equipment sharpened there. . . .

This reference was puzzling. It seemed to suggest that Thomas had seen the tall white man somewhere before, perhaps in the fields. But Hadley let it pass.

Thomas said that he rode back into Oakland with friends he met at the shopping center, that he went back to the bonfire where he had met Mays, and from there to the house of a friend, Cleo Anderson, who was cooking wild game for Christmas dinner. They drank some liquor, and Thomas told Anderson and a woman about what had happened to him at the furniture store.

From Cleo Anderson's house he went back to the fire, and from the fire to a juke joint in Tildenville, a tiny community tucked in between Oakland and Winter Garden. At the bar, around midnight, he heard that there had been four murders at the furniture store.

He went back to Oakland, then with a friend to Winter Garden, where he joined the crowd outside the furniture store. Then back to Oakland again, from where he and his brother-in-law began to drive to Orlando, fifteen miles away, to report what he had seen. On the way to Orlando their car ran out of gas. They walked into a restaurant on Route 50 and Thomas told his story to a black sheriff's deputy there.

Q: Where in Orlando were you going to go?
A: Well, I was going to come over here and report it to some of the officers, you know. I ain't really know where to report it at. So I was coming over here to report it.
Q: What were you going to report?
A: I was going to report that I had been with the man that had got killed.
Q: You knew at this point that Charlie Mays was dead?
A: Well, they say he was in the store.
Q: Who said that?
A: Everybody that was standing around out there.
Q: You stopped and got out at the Zeigler store?
A: Yeah, right. I stopped and got out.
Q: And you found out then it was Charlie Mays?
A: Right. But I didn't tell people—they didn't know I was with Mays when he went up there. And I ain't telling any of the peoples that was standing around that I was with him.
Q: You didn't?
A: No, I didn't.

Q: You didn't tell the police there, either, did you?
A: No, I didn't.

Hadley had pried loose at least five inconsistencies in Thomas's story.

1. According to the route that Thomas drew, Charlie Mays had reached the rear lot of the Winter Garden Inn by driving his van over or through a two-foot wall of concrete block which separates the Tucker Buildings property from the motel.
2. On Christmas Eve, Tommy Zeigler's shirt was rust-colored. His pants were red-and-blue-check, with the dark stain that Edward Williams noted. They were not light-colored clothes.
3. Thomas claimed to have seen a car parked in the driveway where everyone else—including Edward Williams, Curtis Dunaway, the Fickes, and Tommy Zeigler himself—agrees that Zeigler's pickup spent the entire evening. Thomas directly contradicted Williams, who claimed that he parked his pickup truck behind Zeigler's, and who saw no cars except the one that Zeigler was driving.
4. Thomas claimed that Zeigler brought a box out of his garage. Williams would testify that Zeigler's hands were empty.
5. Williams claimed that Zeigler drove into the garage and ran into his house when he arrived with the two passengers. Thomas's testimony was that Zeigler parked in the driveway and walked into the garage, but did not enter the house.

The afternoon deposition with Edward Williams was mostly uneventful. Hadley did elicit some new details of the incident that had convinced Williams that Zeigler wanted to take his life. Williams said that he had parked the truck beside the hallway door, that he had stopped to urinate, and that Zeigler had gone into the store ahead of him.

Williams said he had walked up the dark hallway, opened the door to the showroom, and found Zeigler standing with his back turned, several feet away.

"He turned and he had this thing, holding it, like a cloth

something he had on it. He come to me. He snapped it and it snapped three times. . . . I saw a thing around it. I know it was white, different from his shirt, and he snapped three times . . . pop, pop, pop . . . I said, for God's sake, Tommy, don't kill me, and I ran back outside. When I got there, I run for the gate, and I put a hand on the gate, to open the gate. The gate was locked."

Williams said that Zeigler grabbed him, and Williams kept pushing him off. Zeigler chased Williams around the compound, and finally got down on one knee to beg him to come into the store. At that point, Williams said, he could see blood splattered across Zeigler's face. Williams said that he jumped the fence at the southwest corner of the compound. He ran to the Winter Garden Inn, then ran across Dillard Street to the Kentucky Fried Chicken, where he tried one unsuccessful call to the police.

By now Hadley knew that four witnesses placed Williams at the restaurant after 9:10 P.M., and that three—Ed Nolan, J. D. Nolan, and Madelyn Nolan—claimed to have seen him there after the police cars had arrived at the store.

Q *(HADLEY):* You didn't try again to call the police?
A *(WILLIAMS):* No.
Q: What time was this when you were at the Kentucky Fried Chicken?
A: If I tell you the truth you might not believe me. I didn't check the watch. I was scared and nervous and I was trying to get to the law, police.
Q: You didn't try to call the police again?
A: No sir; I didn't try to call the police again. I got outside. . . .
Q: As you were leaving the Kentucky Fried Chicken, did you see any police cars pulling up at the furniture store?
A: No.
Q: Did you see any lights flashing coming out of the TG&Y?
A: No. If I had seen them, I would have stopped them.

Williams's story stood up after nearly two hours of testimony. To Hadley, though, he seemed vague, defensive, too wary. Hadley thought it was not the demeanor of someone who had only the truth to tell.

Two weeks later, Vernon Davids deposed the young woman named Rogenia Thomas. She and her sister had met Williams outside the restaurant on Christmas Eve. Thomas said that she and her sister had been driving a boyfriend's car; it was a white-and-red 1974 Cadillac with a white interior.

She said: "We slipped over to Winter Garden that night, you know, on December 24th; and he [the boyfriend] didn't know nothing about it. . . . We slipped out to have a nice time, you know. We slipped out and he doesn't know nothing about it yet."

She said that she and her sister had known Williams for several years.

Q (DAVIDS): Where did you first see Mr. Williams that night?

A (ROGENIA THOMAS): Well, I seen him at the Kentucky Fried Chicken. He was standing outside of the Kentucky Fried Chicken. My sister and I drove up and was going to get something to eat and he was standing on the outside. . . . He was standing there nervous-like, shaking. Really, I don't know what was wrong with him. Because it scared me, you know. So he was—my sister got out of the car and she went jiving with him the way you usually do when you're playing around. He keeps saying help me, help me, just like that. I looked at him, like I got afraid of him myself. Like he was shook, nervous, and mumbling with his words. He kept saying help me, help me. . . . We say, what's wrong, like that. And he say I tell you when I get in the car. . . . He was talking like he didn't want to stay around there and tell us anything. He said, just help me. I want you to take me to my car at the Exxon gas station on Route 50. We said okay.

Q: Is that the first thing he asked you to do?

A: Yes.

Q: He didn't ask you to take him to Orlando?

A: No, because his car was at the Exxon gas station. And he asked us to take him there. So we took him. We asked him what was wrong and he told us when we got inside the car, when we were riding along. . . . He was telling us a white man pulled a gun on him and the gun went off three times, snapped three times but it didn't go off. That's what he told us. He told us that when the man pulled the gun and the gun didn't go off, the white man fell on his knees and begged him not to tell the police. That's what he told us. . . .

Q: That's what he said, a white—

A: A white man pulled the gun on him, pulled three times but it didn't go off. The white man fell on his knees and begged him not to tell the police. . . . He pushed him and took the gun and jumped the fence and that's where he wind up at, Kentucky Fried Chicken.

Three times Davids questioned the young woman on this point. *Did Williams say that Tommy Zeigler tried to kill him?* No. *Did he say that the man he worked for had tried to kill him?* No. *Was she sure?* Yes, she was sure: Edward Williams said that "a white man" had tried to kill him in the furniture store.

She added that the time was between 9:00 P.M. and 9:30.

To the defense, this seemed curious behavior. As Williams told it, his friend and employer of more than a decade—a man known to nearly everyone in Winter Garden—had just tried to kill him. Yet Williams said that "a white man tried to kill me." Hadley and Davids thought that something frightened Williams that night. But they didn't believe that a mere three clicks in a half-dark store could provoke such an extreme reaction: trembling, mumbling, help me, help me, help me. *My God, don't try to kill me!*

Some other of Williams's acts that night also were questionable. Why did he stop to urinate outside the building when two restrooms—which he himself had helped to build—were just a few feet away? Why did he not try to call the police a second time from the restaurant? Once he was away from Winter Garden, why did he not call the sheriff, or stop at one of the sheriff's stations?

He claimed to be so shaken that he could hardly drive. Yet he managed to make his way more than a dozen miles to his friend Mary Ellen Stewart, who lived only a short distance from the 33rd Street sheriff's station. The main sheriff's office is within half a dozen blocks of the intersection of Route 50 and Interstate 4; Williams said that he didn't go there "because I got in traffic"—at perhaps two hours before midnight on Christmas Eve. Instead he took the freeway's 33rd Street off-ramp. The sheriff's 33rd Street facility was located within a block of that freeway exit, yet Williams drove on to Stewart's home. Why did he not go directly to the police?

Furthermore, the drive to south Orlando should have taken no more than half an hour; that would have put him at Stewart's house by 10:00 P.M. Williams swore that he and Stewart had only a short conversation inside her house, and that he went outside and waited for her while she made a telephone call to ask advice about what he should do. Then she and her son-in-law drove with Williams to the sheriff's station. This should have required only a few minutes. Yet Williams apparently did not show up at the sheriff's station until well after 11:00 P.M. He appeared at the Winter Garden police station around midnight.

In essence, why did Edward Williams wait nearly three hours to tell the authorities that someone had tried to take his life?

Mary Stewart's deposition of May 7 only muddled the question. She claimed that Williams spoke on the telephone to her pastor and a representative of the NAACP. Williams denied having any telephone conversations. He said that he told Mrs. Stewart only part of what happened at the store. Yet in her original statement to the police, she repeated Williams's story almost verbatim, using many of the same phrases and locutions.

On the afternoon of May 25, Hadley and Vernon Davids deposed Williams a second time in the state attorney's conference room. They also brought Dr. Allen Zimmer, the psychiatrist who had recently examined Zeigler.

Zimmer was seated beside Hadley. Hadley had asked him to observe Williams. If the psychiatrist believed that Williams was lying or discomfited by a certain line of questions, Zimmer was to nudge Hadley with his foot.

Jack Bachman, a state attorney's investigator, represented the prosecution.

Williams seemed unhappy to be there. Immediately after he was sworn he said: "I'd like to ask a question before I get started. Could I?"

"Okay," Hadley said.

"I was here in front of you before."

"Right."

"What else am I coming back again for? Do I know that?"

Hadley explained that he still had some questions.

After a few general inquiries, Hadley asked about a young woman with whom Williams had shared an apartment before Christmas Eve.

Williams bristled.

"Come on now," he said. "I know you've been checking around. Come on now. Bring up something else."

"Beg your pardon?" Hadley said.

"I hear y'all been checking around and finding out this and that, how I live, and where I live, and so on. I try to tell you the truth. You don't believe me. What I don't know, I can't tell you."

Hadley took Williams through every detail of his testimony, sometimes more than once.

Williams became impatient. His voice got loud.

"I don't know now if you're playing me for a fool," he said at one point.

"You're trying to get me mad, aggravate me," he said a few minutes later.

After nearly two hours of testimony, Hadley bored in on the scene in the rear parking compound, when Zeigler was supposed to have given Williams the pistol and begged him to come into the store. Williams mentioned that he saw a black man and a white man near the motel, across the fence.

Q (HADLEY): Why didn't you call for help? There were people in the Winter Garden Inn. Why didn't you call for help?

A (WILLIAMS): I don't know anybody in the Winter Garden Inn. Two people I saw on this side of the fence walking. When I got over on this side of the fence, was a black man and a white man.

Q: Why didn't you say help, I need some help over here?

A: A black man was walking. I think the last time I seen him is in Tildenville. I said, I'll call the man. He [Zeigler] said, Edward, don't call him; no, don't call him.

Q: You had the gun. Tommy couldn't stop you from calling for help.

A: Well, I jumped the fence and ran for help.

Q: When the people were right there and you had the gun, Tommy's on his knees begging, why didn't you just call for help?

A: I jumped the fence and got help. I wanted to get the law. I wanted to get the law.

Q: If you had the gun, why didn't you just hold Tommy prisoner and get them to call the law? . . . Why didn't you just say, help, call the police, and make Tommy stay there?

A: Huh?

Q: You had the gun. Tommy's on his knees begging. Why didn't you just say to those people over there, help, call the police, and you make Tommy stay there?

A: Those two people, them two people were walking and gone. They were gone through the hallway and gone on the other side.

Q: But you had the gun.

A: I had the gun, yeah, and I took the gun and carried it to the law. After he gave me the gun, I take it and carried it to the law. I glad I take the gun when he gave it to me. He could have killed me. He would have went ahead and killed me. He meant to kill me.

A few minutes later, Hadley pressed him on his behavior in the restaurant.

Q: Why didn't you tell the man at the Kentucky Fried Chicken that somebody tried to kill you?

A: What man?

Q: The man who you asked to use the telephone.

A: The only help he could give me is give me the police number. If he give me the wrong number—he give me the wrong number to call.

Q: But you were safe.

A: Huh?

Q: But you were safe.

A: You say I was safe?

Q: Yes.

A: I couldn't say that. I couldn't sit down and be easy and know that a man try to kill me and sit down at the Kentucky Fried Chicken. I couldn't do that.

Q: But you were nervous. Why didn't you have the man call the police for you?

A: What man?

Q: The man at Kentucky Fried Chicken.

A: The young man that give me the phone number?

Q: But you're all nervous. Why didn't you say, call the police, call the police?

A: I asked him to give me the police and let me call them.

Q: Why didn't you call him, hey, man, somebody tried to shoot me, call the police quick?

A: The man was working. The man was working on his job. I asked him a favor to give me the police number. He gave me the number that he know. I didn't get the police. . . .

Q: You mean to tell me that chicken is more important than murder?

A: Huh?

Hadley thought this was the kind of questioning that Williams should have gotten from police on the night of the murders. As Hadley remembers it, Williams now seemed flustered and confused, not combative any longer, but groping for words. He was ready to blurt something.

Q: If you were nervous, why didn't you tell the ladies what happened?
A: Who?
Q: Rogenia Thomas. Why didn't you tell her what happened?
A: Jesus, have mercy on me. Give me patience. Didn't I just tell you that I told [her] that man tried to kill me in the store?
Q: You told them that Tommy did? What exactly did you say to them?

At this moment Don Frye and a state's attorney's investigator, Jere James, walked into the room.

JAMES: That's it. We quit.
HADLEY: Why?
JAMES: Mr. Eagan's orders. You get a court order in the morning, whatever you need to do.
HADLEY: You're terminating the deposition?
JAMES: Yes.
HADLEY: On what grounds?
JAMES: On Mr. Eagan's orders to terminate.
HADLEY: That's fine. I'm just wondering why you're terminating it.
JAMES: I'm terminating on Mr. Eagan's orders.
HADLEY: Certify it.
DAVIDS: You are going to object on the record and request to continue the deposition right now.
HADLEY: Let the record reflect, Jere—Jack, are you terminating it or is Jere?
BACHMAN: That's the word I got from the boss.
HADLEY: Which one of you is terminating it?
DAVIDS: Let the record reflect they have already taken the witness out of the deposition room before we have finished.

Subpoenaed witnesses do not quit depositions. Prosecutors— whose interest in determining the ultimate truth of a matter is presumed greater than any desire to shield witnesses or preserve a case—do not terminate depositions without a protective order from the court.

Yet Williams was gone.

Hadley and Davids immediately went before Judge Maurice Paul. One of Eagan's assistants represented the state, and told the judge that Eagan intended to argue in the morning for a protective order that would prohibit the defense from further deposing Williams.

The next morning, Eagan told Paul that Williams should be protected from further questioning. He complained that Hadley was repeating questions that he had already asked, and that Zimmer actually was conducting a psychological test of Williams.[1] Davids countered that the defense kept asking the same questions because Williams kept giving different answers. Zimmer, he said, was attending the deposition as a consultant.

Paul allowed the deposition to continue, with the limitation that Hadley could not cover any old ground. That afternoon, Hadley resumed his questioning. Eagan and one of his assistants, Steve Thacker, sat beside Williams.

The deposition lasted about two hours. Williams was testy at times, but he stayed composed. The session ended this way:

WILLIAMS: Well, I said like this. I was talking a while ago when he asked me my personal business, I tried to say something different. I didn't approve of that. But everything that I said, you know, what I mean, what I said, if she [the court reporter] type it up how I say it, this is no difference with it. I can't change it. And anything I tell you is the truth. I ain't going to change it.

THACKER: That's all right.

WILLIAMS: I wouldn't lie.

THACKER: Okay.

WILLIAMS: I wouldn't lie.

At the evidence viewing of May 7, Davids and the investigators learned that sixty-odd pieces of physical evidence that the prosecu-

1. Eagan asked an Orlando psychiatrist, Dr. Stuart Bernstein, to read Williams's May 25 and May 26 depositions, as well as Zimmer's deposition of May 27. Bernstein told Eagan that he did not believe that Zimmer could determine whether Williams was telling the truth. "Furthermore, I am extremely doubtful as to how psychiatric examination of Mr. Williams would help to clarify this issue," Dr. Bernstein wrote.

tion claimed were at the FBI Lab actually had never left the 33rd Street sheriff's station. The evidence included Mays's bloody trousers and the pants that Williams surrendered to Denny Martin early on Christmas Day. Hadley and Davids could inspect the items, but the prosecution refused to allow the evidence out of custody.

Hadley wanted to test Williams's pants for gunshot residue. The police and prosecution had not requested any such tests, even though this offered a chance to substantiate Williams's largely uncorroborated story; Williams claimed that he had put the snub-nosed Securities revolver in his right pants pocket after Zeigler gave it to him behind the store. The results of a GSR (gunshot residue) test would be positive if the pants Williams wore at the restaurant were among the garments he gave to Martin.

But Hadley believed that Williams had changed his clothes during the two hours or more between the time he left Winter Garden and when he presented himself at the sheriff's station. Williams swore that he had changed into the green slacks and black cardigan sweater before he left his apartment to meet Tommy Zeigler. But three different witnesses—the apartment manager Mary Wallace, Kentucky Fried Chicken employee John Grimes, and customer Ed Nolan—all claimed that they saw Williams wearing khaki pants and a brown jacket or sweater when they saw him on Christmas Eve.

For the defense, the GSR test of Williams's green slacks was a potential chance to impeach his testimony. It was not a minor point. If he *had* changed clothes, he must have done so, and then lied about it, because he had something to conceal.

At first the state attorney would not release the disputed items. Then Eagan wrote a letter to Sheriff Colman stating that the OCSO "may release" evidence to the defense, and Gene Annan went to the 33rd Street station to pick up the packages. But sheriff's officers told Annan that the word "may" implied that the release was at their discretion, and they refused to hand over the evidence.

TWENTY-SIX

THE DEPOSITIONS OF DON AND RITA FICKE DESERVE EXAMINATION. Their three visits to the Zeigler home on Christmas Eve provide the most detailed observation of what was happening in the driveway at 75 Temple Grove during the time of the crimes.

Typically enough for this case, their testimony is not without controversy.

The Fickes were able to fix the time of these events with some confidence. They knew almost exactly when they left their house and went looking for the Zeiglers: it was 8:05. The *Tony Orlando and Dawn* variety show had just come on TV, and that was a good reason to leave; Don Ficke didn't like Tony Orlando. They stopped first to buy some milk at the Cumberland Farms grocery on Plant Street, near the center of town. Then they drove past the Van Deventer home and went on to Temple Grove, where they arrived at about 8:15.

Both said that they pulled into the driveway and found the garage open, lit, and empty. They saw only Zeigler's pickup, parked to the left side of the driveway.

They swore that they did not see Edward Williams or his truck.

It is a crucial issue. By his own testimony, at 8:15 Williams should have been waiting there, parked behind Zeigler's pickup. Williams never claimed to have been parked in the driveway for any specific length of time, but according to the state's theory he would have had to be there nearly an hour.

However, Don Ficke's secretary stated in an affidavit that he had changed his original statement after showing it to his wife. And

Frye has claimed that Don Ficke originally stated that he did see Williams on this first trip.[1]

Whatever the Fickes saw, they assumed that Tommy and Eunice were gone, so they drove to the Van Deventer home, hoping to find them there.

From this point on, the Fickes' memory of their shuttling around Winter Garden became something less than certain. As Don Ficke said in his deposition, "I didn't know what I was getting involved in, or else I would have taken a pad with me and wrote these things down." However, both Fickes agreed that they drove past the Van Deventer home again and returned to 75 Temple Grove, probably a few minutes before 8:30.

On this second visit they found the garage open and empty, as before. This time Edward Williams's truck was parked behind Tommy's pickup. Don Ficke recognized the vehicle as he got out and knocked on the Zeiglers' door. He saw a black man in the truck whom he assumed to be Williams.

The Fickes drove away and resumed their search for Tommy and Eunice, so that they could avoid walking into the party alone. At some time they drove past the furniture store and found it dark. That was likely after their second visit to Temple Grove, since Don Ficke noticed the cars of Jimmy Yawn and Robert Thompson, who had checked out of service at the Kentucky Fried Chicken at 8:30.

The Fickes returned again to 75 Temple Grove. This time Tommy's truck was alone in the driveway, the garage door was down, and Curtis Dunaway's car was parked inside. By now, according to the prosecution, Zeigler had returned from killing Charlie Mays and was about to attempt killing Edward Williams.

Finally the Fickes gave up on finding Tommy and Eunice, and they went to the party. This was probably no later than 8:45. Their various short trips around town should have consumed no more than forty minutes. Don Ficke estimated that they arrived at the party between 8:35 and 8:40. The Presbyterian minister Herman Fisher thought that he saw them between 8:40 and 9:00. Rita Ficke said that when Zeigler's call came in, at about 9:20, she had been at the party "long enough to meet everybody and get a drink."

All the evidence suggests that the Fickes' last trip to Temple

---

1. Rita Ficke was a legal secretary; her husband said that he showed her his statement only so she could correct the spelling and grammar. Both denied that they had disagreed about what they saw that night, "and we usually disagree about everything," Rita Ficke said.

Grove occurred between 8:35 and 8:45. Frye's time line placed it
at 8:40.

How did their observations at 75 Temple Grove correspond to
Edward Williams's account?

Williams was vague about times. To judge from his testimony,
he looked at his wristwatch only once between the late afternoon
until after he turned himself in at the Winter Garden headquarters. He said that he checked the time when he arrived at Zeigler's
house. It was 7:28.

After ten to fifteen minutes, Zeigler drove up in a car with two
passengers: Mays and Thomas, according to the state. They stayed
two or three minutes; the time now would be no later than 7:45,
by Williams's estimates.

He said that another ten or twelve minutes had passed when
a car pulled up in the driveway: a man and a woman stopped and
then pulled out again without getting out of the car. His mention
of the car pulling in and out of the driveway describes the Fickes'
action on their first visit, around 8:10, when they claim that he was
not present.

However, in his original statement, in his two depositions, and
at trial, Williams failed to mention seeing the Fickes a second time,
around 8:30, when they saw his pickup truck. Yet Don Ficke not
only parked near Williams's truck, but walked past it twice in going
to and from the garage.

The Fickes' depositions posed problems for both Hadley and
Eagan. The statement that only Zeigler's truck was in the driveway
at 8:15 contradicted Williams at a crucial point. If correct, it meant
that he must have been elsewhere at a time when he claimed to be
waiting for Zeigler. It raised two questions: where had he gone,
and why would he conceal it?

But the Fickes' second visit approximately fifteen minutes
later was consistent with Williams's testimony. Neither Felton
Thomas nor the neighbor, Ed Reeves, saw Williams's truck when
Williams claimed it was there, so the Fickes' second visit was the
only independent corroboration of Williams's testimony about the
hour or more when he should have been parked in the driveway.
(In fact, no other witnesses supported Williams's account of where
he was and what he was doing on Christmas Eve, until he appeared at the Kentucky Fried Chicken.)

But Eagan could not get into that testimony without also ad-
mitting the damaging observations from their first visit.

If Hadley called the Fickes, he would risk having them compromised by the controversy over whether Don Ficke had changed his original statement.

For both sides, the risk was too great. Neither Don nor Rita Ficke was called to testify: no jury ever heard the most pertinent independent testimony about the whereabouts of Edward Williams during the crime.

Table Five

TIME SEQUENCE: 75 TEMPLE GROVE DRIVE

Incorporating Ed Reeves's statement, the depositions of Don and Rita Ficke, and elements from Don Frye's time line study.

7:28 P.M.	Edward Williams arrives at Zeigler's home, finds the note (Williams testimony).
7:50	Zeigler, Mays, and Thomas arrive at Temple Grove Drive (Frye estimate). Williams sees Zeigler and two passengers in Dunaway's car. Zeigler tells Williams to wait a few more minutes (Williams testimony). Zeigler, Mays, and Thomas return to the store.
8:05	Reeves sees dark car parked behind Zeigler's pickup.
8:10	Don and Rita Ficke stop in driveway and back out. They see Zeigler's pickup truck alone, no car in garage.
8:20–8:30	Zeigler arrives home and parks the Dunaway car in the garage. He wipes down the front seat and the outside door handle. After closing the garage door, Zeigler gets into Williams's truck, carrying a paper bag (Williams testimony).
8:35	Fickes park in driveway, see Williams's truck behind Zeigler's in driveway; no car in garage.
8:45	Don and Rita Ficke drive in a third time. Williams's truck is gone. Dunaway's Olds is parked inside the garage. Ed Reeves sees dark car again.

TWENTY-SEVEN

SEVERAL OTHER DEPOSITIONS PROVIDE SOME INSIGHT INTO THE EVENTS on Christmas Eve of 1975.

The Police. From Jimmy Yawn, Robert Thompson, and others, the defense drew out details of the three police search parties that entered the store while the lights were off. Of the five who first went in the store, only Yawn and Thompson had flashlights. The others walked around the crime scene, apparently for several minutes, with no illumination except the faint light from outside.

Had any evidence been disturbed? Yawn admitted that he first saw the shoulder holster several feet away from where Don Frye eventually found it. The implication was that it had been kicked or otherwise inadvertently moved before the scene was photographed. This was the holster that provoked Frye to speculate about Zeigler's guilt, because it lay on top of dried blood splatters.

Yawn also testified that Mays's pants were up around his waist in a normal manner. He said that he didn't believe that the crank was lying on Mays's arm, where the crime scene photographs showed it.

Amy Crawford. Amy Crawford said she had arrived at the Kentucky Fried Chicken between 8:55 and 9:00; she had hurried in after calling and learning that they were about to close. She was sure of the time, because she knew that she left home at 8:50, and the drive from her house to the restaurant usually took between five and ten minutes.

She placed her order and was told that it would be ready in

approximately twenty minutes. She apparently saw Ed Nolan, whom she recognized from around town but did not know by name. In the meantime, one of the two female employees finished her shift and left. After about ten minutes, a group of three men was let into the store, and they placed an order. The employee told them that the batch would be ready in twenty minutes.

Her twenty-minute wait now was turning into half an hour. The three men made her nervous, too. She was anxious to get home: she was nine months pregnant, and overdue.

Less than five minutes later, a "black gentleman" came in and wanted to use the phone. He was dressed in a dark conservative suit and a white shirt. The store had no pay phone, and he had to wait for permission to use the store's private line.

Mrs. Crawford got the impression that he wanted to call the police. She thought that he seemed "very uncomfortable, restless or watchful. . . . He also had a hand in his pocket from time to time." She thought that he might be carrying something in the pocket.

"He was hesitant," she said. "He seemed hesitant about what his action should be. Of course I was expecting him to go right to the counter and order chicken, you know. But instead, he came over to the left of where I was. So, he was hesitant. I could not say that he looked over his shoulder, but I felt that he was being observant as to what was happening, you know, in the chicken place, and trying, you know, without being too obvious, to see what was going on around him."

He used the phone and left; he had been in the restaurant around five minutes. Less than ten minutes after he left, she heard someone in the restaurant remark, "What are the police doing over there?"

She said that eventually she waited more than half an hour for her order. This would place her departure at 9:30 or later. She said that she did not see any police cars or flashing lights. However, the defense regarded this as insignificant, since Don Ficke's unmarked car and the Edwardses' sedan were probably the only two vehicles at the front of the store during the first ten minutes after the police arrived. Robert Thompson was at the hospital with Zeigler, Yawn took his unmarked car down the driveway along the north side of the store, and Cindy Blalock had driven her cruiser into the parking lot of the Winter Garden Inn, past Charlie Mays's van.

The Nolans. Ed Nolan said that a clerk locked the front door of the restaurant at 8:55, and shortly afterward the cook started a last batch of chicken. Nolan knew that a tray of chicken needed twenty-two minutes to cook.

His testimony about time was somewhat unclear. He said that around eight or ten minutes after the store closed he unlocked the front door to let out two customers. He opened the door and found a black man outside, asking to use the telephone to call the police. Nolan let him in.

By Nolan's estimate, this would be about 9:05. But what he next said placed the time nearly twenty minutes later:

"[The black man] asked me what the police number was. I said, are you local, sir. He said, I am. I said, dial 3636.[1] It wasn't no use telling him a half-dozen numbers. Then he turned his back to me. I got the profile of how he was dressed there. Just slipped my mind. Wasn't interested in the call. When I turned back around, my brother [J. D. Nolan] was knocking on the door. He wanted me outside because he had done seen this commotion going on across the street. He had just liked to have run into—the statement I made here, somebody driving pretty fast around the corner, a police car."

Q (HADLEY): So your brother called you outside?
A (NOLAN): He went like this [indicating] to come outside.
Q: Would you describe the man that used the telephone? Was he a white man or a black man?
A: Black man.
Q: How was he dressed?
A: He was dressed, the best I can recollect, in a light brown sweater, the kind that old people wear that buttons all the way down. . . . He had a hat on. It was a dark brown or light brown. . . . Sort of a squatty man, wasn't too tall. I would say he would have weighed 160 pounds. . . .[2]
Q: Did he use the phone?
A: Yes, sir, he used the phone and I reckon he was on it about two minutes maybe.
Q: What happened then?

1. The prefix did not have to be dialed from within the town's single telephone exchange.

2. This generally described Edward Williams.

A: All right, when I let him in, most of the crowd had done gone out the door. I had left it unlocked and directly I turned around and I saw my brother. . . . I walked out the door and backed up against the door to where you couldn't get in. And directly talking to my brother a little bit. This guy gets through on the phone. He come out by me. My brother heard him. Two women approached him. Three cars were parked and they must have been in the last car over. . . . He said to the women, let's get the hell away from here, the best I can remember. . . . I was talking to my brother. He was excited; said there's something happened over there.

Jimmy Yawn, Ficke, and Robert Thompson had arrived simultaneously at the furniture store, at 9:21. J. D. Nolan, after the near collision with Yawn's car, made a U-turn on Dillard Street and parked at the Tucker Buildings, just south of the store and directly across the street from the restaurant. J.D. and his wife watched the goings-on at the furniture store for several minutes before they went across to the Kentucky Fried Chicken, and they arrived within moments after Ed Nolan unlocked the door for Williams. If the Nolans' testimony was true, this meant that Williams must have walked into the restaurant near 9:25.

Ed Nolan had further startling testimony. He claimed that later he spotted the same black man whom he had let in to use the telephone. Now, he said, the man had changed his clothes, and stood near Mattie Mays in the crowd that was gathering in front of the furniture store.

NOLAN: . . . I said, gentleman, I want to ask you something. Ain't you the guy I let in the Kentucky Fried Chicken to call the police. He said, I ain't called no police. Well, I could see his point, touchy a little bit, thinking I done him a favor. I backed off again to look at him to see if I was right. I can see his point.

Q (HADLEY): But you stood back off and studied this man?

A: Studied him out.

Q: In your own mind, were you convinced he was the same man at the Kentucky Fried Chicken?

A: He was the same man. I don't know whether it was Williams or not. It sort of burns me. I was as interested as the rest of them was.

Q: He denied it?

A: Denied it right then because he knew who I was. I suspect he was under shock enough. I bet he could recognize me right now. . . . I still have been asking myself. I don't know Williams. I didn't even know him then. All I want [is] to see him in the clothes he dressed in. You can change your clothes in thirty minutes. When you get out, you look different, especially a nigger. They're hard to identify.

Q: Yes sir; black people.

A: Yes, they're harder than we are.

Q: Mr. Nolan, thank you very much. I don't have any further questions. . . .

Ed Nolan died before the trial began. Ordinarily, Hadley would have introduced the deposition, to be read from the stand as sworn testimony. It would have been invaluable: Nolan's statement corroborated the accounts of J. D. and Madelyn Nolan. It also directly contradicted Edward Williams, who swore that he went directly to Orlando after he picked up his Camaro at the Texaco service station. Nolan placed Edward Williams in front of the furniture store at a time when both Williams and Mary Ellen Stewart swore that he was in Orlando. Nolan also implied that Williams had changed his clothes before he went to the police.

But Hadley kept the deposition out of the record. Zeigler's jury of twelve included six black men and women, and Hadley could not afford to risk alienating at least half the panel. With a single obnoxious comment, the dying man not only demolished his own identification of Williams at a time and place where Williams should not have been, he rendered his own testimony virtually useless.

TWENTY-EIGHT

HERBERT MACDONELL FLEW TO ORLANDO ON MAY 11 AND GAVE A deposition that began at 1:45 P.M. the next day in the state attorney's office. Hadley and Davids had a long list of questions. This was their first chance to probe the technical details of the state's theory. Davids had learned what he could about blood-splatter evidence, most of it from a booklet that MacDonell had written several years before.

The going was slow. Davids was debriefing the country's foremost authority on this relatively new branch of forensics, and at times the deposition was less testimony than a lecture. After about an hour and a half, Assistant State Attorney Steve Thacker told Hadley and Davids that MacDonell had to leave the building at 6:00 P.M. to catch a flight to St. Louis, where he was supposed to testify the next day.

HADLEY: Professor MacDonell, our problem is they didn't make you available today until 1:30. We've been prepared and asked to start this morning, but they wanted to have conferences with you. We have a pretty weighty responsibility. . . . We have to go through this as thoroughly as possible. I'm in total sympathy with your scheduling problem. But we've got a side we have to look after, also.

THACKER: Let's just say I think we could step it up, though.

HADLEY: Steve, with all due respect, what you think frankly doesn't make any difference because we're going to go through this as thoroughly as we need to.

THACKER: Okay, but he's going to get on a plane at 6:00 and that's what it is.

154

MacDonell told the defense that police and prosecutors had not briefed him before he inspected the store. His findings were independent, although as far as he knew, there were no differences between his conclusions and the prosecution's.

He said that Eunice Zeigler had been shot from behind as she stood in the west doorway of the kitchen, her body facing east toward the front counter. Her assailant had stood behind her, in the showroom, as he fired the fatal shot. To have fallen where she was found, her body would have had to turn half a revolution, then collapse in such a way that it was laid out with the spine perfectly aligned, her legs straight, and the left hand still in her pocket. Hadley thought it was improbable, but MacDonell insisted that the energy of the bullet could have accomplished it.

MacDonell admitted that he had written his report without examining the victims' clothing and without reference to the results of the blood examinations, which were not available. Hadley asked him about his conclusion that Zeigler had left the blood trail from the counter to a chair near the front door. MacDonell had noted that there was no blood trail to the phone on the counter; the implication was that Zeigler had called the Van Deventer home, then moved away from the counter and shot himself and walked to the front door, where he sat to wait for the police.

Q (HADLEY): Professor MacDonell, if you don't mind my throwing a monkey wrench in at this point, in your report you indicated you felt that blood trail was caused by Mr. Zeigler, Tommy Zeigler, the defendant?

A (MACDONELL): Yes.

Q: What did you base that conclusion on?

A: The fact that he was here in this chair or so I was advised. That he was in the chair and it led up to that point and the fact that no one else apparently had gone in that direction.

Q: If I may now throw the monkey wrench. I wish to advise you you were erroneously advised as to which chair he was sitting in. In addition, the blood trail is the type of blood that could not have come from Mr. Zeigler.

A: Then it obviously was not his blood. But it doesn't mean he could not have switched chairs.

Q: Sir?

A: It doesn't mean he couldn't switch chairs. But if it isn't his blood, then it's not his blood trail.

Q: It's Type A and he's Type O.
A: Hmm.

The bloodstain tests had completely failed to support Mac-Donell's contention that Zeigler had made the blood trail: *"Mr. William T. Zeigler left a rather well-defined trail of blood from the general area of the telephone on the counter to the front of the store,"* MacDonell had written. Only three persons found in the store had Type A blood: Eunice Zeigler, her father, and Charlie Mays. MacDonell and Frye were certain that Eunice had died at once, where she was found in the kitchen. According to the state's theory, Charlie Mays had been attacked and killed nearly at the spot where he was found at the back of the store. This left Perry Edwards, who must have run to the front door, wounded and bleeding, before he somehow ended up nearly one hundred feet away in the back of the showroom. Neither Frye nor MacDonell had taken this possibility into account.

The blood on Charlie Mays's sneakers and the heavy bloodstains around the cuffs of his pants also suggested that MacDonell and Frye had failed to address some important questions. The defense felt that Mays could not have innocently picked up that quantity of blood.

MacDonell told Hadley and Davids that the more severe of Mays's wounds, a gunshot in the abdomen, "possibly" could account for the blood. But he admitted that the stains around the cuffs of the pants were "an awfully heavy stained area."

Davids suggested that Mays had picked up the blood while hunkering down in a pool of blood.

"Possibly," MacDonell said. "I haven't examined these pants so I don't want to give an opinion."

But the single most critical line of his testimony passed without comment at the time. They were discussing the photographed footprint that MacDonell had identified as being the footprint of the perpetrator.

Hadley asked: "Did you do any testing, photographing in reference to the shoe print?"

Professor MacDonell answered: "No; I did not."

His four words would reverberate in the verdict.

Don Frye gave two depositions. The first was routine; Hadley and Davids were still trying to sort out the evidence and the state's theory of the crime. The second deposition was on May 14, and Hadley spent much of the time focusing on Frye's grand jury testimony.

There had been inaccuracies. In some cases Frye had presented as fact what he merely believed to be true: identifying the blood trail to the front door as having dripped from Zeigler, for example, or stating that he could "prove scientifically" that the kitchen door was closed after the incident with Edward Williams.

Other errors were more serious.

"He collected $2,000 worth of insurance," Frye told the grand jury, referring to a fire in a storage shed behind his parents' house. The implication was that Zeigler had previously committed a crime in order to collect insurance benefits, albeit in a minor way. In fact, the shed belonged to Tom senior, and Tommy collected no money.

"There is one occasion when Tommy and his father were out in the lake, and Tommy was trying to drown him," Frye told the grand jury. But now he admitted to Hadley that he could not validate it. He was not even sure who had told him the story.

"He was vicious as a boy," Frye told the grand jury. *"One time, he cut the leg off a dog to play a joke."*

Q *(HADLEY):* Did you check with Dr. Gibbs, the physician who had surgically operated on that dog?
A *(FRYE):* No; but I heard somebody had contacted him and said, I believe, it wasn't true. He had been hit by a car or something. He tried to reset the leg and it wouldn't, so it was amputated.
Q: That is correct.
A: For that particular dog.
Q: The one that went around for about twelve years as a three-legged dog?
A: That rumor is still kicking around.[1]

Frye told Hadley that two confidential informants were his sources for some of the rumors, including the homophilia. He refused to identify the informants. The rumors had extended to include most of Zeigler's friends and close associates. Hadley rattled off several names, and Frye said yes, he had heard that these men were closet homosexuals.

1. There is no evidence that the Zeiglers ever owned more than one three-legged dog.

Q: Anybody else? Spit it out.
A: No.
Q: I didn't get tagged with that rumor?
A: No.
Q: Do you have firsthand information to substantiate any of these rumors?
A: No; I do not.
Q: Has anyone advised you personally that they have had homosexual relations with W. T. Zeigler, Jr.?
A: No, they have not.

Frye told Hadley that one of the confidential informants was the source of the story about Tommy vandalizing a house that his parents had sold. But he admitted that he had not verified it.

"I planned to go talk to her," Frye told Hadley, "but I was advised from my office that was not necessary, to discontinue that. It was at this stage of the investigation that my office had informed me that I had done enough on the case. So, for a few days, there was a lag time and I just never got back to it."

Frye again refused to identify the informant. But he told Hadley: "I will clarify one thing; just about everybody that I'm talking to out there says he's capable. Anybody who has known Tommy for a long time—whether or not they would reveal this to you under oath, I don't know. . . ."

TWENTY-NINE

IN EARLY MAY, VERNON DAVIDS AND PETE RAGSDALE SPENT FOUR DAYS in Washington, D.C., interviewing the FBI experts who had tested the physical evidence. It was the defense's only chance to interview these witnesses before they testified at trial. Frye, Jack Bachman, and Steve Thacker represented the prosecution.

William Gavin, the serologist and chief examiner on the case, said that he had used a spot-checking method in testing the bloodstains on clothes. Therefore he could not say positively that a certain type of blood did not occur on a garment, only that he had not found it in the places he sampled. This was especially important in the case of Zeigler's shirt and trousers, which seemed to show a preponderance of Type A blood, rather than his own Type O.

(Further, Type A blood contains A antigens, while O blood is identified by the absence of both A and B antigens. Therefore, when A and O blood are mixed, even a relatively small proportion of A antigens will type the mixture as A blood. A deeper subgrouping would likely have eliminated this ambiguity.)

Gavin suggested that the blood samples the OCSO had submitted were too slight to be subgrouped. His explanation for the failure to subgroup did not satisfy Davids. Not even the large "known" samples drawn from Tommy Zeigler and the four corpses had been subgrouped beyond a basic Rh factor (Tommy Zeigler's blood was Rh-negative; all the others were positive). This seemed to imply that Gavin never intended to subgroup the evidence, however large or small the dry blood samples might have been.

Ruby Lee Ross, a fingerprint expert, told the visitors that she had identified Zeigler's palm print on one of the cabinet bags. She said that she had photographed some partial prints on the .357 magnum, but that they contained too few points for positive identification.

And then, she said, she had burned the photographs of those partials.

Davids was aghast. The prints might not have been valid for positive identification, but they could conceivably have shown a unique feature that eliminated Zeigler as the source of the prints. And that would virtually exonerate him, since the prosecution maintained that he alone had fired all twenty-eight shots in the store. But the evidence, whatever it showed, was now gone forever.

Davids asked why had she destroyed the photos.

She answered: because they were of no value for identification.[1]

Davids thought that a third examiner, ballistics expert Robert Sibert, "turned red and flashed like a neon sign" when Ragsdale asked him if he had performed a sodium rhodizonate test for the presence of GSR—gunshot residue—on Zeigler's trousers.

Sibert said yes, he had tested the pants, but had neglected to note it in his written report. The result, he said, had been negative. It meant that if Zeigler actually had run around the store, firing more than two dozen shots from several different weapons, he had done so without ever putting a gun in one of his pockets.

Davids also learned that Zeigler's trousers were the only piece of clothing on which the GSR test had been requested, and that both the request and the results were given orally. The defense would never have learned of it if Ragsdale had not thought to ask.

Davids wondered what else was missing from the written reports.

"The FBI sandbags like hell," he told Hadley and the others when he returned to Winter Garden.

Davids had reached another conclusion during his trip to Washington. It came from the days he spent with Ragsdale, whom he considered brilliant. They were immersed in the case. They talked about it on the airplane, they talked about it over dinner.

---

1. From a 1981 FBI handbook for police departments submitting material to the FBI Lab: "All original evidence will be returned to contributing agency unless directed to make some other disposition by the contributing agency."

They talked about it every morning when they walked to the FBI headquarters, crossing the 14th Street Bridge from their motel in Virginia, and they talked about it in the evening when they walked back; for four days they talked of little else. By now they knew the state's evidence against Zeigler, and they would take turns trying to construct a conclusive, indisputable case for his guilt.

They could not do it. No single fact proved Zeigler's guilt. No combination of facts and witness statements and test results proved his guilt. The state had a case, but it did not have proof. Take away the unsupported testimony of Edward Williams—who could hardly be called a neutral party—and there was not even much of a case, so inconclusive was the physical evidence. Davids was forced to admit it: he had begun to accept that his client might actually be innocent.

THIRTY

A SERIES OF COURT HEARINGS LAID THE GROUND RULES FOR *FLORIDA* V. *Zeigler*. Judge Paul consolidated the trials of the two counts into a single proceeding, which he set for June 1.

On April 7, Hadley argued that the trial should be moved from Orange County. Paul denied the motion.

On May 3, Hadley argued a second time for the change of venue. He believed that publicity in the case would prejudice any local jury. To support the motion, Hadley submitted articles from the *Sentinel Star*. He told Paul: "Constantly it's Tommy Zeigler, $520,000 or other miscellaneous figures used in insurance. Charlie Mays, a long-time customer of the store, lured to the store, things of this nature."[1]

---

1. A *Sentinel* editorial criticized Hadley for having created much of the publicity.

Hadley also alluded to the rumors about Zeigler that had surfaced during Don Frye's grand jury testimony: "Scandalous matter, matter which no reasonable human being would like to have said about him . . . incidents about the dog and many others which do not have foundation. In fact they are founded in rumor. . . ."

Hadley also asked for a continuance until June 21, a date that was within the limits of the speedy-trial statute. The defense was swamped with work. Hadley and Davids were conducting depositions, staying current on evidence, arguing motions, and preparing their case. They had hired two more investigators, but Eagan's office continued to add to the state's witness list. Each person on the list had to be interviewed, perhaps deposed. And, seemingly, each interview and deposition suggested the name of someone else who should be interviewed.

Hadley told Paul that he could not be ready by June 1.

Eagan argued that the FBI experts were committed to a June 1 trial, and that they could not easily appear if the trial was postponed.

Hadley countered that the sheriff had chosen to send the evidence to Washington, rather than use a local crime lab, and that the slow work of the FBI had forced the prosecution to postpone a grand jury hearing, which had delayed Zeigler's opportunity for reciprocal discovery.

Paul denied the motion for a change of venue, denied the motion for a continuance.

On May 20, Hadley and Eagan again were before Judge Paul for a hearing on several motions, including Hadley's request to suppress the evidence seized during the warrantless searches at the store and at 75 Temple Grove. Jimmy Yawn testified that on Christmas Eve, he and Thompson broke into the house "looking for hostages or bodies." Frye, Ficke, and Zeigler, among others, testified about the handwritten consent form that Zeigler had signed on Christmas morning. Zeigler swore that he did not remember the nurse asking him to sign it.

Hadley again requested a continuance. He told Paul that the late pace of discovery made it impossible for him to prepare for trial. The state had still not relinquished some physical evidence for independent testing.

Hadley argued that Zeigler was being forced to choose between his right to a prompt trial and his right to discovery.

"We worked on this case three months without the benefit of the state's witnesses, statements, testimony, or anything else, without the benefit of viewing the state's evidence," Hadley said. "We keep stumbling onto more evidence. We find out work that was not done by the FBI. We have got to try to do it. . . .

"Your Honor, Mr. Eagan would like it very much if I stood here and said we waive speedy trial. That is what he wants to hear. That is the magic word. He wants me to waive the constitutional right to a speedy trial when my client sits up there in jail held without bond. . . . The defendant did not delay the presentation to the grand jury and cause a speedy-trial problem. . . .

"We are in good faith asking for this. We desperately need the time. My client should not be compelled to choose between two equal rights simply because the state fouled up and arrested him too soon or indicted him too late. That is the state's problem, Your Honor. The state is trying to make it the defendant's problem."

Paul denied the motion for continuance. He denied the motions to suppress. The consent form was valid, he said. The evidence that Yawn seized on Christmas Eve, before the consent, was admissible because Yawn was in the house on what he perceived to be an emergency, which overrides the need for a warrant. As for the search of the store, he noted that Zeigler himself had called them to the store, and cited a "crime scene exception" to the Fourth Amendment.

". . . [T]he police were conducting a crime scene investigation which, due to its complexity, continued for more than a week . . ." he said. "The police were legally upon the premises carrying out their required duties."

One of the two minor motions that Paul did grant was Hadley's request that the state turn over physical evidence for testing. The next morning, Annan signed for the evidence at the sheriff's station, and he delivered it to a private crime lab in Sanford, Florida. The defense would finally be able to test Edward Williams's trousers, and his story.

On May 22, Hadley filed a motion to recuse Judge Paul: a request that the judge remove himself from the case. Paul's presence on the bench, after his involvement in the Andrew James matter, was a defense attorney's nightmare made real: not only had Paul and Tommy Zeigler testified on opposite sides of the Andrew James case, but it had been a rancorous, bitter case, and Zeigler was closely identified with James.

Attached to the motion were affidavits by several of Zeigler's supporters, including Mary Van Deventer, claiming that Paul's courtroom demeanor, his voice and manner, showed prejudice against the defendant.

Hadley agreed. He thought that at times the judge was palpably hostile to him and his client. If that was bothersome now, it might be disastrous before a jury. Hadley knew that a smart judge could influence the outcome of a trial in ways that never showed up on a transcript, partly through his rulings from the bench, but mostly through his expressions and tone of voice: jurors take a cue from how a judge listens to evidence or arguments.

Hadley also knew that a motion to recuse is a good way to provoke a judge's latent ill will. But he felt that he had no choice; he thought the situation could hardly get much worse.

On May 24, Judge Paul denied without discussion the motion to recuse. On Tuesday, June 1, he denied Hadley's fourth motion for a continuance, and the two sides began screening jurors in groups of twenty-five. An article in the *Sentinel Star* described Zeigler as "pale, emotionless, almost withdrawn."

The defense team had retained Stephen Robertson, a Florida psychologist, to advise on jury selection.

Some attorneys believe that this is the most important phase of a criminal trial. Both sides can probe the background and opinions of prospective jurors, in a process known as voir dire. Usually the questions are straightforward; they might touch on whether the juror truly believes in presumption of innocence, for example, or has ever been the victim of a crime.

But by 1976 some defense attorneys had begun hiring psychologists to devise more subtle tests that would develop a psychological profile of each juror. The defense used this method in the trials of black radical Angela Davis and former U.S. Attorney General John Mitchell.

Robertson was a college friend of Hadley's. He had read most of the literature on the technique. He tried to help Hadley find an expert, and he consulted with the specialist from the Angela Davis trial. But as June 1 drew near, Hadley still had found no one, and asked Robertson to join him.

Robertson was reluctant to suspend his practice, but he agreed to interview Zeigler informally in the Orange County Jail. He found Zeigler affable and cooperative, and he left thinking that Zeigler might well be innocent. Robertson agreed to help. He composed a series of questions for Hadley to ask during voir dire.

By Thursday evening, eight jurors had been tentatively seated, although neither Hadley nor Eagan had yet used any of their forty peremptory challenges, by which they could reject a juror without cause. Hadley intended to reject nearly all of them. He thought that Zeigler's prospects in Orange County were grim.

On Friday morning, June 4, Hadley and Eagan met Paul in the judge's chambers. Eagan said that he would not oppose a change of venue if Hadley finally would waive Zeigler's speedy-trial rights.

Hadley agreed. With apparent reluctance, Judge Paul ordered the trial moved out of Orange County.

Then he denied for a fifth time Hadley's motion for a continuance. The trial would begin again on Tuesday, June 8, at the Duval County Courthouse in Jacksonville.

The defense booked rooms in a moderately priced, slightly shabby hotel in Jacksonville. Five and a half months of a spare-no-expenses defense had depleted the Zeiglers' cash reserves, and business was poor at the furniture store. Tom and Beulah had put one of their apartment properties in trust to the law firm, to cover the costs of what was expected to be a month-long trial.

Hadley's team arrived in Jacksonville on Sunday, dispirited by the series of denied motions. What they learned that evening was even more discouraging.

Steve Robertson tacked a street map of Duval County up on a bulletin board. He and Leslie Gift placed pins at the addresses of each of the prospective jurors in the pool. They found that the majority were in black neighborhoods. At that time in Florida, juries tended to be overwhelmingly white. Yet Vernon Davids thought he had never seen such a preponderance of black men and women in a Florida jury pool.

Given the loathing that the murder of Charlie Mays inspired among black residents in Orange County, Hadley and Davids knew that this could not bode well for their client.[2] The trial would have

---

2. Ordinarily Hadley and Davids would have welcomed a black majority on a jury; in 1976, many trial attorneys accepted the idea that black jurors were suspicious of authority and

racial undertones, if only by implication. Zeigler was about to become that rarest of rare birds: a white citizen tried in a Southern court for the first-degree murder of a black man.

At about this time, the prosecution furnished Hadley a copy of Don Frye's taped interview with Cheryl Clafler, in which she claimed that Eunice was in fear for her life after discovering Tommy in a homosexual act with one of his friends.

He believed that the testimony was rank hearsay, and not admissible. If it was admitted, he was sure that he could demolish it. He believed that the only significance of the tape was that Frye finally had persuaded someone to go on record with the slanderous rumors that had become current since the police investigation began.

Clafler's account contained numerous inconsistencies: the insurance polices were applied for in September, not in December; Eunice had signed the applications and thus knew about them immediately; Perry Edwards, Jr., would testify that his parents had gone to Florida to spend the holidays with Tommy and Eunice, not for a rendezvous in which they would snatch her back to Georgia. Eunice was close to the wife of Zeigler's supposed homosexual infatuation, yet the wife said that she knew nothing about it, that Eunice had never mentioned such an incident to her. Nor to anyone else, apparently: none of Eunice's many friends ever claimed to have heard such a story, or anything like it. If Clafler was telling the truth, Eunice had confided in a near-stranger to the exclusion of everyone else. And why had Clafler waited nearly five months to tell police that Tommy Zeigler had threatened his wife's life?

Above all, nobody who had seen Eunice on Christmas Eve had suggested that she was under any such tension. A woman who plans to leave her husband because she fears for her life does not take a cat to a vet, or bake a cake, or routinely plan to attend a Christmas Eve service. Eunice was alone with her mother and father during most of the day on Christmas Eve. She had every opportunity to leave with them while Tommy and his parents were at the store on Christmas Eve.

---

therefore sympathetic to a defendant. That notion has since proved false. Previous victims of crime are considered ideal jurors for the prosecution, and the percentage of blacks who have been victims of crime is greater than for any other racial group.

Gene Annan and another defense investigator interviewed Clafler at the mobile home where she lived. She appeared to back away from some of her allegations.

Hadley had other reasons to discount the tape. He believed that Clafler was closely involved with a potential prosecution witness, a man who had already given some questionable and highly damaging statements against Zeigler. This man, they believed, was a source of some of Don Frye's discredited grand jury testimony.

Leslie Gift had seen Cheryl Clafler and refused to believe that Eunice Zeigler associated with her, much less confided in her.

Hadley and Davids debated whether they should depose Clafler. So far the rumors of homosexuality had not been published. But any deposition would become public record, and although the local media generally did not search out depositions, Hadley feared that someone in the prosecution would leak the story. Vernon Davids put it more bluntly: if they deposed Cheryl Clafler, he said, they would read about it the next morning in the *Sentinel Star*.

Hadley decided against the deposition. If Clafler's story reached the public, it would have to be from the witness stand.

III

THE

TRIAL

THIRTY-ONE

DO YOU READ NEWSPAPER HOROSCOPES? HADLEY ASKED PROSPECTIVE
jurors when voir dire began on Tuesday, June 6, in Jacksonville.
*Can one voter make an impact on the system? Do businessmen and
scientists provide a greater service than artists, musicians, and
professors? Do you support the Equal Rights Amendment?*

Voir dire was the defense's first chance to learn something
about the jurors who would judge Tommy Zeigler. Robertson
would have liked to interview their neighbors, at least drive by
their homes to see how they lived, but there was no time. He was
dismayed at the speed with which Zeigler was being brought to
trial. Bam, bam, bam, he thought, suddenly they were in a courtroom, about to decide a man's fate. The atmosphere was almost
chaos, he felt; the defense was not prepared, too many loose ends.
It didn't seem fair. Zeigler's life was at stake—what was the hurry?

Robertson's questions were designed to identify independent,
free-thinking personalities. This was predictable: defense attorneys are always looking for the confident, self-possessed juror who
may stubbornly hold out when the majority of the panel wants to
convict.

But he and Hadley had also decided that they wanted the
most intelligent, analytical minds they could find. They wanted
jurors who would not be overwhelmed by the imposing quantity of
the state's physical evidence. Voluminous as it was, the collection
of clothing and photographs and fingerprints and blood samples
contained nothing that positively identified anyone, including Zeigler, as the murderer.

A dozen scientists would be perfect, Robertson thought. But
there was no chance of that. The kind of juror he wanted was the

least likely to be available for a long trial, and the most likely to find a way of being rejected by one side or the other.[1]

Robertson thought that the state also knew what it wanted. Eagan used one of his challenges to remove a man with a scientific background. Another had served on military courts-martial. Ordinarily this background would be anathema for the defense, but he fit Robertson's profile in this case. Eagan rejected him, too.

By Wednesday afternoon, fourteen potential jurors remained unchallenged by either side. Hadley still had challenges to use, but Robertson believed that the rest of the pool was no more promising. A drawing of lots selected twelve jurors and two alternates. Tommy Zeigler's jury of his peers was composed of three men and nine women, six black people and six white. It was not the panel Hadley and Robertson wanted. But it was the best that they could do.

THIRTY-TWO

ALMOST ANY CRIMINAL TRIAL IS A BATTLE FOR THE PERCEPTIONS OF the jury. That was especially true of *Florida* v. *Zeigler*, in which most of the undisputed facts are trivial and most of the critical points are ambiguous.

The two opening statements on the morning of June 8 offered two versions that hardly seemed to describe the same crime.

Robert Eagan's opening was a précis of the state's theory: life insurance; a murderous plan; an attempt to take advantage of two trusting black men ("Edward Williams practically worshiped

---

1. This is the opinion of Steve Robertson, as expressed in an interview in 1991. It should be noted that one of the jurors, a young black student named Leatrice Williams, later passed the bar and is now a practicing attorney in Jacksonville.

Tommy Zeigler," Eagan told the jury); four murders and a botched try at a fifth; the dramatic scene with Williams in the back parking lot, and the self-inflicted wound.

In transcript, Eagan's words read as a dry summary, almost perfunctory. But the jurors were hearing this story for the first time. The impact must have been considerable.

Hadley, in his turn, told the jury that Tommy and Eunice were "in love and in an enviable position." The family had wealth that it wanted to protect with insurance. On Christmas Eve, Tommy Zeigler had everything. He awoke on Christmas Day having lost nearly all of it, and "this young man who lost so much is still losing." Charlie Mays was in the store as a perpetrator. Eunice and her parents "came into the wrong place at the wrong time and the first part of the tragedy occurred. They were killed, murdered brutally, but not by Tommy Zeigler."

Eagan began his case with Arthur McGraw, an OCSO crime scene technician, who identified photographs that he took in and around the store on Christmas Eve. This began a shuttle of technical witnesses who identified items of physical evidence and testified to their own part in the chain of custody.

The trail could be bewildering. A typical item of evidence was a .38 caliber lead slug that the associate medical examiner, Dr. Ruiz, recovered from Perry Edwards during his autopsy. From Ruiz it went to technician Harry Park, who gave it to Alton Evans, who packaged it for the FBI. At the FBI Lab it went from examiner William Gavin to ballistics expert Robert Sibert, then back to Gavin, who returned it to the OCSO, where it went into the care of Evans, who brought it to trial. Each of these individuals had to testify how he received it and to whom he passed it on. The slug also received four different identification numbers before it joined the collection of trial evidence. Originally the OCSO designated it Q-71.[1] At the FBI Lab it became Q-99. At trial the slug was marked for identification as item VVV, and became State's Exhibit 117 when it was admitted into evidence.

---

1. It is standard investigative procedure to designate unidentified specimens by a Q number. A Q specimen is a "questioned" item. Evidence of known origin, such as liquid blood samples drawn from a body, are "known" items and are given a K number. In the Zeigler case, the FBI Lab changed the numbering key because several of the state's K numbers actually were questioned items. This caused some confusion, especially for the defense, which was not supplied the revised key system until late in discovery.

Identifying evidence and tracing custody is a legal necessity that can become tedious. The number of state's exhibits reached 171; 98 were admitted for the defense. Many exhibits made multiple stops along the chain of custody and had to be accounted for at each destination along the chain. Alton Evans eventually testified nine times, for both the state and the defense. His testimony, dealing almost exclusively with chain of custody, totaled more than 180 pages. Taken together it would compose nearly one volume of the fourteen-volume trial record. Deputies Harry Park, James Shannon, Toivo Nasi, Robert Gosselin, and John Fischer all testified on collection and custody of evidence, as did defense investigator Gene Annan and each forensics expert on both sides.

In all, nearly 500 pages of the 2,800-page trial record are devoted to this kind of procedural housekeeping, or to the minutiae of forensic evidence. It is difficult to follow even in printed form. At trial, it must have been beyond the comprehension of the most alert jurors. Most of that testimony did not bear on Zeigler's guilt. But, combined with the lengthy and often complicated opinions of the experts, it served to lend gravity—importance by virtue of sheer mass—to the fingerprint cards and the dry blood samples and the firearms and the clothing and the swatches of carpet and the lead slugs and the ammunition and all the rest that eventually filled two large tables.

In the midst of these formalities, Eagan built the state's case.

Jack Bachman, the state attorney's investigator who happened to have been at the scene on Christmas Eve, introduced a detailed model, which he had built by hand, of the furniture store and its surroundings. Both the prosecution and the defense used the model for reference throughout the trial.

George Daniels, the manager of the TG&Y store, testified about the arrangement of lights on poles in the parking lot of the Tri-City shopping center, across Dillard Street from the furniture store. These lights, shining through the display windows in front of the store, provided much of the illumination by which Edward Williams, so he said, had seen Tommy Zeigler holding a revolver.

Lynn Churchwell, the nurse who cut the clothes off Zeigler in the emergency room at West Orange Memorial, testified somewhat out of sequence because of scheduling problems. She said that she saw "markings, some black markings, and a certain amount of blood" around the edges of the bullet hole in the front of Zeigler's shirt. As she cut the shirt away, she said, Robert

Thompson kept asking Zeigler, "Who did it?" to which Zeigler mumbled the answer, "Charlie, Charlie." He was not in shock, she said.

Under Hadley's cross-examination, she said that Zeigler's shirt was dry when she cut it off.

"I didn't get any blood on my hands," she told Hadley.

Curtis Dunaway said that he had seen surgical gloves around the furniture store, but that they weren't used for anything, as far as he knew. Dunaway had been very cooperative with the defense during the days immediately after the murders, but his relations with the Zeiglers deteriorated, and he quit his job around the end of January. Now, on direct examination, he repeated his grand jury testimony about the exchange of the automobiles. He identified the four bodies and the linoleum crank in the state's photographs. He identified Zeigler's shoulder holster, and the wall clock, and the photograph of his own Oldsmobile.

Dr. Ruiz testified for several hours the next day, on the wounds and the cause of death of each of the four victims. He used graphic slides, which Hadley tried to keep out of evidence, arguing that their emotional impact outweighed their probative value. But Paul denied the motion. Zeigler looked away from the screen as Ruiz pointed at details in the photos. Perry Edwards, Jr., who attended every day of the trial, stood up and left the courtroom.

In cross-examination, Ruiz told Hadley that he found one empty socket in Mays's mouth: an upper canine. This was a foundation for the defense's argument that *two* teeth were found in the store, with the implication that one of them must have come from the mouth of another perpetrator. Eagan, on redirect, brought out that other teeth were missing from Mays's mouth; but these, apparently, were long-gone molars.

Ted Van Deventer's testimony on Friday afternoon ended the first week of the trial. He described Zeigler's telling him on the telephone that he had been shot. He said that shortly afterward, at the hospital emergency room, he and Mickey Fisher recovered a small key pouch from Zeigler's pants; these were the keys to the Dunaway car.

Monday morning, Robert Thompson told how Zeigler had approached him about attending the Van Deventers' party. He picked up the chronology of Christmas Eve: seeing the Edwardses' car in front of the furniture store at 8:30, after his meeting with Jimmy Yawn at the Kentucky Fried Chicken; his visit to the party as Zeigler's emergency call came in; seeing the blood splatters on Zeigler's face after he unlocked the door of the store. Zeigler's clothing bore dry and damp blood, he said. The blood around the exit wound was almost dry; the wound was not bleeding.

He said that at the hospital, when he asked Zeigler who had shot him, the answer was "Charlie, Charlie Mays."

Thompson described how he entered the dark store with Yawn and Ficke and the two volunteers, looking for Mays. Shown photographs of the bodies that the OCSO took later that night, he said that he could not remember Mays's pants being down, and that he had thought that Perry Edwards's head was turned in the opposite direction.

Under cross-examination, he said that he believed some of the light switches were in the "up" or "on" position when he and Yawn began flipping them to get lights. He agreed with Hadley's description that the blood around the entrance and exit wounds was "somewhat caked" and "dry or almost dry." He was certain that Zeigler, in the emergency room, had mentioned the full name of his assailant: "Charlie, Charlie Mays."

Q *(HADLEY):* At the time you were trying to ascertain what happened to Mr. Zeigler, Chief, did he speak some names to you that were unfamiliar to you?

A *(THOMPSON):* I didn't recognize any names per se. The only other name I heard mentioned was Don, Don's plant, Mama and Daddy's Christmas present, and things of this nature, which were kind of babbling. At this point I discontinued trying to ask him anything and hurried back to the store.

Q: Chief, do you recall on January 12, 1976, giving a statement at 11:20 A.M. to the state attorney's office in Orlando, Florida?

A: I remember giving a statement, yes, sir.

Q: I am going to read a portion of that statement and ask you if you recall making that statement, sir. "At this point Mr. Zeigler began to mumble about Don's plants, Don Ficke's plant at the store. I didn't know what he was talking about. Mommy's and Daddy's Christmas present at the store, and then he mentioned several names that were unfamiliar to me." Do you recall giving that statement, sir?

A: Yes, sir.

Q: Did you make any note of the names Mr. Zeigler mentioned that were unfamiliar to you?

A: No, sir, I didn't, because the whole gist of the statement at that time appeared to be rambling and incoherent and I couldn't understand them plainly and I just assumed that he was confused and I left.

Q: You were asked on page fifteen of your statement, "Chief, did you get the impression that the people he named were back in the store also?" Answer: "No, I got the impression that they may have been people involved. I just don't know who they were." Do you recall making that statement, sir?

A: No, sir, I don't remember.

Q: It was on examination by Mr. Eagan.

A: May have.

Byron Rhodes, a paramedic, testified that in the emergency room Zeigler noticed his name on his shirt and asked about his mother, whom he apparently knew. Rhodes said that Zeigler told his physician, Dr. Albert Gleason, that he did not want to be transferred to another hospital. Phillip Wymer, a second paramedic, said that Zeigler "seemed mildly upset" in the treatment room. His wounds were not bleeding.

Dr. Gleason described Zeigler's wound, and noted that the bullet had passed to the right of any vital organs. He said that Zeigler had a contusion on the right side of his skull, a small abrasion and bruising to the front of his right leg, a black-and-blue area over his left kneecap, and a superficial abrasion of his left cheek. He said that he complained of pain and soreness in both index fingers, but that X-rays showed no fracture. Gleason told Terry Hadley in cross-examination that the contusion behind Zeigler's right ear was still swollen on December 28, four days after the injuries. On the 29th, Zeigler still had "deep tenderness" around that area.

Hadley asked if that injury was consistent with Zeigler's having been struck a blow to the back of the head.

"I believe it is," Gleason said.

Hadley asked whether anyone could shoot himself in the right abdominal area and be sure that he would not hit any vital organs.

"Not that I know of, sir," Gleason said.

The next morning—now Tuesday, June 15—Jimmy Yawn described answering the radio call to the store. He said that he drove beside the north side of the store. He believed that the gate was locked.

Q *(EAGAN):* In what way was the gate secured?

A *(YAWN):* There was a lock, padlock, on the gate and I pulled the gate as you would pull a sliding gate and the gate did not move.

Q: Did you shake it back and forth?

A: No, sir, I did not shake it back and forth.

Q: Did you have your flashlight on it?

A: No, sir. The headlights of the car.

Yawn told Hadley that the bolt was open on the rear storeroom door. He said that Mays's van was parked beside a "a heavy trailer with a—some type of heavy equipment tractor sitting on it." He said that the trailer and the tractor would have hidden Mays's van from Dillard Street.

Hadley showed Yawn one of the OCSO photos of Mays's body on the terrazzo floor, in which his pants were down and the crank lay across his outstretched right arm.

Q *(HADLEY):* . . . Is it accurate to say that Mr. Mays was in this position, either as to the crank or to his pants, at the time you observed him?

A *(YAWN):* That would be—that's not the state that he was in when I observed him.

Q: Okay. This picture is inaccurate as far as his position had changed between the time you observed him and the time it was taken?

A: Yes.

Following Yawn, Barbara Spencer Tinsley[2] became the only witness to describe what may have been the gunfire on Christmas Eve. Questioned by Eagan's assistant, Steve Thacker, she said that she arrived at her parents' house, which was west of the furniture store, at about 7:10 that evening:

Q *(THACKER):* Upon arriving at your parents' house, Mrs. Tinsley, what transpired?

A *(TINSLEY):* . . . It was maybe approximately twenty-five after, right in there, and I heard a set of what I thought at that time

---

2. She had married since Christmas Eve, and had taken her husband's name.

was firecrackers. There was maybe three or four of these explosions and I commented on it at that time to my daughter who was there also and about fifteen minutes later I heard another set of these explosions.

Q: With regard to the first set of explosions you heard, were you able to determine from what direction they were coming?

A: Yes, sir. They would have been coming from the east because my mother had the front of the house closed up and the back window open which I was sitting at in a chair and the window was to the east and it was very loud. . . .

Q: Are there houses in between the back of your house and the furniture store?

A: There are some there, sir, but they are not in line, you know, they are sporadic so there is open space there.

Q: With regard to the first set of explosions you heard, approximately how many explosions did you hear?

A: Three or four.

Q: Okay. And you say this was approximately how long after you first arrived?

A: I'd say between ten and twelve minutes.

Q: And with regard to the second set of explosions, how long after the first set did they come?

A: It was about fifteen or twenty minutes after that.

Q: And do you recall now approximately how many explosions you heard on the second occasion?

A: Well, I didn't count them but I know there were more than the first time. I would say probably six or seven.

Barbara Woodard, who had stopped at the Tri-City shopping center on Christmas Eve, testified that she and a friend happened to look across Dillard Street before she pulled out. She said she saw a tall, short-haired white man standing in the door of the furniture store. Two cars were parked in front of the store, one of them a large Ford with the parking lights turned on. She estimated that the time was about twenty minutes before eight.

Terry Hadley reminded her that in her original statement to the police she had said that the man at the door was wearing a dark jacket, blue or black. She did not dispute that description now. Hadley pointed out that in her deposition she had placed the time of this sighting simply between 7:00 and 8:00, while in her sworn statement to Frye she had given the time as 8:00 to 8:30. She explained the discrepancy by saying that Frye made her nervous, "same way you are doing."

Kathy Clark, the intensive care nurse, testified about the handwritten consent form that Zeigler signed in her presence on Christmas morning.

Now Eagan shifted from eyewitnesses. Three OCSO technicians testified about finding and seizing evidence at the store, and making fingerprint lifts. The next day—Wednesday, June 16—was spent almost entirely on technical matters and arguments on the admissibility of fingerprints found in the store and on the Dunaway automobile. James Murray, the OCSO's latent print examiner, testified that he did not identify any fingerprints of Edward Williams or Felton Thomas among prints lifted in the store.

Murray ended the first week of testimony. In that time, the most damaging evidence against Zeigler had been Barbara Woodard's, and she had not positively identified Zeigler, but only described seeing a man who generally resembled him. The state had not remotely connected Zeigler to the murders. On Thursday morning, the lead witness would be Tom Delaney, the FBI Lab's shoe print expert, who had found that the ripple-sole prints in blood, near the body of Perry Edwards, were not made by Zeigler's shoes. Hadley expected Delaney to put even more distance between his client and a guilty verdict.

The momentum of the trial was about to change, irreversibly.

THIRTY-THREE

TOM DELANEY WAS GOING TO TESTIFY OUT OF TURN. AS A DEFENSE witness, he should not have been heard until after the prosecution rested. But he was not subject to a subpoena. He could testify for the defense only through an arrangement with Eagan and the FBI, and this was the day when he had been made available.

He had arrived in Jacksonville the evening before. Thursday morning, Hadley met his star witness for the first time. Hadley and Vernon Davids briefly reviewed his testimony, and the court was called to order.[1]

His direct testimony was succinct. He said that he had made footprint tests or examinations in a thousand or more cases. Comparing Zeigler's shoes to one of the photographs of the bloody footprints—Defense Exhibit 1—he had found some general similarities, but not enough to make a positive identification. Comparing the shoes to a second photograph, Defense Exhibit 2, he found that Zeigler's shoes did not make the print. The bloody print showed a border around the edge; Zeigler's shoe did not have that border.

Eagan asked Delaney if he had used liquid blood in making his comparisons. Delaney said no, that his usual method was to press the sole of the shoe on an inked pad, and then make a print of the sole on a piece of onionskin paper, which he could place on the photograph of the unidentified print.

---

1. Hadley now says that years after the trial, he learned that Bob Eagan had met with Delaney after he arrived on Wednesday, in an attempt to shake his testimony, but that Delaney would not budge. This would have made an excellent point on rebuttal, but Delaney never mentioned the meeting to Hadley.

Eagan finished his cross-examination, the defense had no redirect, and Delaney was excused. He left the courtroom.

Eagan now called Mattie Mays to the stand, but then told Judge Paul that she had not arrived from Orlando. He asked for, and was granted, a ten-minute recess to prepare another witness.

The witness was Herbert MacDonell. The professor began by describing the work of a criminalist, and his own background and qualifications. He said that in the case at hand he had examined the store, studied OCSO photographs, and made his own photos.

Eagan asked the clerk for Zeigler's shoes in evidence and the two photographed prints that were now Defense Exhibits 1 and 2. MacDonell said yes, he had tested the shoes to compare them to the photographs.

"Was that to determine whether the shoes . . . made the prints in the photographs?" Eagan asked.

"That was the purpose, yes," MacDonell answered.

Hadley immediately asked for a hearing. With the jury out, he protested that the defense had never been informed of MacDonell's tests of the shoes. By reciprocal discovery, he said, he should have been furnished the results.

Eagan replied that there were no written results, hence nothing to furnish. Furthermore, he said, the defense itself had its own ongoing tests:

"I received last night a telephone report from Mr. Hadley of experiments they are conducting even now. . . . Everything they are doing in the way of fiber comparisons, fingerprint comparisons, blood comparisons or anything of that nature is just absolutely unknown to us and yet they call us on the phone late last night and say, hey, we have made this and we have made that. . . . We have no way of getting that evidence to conduct our own investigation."

Eagan was referring to defense tests on items of evidence that the state and police did not release until shortly before the trial. Having withheld that evidence as long as possible, having declined to do some of the same tests the defense now was conducting, and having opposed Hadley's motions for a continuance, the state was now complaining of insufficient time for discovery.

HADLEY: I'm anticipating the state didn't like the results of their expert [Delaney] so they have gone to another one—and without advising us that the tests had been run or the nature of the results. . . . Therefore, we do object. We claim surprise and feel that it would be substantially prejudicial.

JUDGE PAUL: Well, I don't know how you can hold the state to fault if they have no reports and that they do, I assume, have ongoing investigations, which evidently is what happened here, right?

EAGAN: Yes, sir.

JUDGE PAUL: I have no knowledge, I have read his deposition, as you know—

HADLEY: Yes sir.

JUDGE PAUL: —at your request. And I don't think your objection is a well-founded objection to that portion of it. I overrule it.

MacDonell began to testify again. He said that he had "examined" Zeigler's shoes on May 12—the morning before his deposition to Hadley and Davids. He said that the inked impressions he had made did not constitute testing, as Hadley had phrased the question during the deposition.

MACDONELL: . . . I examined the shoes and compared them to the prints, Defense Exhibits 1 and 2. I then made replicas of the shoe patterns using printer's ink, ordinary fingerprint ink. This was a secondary choice to using human blood since the medium in the photographs is apparently blood. . . . I wanted to use blood and did later last week when I was down. I took the ink impressions or prints, rather, back to my laboratory. I did not have an opportunity to examine them prior to the deposition and, therefore, was not withholding any information. I simply hadn't made prints or latent comparison. I went back to my laboratory and spent several hours comparing the prints that I had from the two shoes . . . to the photographs of the evidence on the floor of the furniture store. I then last week repeated the same tests by making prints in human blood. . . . These were made in the crime laboratory in this building.

Hadley and Davids were stunned. They realized for the first time that MacDonell's deposition had been delayed on May 12 because he had been examining the shoes and making the new inked impressions. Now MacDonell obviously was about to refute Delaney's conclusion that Zeigler had not made the bloody footprints in the store.

Davids asked for another hearing. When the jury was out, he

complained that the defense had never obtained copies of Mac-Donell's inked prints, made on May 12.

DAVIDS: At the deposition . . . we requested photographs, copies of all the photographs and slides and notes. . . . We were not supplied any of these items that he is presently going to testify about. . . . Nothing was disclosed to us about this man, and this is a blatant attempt to prejudice us on this, to surprise us at trial. They knew what they were doing at that time. It is obvious from the thrust of this examination and the preparation for it on May 12th. . . . They set this whole thing up to get us here today unprepared and surprise us with this type of testimony and we strenuously object, Your Honor, to this type of tactics.

EAGAN: That's absolutely untrue. . . . There were photographs of these bloody footprints about which he was examined. The inked impressions that he took have been replaced by these which are made in blood and I submit that the defense is not surprised. . . . They have made this footprint an issue and we are prepared to rebut it. We are prepared to go forward, sir.

JUDGE PAUL: You will have an opportunity to inquire of Professor MacDonell.

DAVIDS: Your Honor, in this posture we are now faced with a witness—

JUDGE PAUL: I mean outside of the courtroom.

DAVIDS: Yes, sir. Okay. Mr. Delaney has now apparently grabbed his airplane with the intervening delay and left. . . . We were lulled into allowing him to leave his subpoena and take off. We have him and the FBI in Washington with a virtual impossibility of ever getting him back down and we have not yet ever looked at [MacDonell's test prints in blood]. . . . They should be made a part of the evidence, but we have not ever been afforded an opportunity to look at these prior to—we have not seen them yet.

JUDGE PAUL: You are about to see them.

DAVIDS: Okay.

JUDGE PAUL: How long would you like a recess? Tell me. I'm sure Professor MacDonell would make it available to you during the recess.

DAVIDS: At least thirty minutes.

JUDGE PAUL: We will recess until 11:00.

Tommy and Eunice Zeigler on their wedding day, July 25, 1967. From left to right: Perry Edwards, Virginia Edwards, Eunice Zeigler, Tommy Zeigler, Beulah Zeigler, Tom Zeigler, Sr. (*Beulah Zeigler collection*)

Tommy and Eunice in 1973. (*Beulah Zeigler collection*)

Tommy and Eunice Zeigler's house, 75 Temple Grove Drive in Winter Garden, as it appears in 1992.

Dillard Street and the Zeigler Furniture Store. Note the fenced rear compound and Edward Williams's truck parked at the rear bay door; to the right of the building are the twin Tucker buildings; the Winter Garden Inn is the large L-shaped building in the lower right. The Tri-City shopping center and the Kentucky Fried Chicken are across Dillard Street. (*Police evidence photo*)

The furniture store as it appears in 1992. The pickup truck is parked in the same place the Edwards's sedan occupied on the night of the murders.

Don Ficke (hand on head) standing outside the furniture store after the murders while a deputy collects evidence from underneath a car. (© *The Orlando Sentinel*)

The bloody footprint found near Perry Edwards's body. In order for the state's case to hold up, this footprint had to have been made by Tommy Zeigler—but the FBI laboratory refuted this. (*Police evidence photo*)

Charlie Mays's body. Note the heavy caking on the soles of Mays's shoes and the amount of blood soaked into the bottom of his pants, yet the curious absence of blood swipes around his feet. (*Police evidence photo*)

Davids and Hadley interviewed MacDonell through the recess. But when court was back in session, Hadley continued to argue that the professor should not be allowed to testify about the tests or the prints that he had made without their knowledge.

HADLEY: . . . We would object to the introduction into evidence of those items that were not furnished to the defense pursuant to discovery, the ones on May 12th or the ones that were prepared last week. . . . We would claim surprise and would claim prejudice.

JUDGE PAUL: Anything further, Mr. Eagan?

EAGAN: No, Your Honor.

JUDGE PAUL: Did you say earlier, Mr. Eagan, that those reports were furnished to the defense or were available?

EAGAN: The only report that I have obtained from Professor MacDonell was furnished Counsel, Your Honor, prior to their taking his deposition.[2]

HADLEY: Your Honor, that is correct. We have a complete report on Professor MacDonell which was given to us by Mr. Eagan prior to taking his deposition. However, these matters were not covered in the report or the deposition. . . . We have never been furnished with either the ink prints that he made or the bloody ones that he intends to testify to today, and that's what we object to. . . .

JUDGE PAUL: It appears from everything that has been said that the state has complied with the discovery rules as it became known to them, Mr. Hadley. I overrule the objection and will permit him to testify on these areas.

MacDonell's testimony was poised and thorough. He said that the first of the two photographed footprints from the store shared several characteristics with Zeigler's shoe, but that he could not make a positive match. This was also Delaney's finding. But on the second photograph, the two experts disagreed. Delaney had said that Zeigler's shoes did not make that print; MacDonell said that

---

2. A document found in the state attorney's files in 1991 seems to contradict this assertion. The one-page paper captioned "Points of Testimony of Professor Herbert Leon MacDonell" enumerates eight of the professor's findings, including a discussion of the bloody shoe print and other observations that do not appear in his official report. This one-page document, apparently written by MacDonell, was never released to the defense.

he found "great similarities with an apparent individual characteristic" between the photographed footprint and his test print in blood, although he could not say positively that Zeigler's shoe had made the print in the store.

Eagan interrupted MacDonell's testimony to put on William Tobin—another FBI examiner with a scheduling crunch—who found that the store clock had been in working order when its works were jammed by a bullet that passed through the wall. But he could not say whether the clock was running at the time—that is, whether there was any electricity in the line.

Then MacDonell resumed. He noted that the left underarm of Zeigler's white T-shirt showed both soaked-through stains and "transferred stains," where another bloody garment apparently had brushed it. They had not been caused by anyone bleeding from the inside, but rather had been applied from the outside. They corresponded to the heavy Type A blood that was in the same location on Zeigler's long-sleeved outer shirt.

MacDonell noticed dark staining, which he called "gunshot residue or grease," at the entrance hole in the front of the T-shirt. Around the exit hole, he said, were "bloodstains below it quite heavy from the inside. They are internally generated from bleeding inside this garment. They don't even hardly come through."

The blood splatters on Mays's sweatshirt suggested that his right arm had been stretched out, as it was found, when he was beaten.

No bloody footprints similar to Mays's sneakers were found in the store.

MacDonell said that he had examined Mays's clothes only a week before, and had discovered fine splatters on the inside of Mays's undershorts. He now believed that Mays's undershorts had been down around his knees, pulled inside out over the top of his pants, when he was being beaten.

Vernon Davids cross-examined MacDonell closely on the bloody clothing. MacDonell said that he could not preclude the possibility that Mays was wearing the undershorts inside out, which would mean that they had not necessarily been pulled down when he was beaten.

MacDonell told Davids that he could not explain the blood splatters on the back of Zeigler's shirt. They had not been transferred from the floor. Davids asked him whether the blood could have been thrown there from a beating that occurred nearby: the defense contended that someone else had beaten Mays to death after Zeigler was shot. MacDonell said yes, it was possible. The spots were irregular; they had not dripped down from above, and they were not typical cast-off blood from a beating, but they had not occurred from Zeigler's pressing his back against a bloody surface.

Davids asked about the blood droplets on the inside of Eunice Zeigler's buttoned overcoat. MacDonell admitted that the coat probably would have had to be open when the blood fell there.

Davids did not ask a single question about MacDonell's footprint tests, or his conclusions. The defense was unprepared to confront any evidence that contradicted Tom Delaney.

Mattie Mays and Thomas Hale followed MacDonell.

Mrs. Mays's testimony was virtually the same that she had given before the grand jury. Once again she said that her husband had left home between 6:30 and 6:45 when he drove to the furniture store that evening.

Hale repeated his statement that he was parked at the intersection of Dillard Street and Route 50 around 7:05 when he saw Tommy with Eunice, turning north onto Dillard. He admitted to Hadley that he had identified Zeigler's old car as the one Tommy was driving that evening.

That evening, Hadley and Davids realized that they had erred in accepting a half-hour conference with MacDonell during the recess. An appeals court might construe the conference as a fair remedy of the state's failure to disclose the tests and the results.

Half an hour had not been nearly enough, and it showed in their cross-examination of MacDonell: they knew nothing about testing footprints. Were there any other differences between using ink and blood for the test prints? Could a print be altered by varying the amount of blood and the pressure applied to the shoe? If so, did MacDonell try to simulate Zeigler's weight in making the test prints? Did he try to duplicate the temperature and humidity inside the store? Wasn't the paper MacDonell used for the print actually more porous than the terrazzo floor?

Thirty minutes was nothing. They had needed days. They had needed to find an expert, get answers to these questions and others, before they would have a chance of seriously challenging Mac-Donell's results, or at least his methods.

The day had been a disaster. MacDonell's virtual impeachment of Tom Delaney's testimony was especially effective because of the sequence. MacDonell, as a prosecution witness, would ordinarily have taken the stand before Delaney. But his erudite testimony, coming minutes after the FBI expert, was crushing. If Delaney had belonged to any other crime lab, he would have been available for recall, to defend his work. But with Delaney beyond reach in Washington, MacDonell's damaging conclusions would go unchallenged.

THIRTY-FOUR

FRIDAY, JUNE 18: AS THE TRIAL'S SECOND WEEK ENDED, EAGAN APproached the heart of his case. Before the day was done, Felton Thomas and Edward Williams would add two huge pieces to the Christmas Eve mosaic that the state had been building since the first day of testimony.

First Eagan had another forensic witness. Ruby Lee Ross, the fingerprint expert whom the FBI Lab assigned to the case, testified to finding Zeigler's palm print on a grocery bag that the OCSO's investigators had found in the storage room cabinet, containing bullets and cartridge hulls and the two empty revolver boxes.

Hadley cross-examined her. The bag she examined was one of a double bag found together inside the cabinet, and she admitted that she didn't know whether the bag with the palm print was the outer or inner bag. She said that fingerprints on that paper might persist for as long as ten months, and that she had no way of knowing when that print was put there.

Hadley asked about the .357 magnum that was found beside Perry Edwards near the back of the showroom. She said that she had photographed a partial "visible latent" fingerprint she found on the weapon.

Q *(HADLEY):* What did you do with the photographs?
A: *(ROSS):* After they were of no value they were torn up and thrown away.
Q: I understand you to say of no value for identification?
A: That's correct.
Q: Do your notes reflect how many points of comparison were in those?
A: Any latent that turns out to be of no value we make no notes as to it.
Q: Were you saying that was of no value in a comparison with the palm prints or hand prints of the defendant Tommy Zeigler?
A: It means that in order for me to think that a latent would be of value that I would have to have at least seven points of identity, of which these impressions that appeared on the weapon did not contain seven points of identity.
Q: That is to make a positive ID?
A: That is correct.
Q: But, Miss Ross, don't you sometimes have elimination, or can have elimination by fewer points?
A: No, sir, not for me.
Q: Not for you?
A: Right.
Q: What about other people?
A: Well, they have to testify to that, not me.
Q: But you did not preserve that evidence?
A: No, I did not.
Q: Because it was of no value to you?
A: That's correct.

Once again Felton Thomas pointed out the man who had driven up while Mays and Thomas sat in the van in the motel parking lot on Christmas Eve. The car "looked like a Cadillac," Thomas said. The man he pointed out was Tommy Zeigler. His story under direct examination remained the same: the trip to the orange grove, Zeigler's attempted break-in at the store, the trip to what apparently was Zeigler's house, the trip back to the furniture store, where Thomas ran away after watching Charlie Mays enter the front door with Zeigler.

Thomas said that he had met Mays that night "after 6:00." It was dark, he said. This became the first major point that Hadley covered in cross-examination. In his deposition, Thomas had testified that "it was starting to get dark" when Mays drove up in his van.

"Is that correct?" Hadley asked now.

"That's correct," Thomas said.

Hadley asked Thomas what path Mays took to the motel parking lot. Again Thomas traced a route through the concrete-block wall behind the Tucker Buildings. Hadley ended his cross there, convinced that the wall had put a significant dent in Thomas's credibility.

Edward Williams was the first witness after the lunch break. He told the story that he and Hadley had covered twice before under oath. Williams added some new details to the key moment when he claimed that Zeigler had tried to kill him in the back of the showroom: he said that Zeigler had held the gun to his chest when he pulled the trigger, and that when the hammer fell three times "I stopped for a couple of seconds, I was so scared. . . . I ran out the door."

Mostly Williams used the same words and phrases—*snap, snap, snap . . . Please don't kill me, Mr. Tommy . . . Edward, if you don't go in there you're going to frame me*—that by now were familiar to anyone who had followed the case.

But they were not familiar to the jurors. They listened with an interest that was obvious to Terry Hadley. Williams was a convincing witness, Hadley thought, and this jury believed him.

Eagan ended his questioning after more than an hour of testimony. After a short recess, with the jury still out, Hadley put Williams's impounded clothes into evidence. Eagan asked whether the defense had any results from its late tests of the clothes. Hadley said that he had been told only that tests for blood were negative. But results were not yet available for the gunshot residue test on the pants pocket.

The clothes were marked in evidence, and Hadley got his last chance to question Edward Williams.

Hadley began with inconsistencies on what seemed to be minor points: whether the paper bag containing the two RG pistols was open when he got it from Frank Smith and delivered it to

Eunice, whether he quit work at 4:00 or 4:30 on Christmas Eve. Hadley's questioning was crisp and pointed, but not as aggressive as it might have been. He was aware of the six black jurors, whose sympathies he needed. He would lose any benefit if he was perceived as trying to trick or badger Williams.

Williams denied speaking to anyone that evening when he left his apartment and drove to meet Zeigler. He said that "it wasn't dark, quite dark" when he drove from the apartment complex, which is less than two miles from Temple Grove Drive. "The sun was down, but it wasn't dark as yet. . . . The daylight didn't darken yet." He said that the truck he drove that night had a carburetor problem that sometimes caused it to stall.

Hadley pressed him on what he saw at the store, when he claimed that Zeigler left his truck and went in the front door carrying a bag.

Q (*HADLEY*): Did Mr. Zeigler walk through the light of your truck when he got out?

A (*WILLIAMS*): He walk around the front of the car, yeah.

Q: Did you see any blood on his shirt or anything?

A: I wasn't paying no attention.

Q: Did you see the color of the bag when he walked in front of your headlights?

A: I didn't pay no attention.

Q: Did you see any blood on his face when he walked in your headlights?

A: I didn't pay no attention. I didn't see no blood; I didn't pay no attention.

Williams repeated what he had said at his first deposition, that at Mary Stewart's house he had talked to nobody on the telephone. He said that after Zeigler clicked the gun at him, he ran out and tried the back gate of the store, and that the gate was locked in place. He said that the telephone at the Kentucky Fried Chicken was not a public phone and that he did not have a dime to use a pay phone. He said that he had stayed with his truck from 7:28, when he arrived at the Zeiglers' home, until he drove to the store with Tommy.

Eagan had no redirect: a sign that Hadley's cross-examination had done no serious damage. Edward Williams walked out of the courtroom, having testified for the last time.

The day and the week ended with the brief testimony of six witnesses. John Grimes, the seventeen-year-old clerk at the Kentucky Fried Chicken, said that on the night of Christmas Eve, a frightened black man came into the restaurant and asked to call the police. Grimes testified that he told him that the number was in the front of the phone book, and the black man made a call that lasted about two minutes. Grimes said that he did not overhear the conversation, and that as far as he knew, no police cars had arrived across the street.

Grimes was a necessary witness for Eagan. The jury had to hear some corroboration of Williams's appearance at the restaurant. For the prosecution's purposes, Grimes was the best choice of a bad lot, since he was vague about the time that Williams arrived; all the other possible witnesses placed Williams at the store after 9:00. But Grimes was not without a price for the prosecution. Hadley's three questions on cross-examination brought out his testimony that Williams was wearing a brown jacket or sweater.

James Lee Bryan, an Orange County deputy, described how a work party of jail trusties had recovered the bullet from the grove south of Route 50, where Felton Thomas said that Zeigler had taken him and Mays to shoot pistols.

Fred Crawford, a firearms dealer (and brother-in-law of Zeigler's cousin Connie Crawford) testified that he had sold Tommy the .22 Beretta pistol that had been found, unfired, in the office desk drawer.

Two uniformed OCSO officers, James Pearson and Frank Hair, described the puzzling sequence at the back gate of the fenced rear compound when Pearson found the gate locked and Hair, moments later, found it open. This incident occurred shortly after police arrived at the store on Christmas Eve. Pearson said that he inspected the lock, but he admitted to Hadley that he might have been mistaken about whether the gate could be opened.

Finally, Alton Evans gave brief chain-of-custody testimony about the orange grove bullet, and Judge Paul recessed for the weekend.

Attorneys at a jury trial usually try to end the day on a high note, to give the jury some favorable evidence to ponder until the next session. By that standard, and by any other, the day belonged to Robert Eagan. The overwhelming impression was Edward Williams's story of an attempted murder in the dark furniture store, and Hadley had been unable to contradict it. After a preliminary hearing, two long depositions, and nearly a full afternoon at trial, the most important testimony against Tommy Zeigler remained unshaken.

THIRTY-FIVE

THE THIRD WEEK OF THE TRIAL BEGAN ON MONDAY MORNING, JUNE 21. Ray Ussery, the owner of Ray's Bait and Tackle in Winter Garden, testified that a clerk in his shop had sold Tommy Zeigler the Securities .38, the Smith & Wesson .38, and the Colt .357 magnum that now were in evidence.

Ussery first testified that the transactions took place on January 9, 1975. He said that he himself was busy at the time—"I was in and out, but I did know the transaction was transpiring"—so a clerk made the sale to Zeigler.

Ussery also identified the two empty pistol cartons that were found bagged with bullets and empty cartridge hulls in the storeroom cabinet. They belonged to Zeigler, he said. He could identify them because each gun carton was marked with the serial number of the firearm it originally held. According to Ussery, the original pistols from those two boxes were sold to other customers in 1972 and December 1974.

Q (EAGAN): . . . On the day that Mr. Zeigler made his purchase, sir, do you recall any matter concerning gun boxes?

A (USSERY): Well, the best of my knowledge, when we sold the two guns in question [the Smith & Wesson and the Colt] there was no box available at the time in the case or near the case.

Q: Do you have a place where you accumulate these boxes?

A: And Mr. Zeigler wanted a box to put the gun in, so Mr. Walker, the guy working for me, produced two boxes at random that we had thrown back or put on a shelf someplace that the people—the other two parties did not care for when they bought the guns, they just threw them back, and he [Zeigler] did want the boxes to carry the guns in.

Hadley showed Ussery that the firearms transactions slips for Zeigler's purchases were dated October 31, 1974, beside Ussery's signature. Ussery called the discrepancy a "clerk's error."

Hadley asked again about the empty cartons that Ussery connected to Zeigler.

Q: (*HADLEY*): As I also understand your testimony, although Mr. Zeigler did get some boxes, you cannot state positively that these are the boxes he got, can you?

A (*USSERY*): Yes, I can, because I have a record of the people we sold—the gun was sold to.

Q: Yes, sir, but my understanding is that boxes generally are thrown back someplace and accumulated. Is that right?

A: Right.

Q: So these boxes could have been given to someone else for the purpose of putting their weapons in a box somewhere along the line between 1972 and—

A: No. I don't think that happened.

Q: You don't think so?

A: I'm positive that it didn't.

Q: Now, my understanding further is that Mr. Walker of your firm is the one who actually handled the transaction. Is that right?

A: Right.

Q: So, he would be the one to place the guns in any boxes, is that correct?

A: Right.

Hadley let the matter drop. He did not ask how Ussery could be so positive about which particular empty boxes Zeigler had randomly received.

Eagan's next witness was Frank Smith, the friend of Edward Williams and key link between Zeigler and the two RG revolvers.

Smith was a tall, slim young man who had served as an Air

Force MP. After driving a cab in Orlando, he now was attending college on the GI Bill.

According to Smith, he had bought the weapons the previous June, after speaking by telephone to a man who Williams said was Tommy Zeigler. According to Smith, the man on the telephone told him that he wanted two "hot" (untraceable) pistols, and gave him a telephone number where he could be reached. Smith said he used his own money to buy the two new RG revolvers at a pawn-shop in Orlando. He called Zeigler at the number he had been given and told him that he had the pistols. (He did not remember what this number was, and had thrown away the slip where he wrote it down.) The next day Edward Williams brought him a sealed envelope containing $150, and Smith gave Williams the two pistols in a bag.

Smith said that the two RG pistols in evidence seemed to be the same ones he had bought, except for the bent trigger guard on one of them.

He admitted to Hadley that Edward Williams had initiated this transaction.

Q *(HADLEY)*: I'm talking about June at the time of this alleged telephone conversation. It was Edward Williams who con-tacted you at this time, wasn't it?

A *(SMITH)*: Edward Williams came to my apartment that morning.

Q: Right. That's what I'm trying to get at. Was it Edward Williams and he made a telephone call?

A: Yes.

Q: He dialed the number himself?

A: Yes.

Q: Did you see the number he called?

A: No.

Q: Do you know what that number was?

A: No.

Q: Now, at that time and the placing of that telephone call, had you ever met Tommy Zeigler?

A: No.

Q: Had you ever talked to him?

A: No.

Q: Did you know at that time what his voice sounded like?

A: No.

Q: So, then would it be a fair statement, Mr. Smith, that you have no way of personally knowing that that was Tommy Zeigler you talked to on the telephone?

A: Yes, that would be a fair statement.

Mary Ellen Stewart was the state's last witness with personal knowledge of what happened on Christmas Eve. In her brief direct testimony, she told Eagan that she had been a customer of the furniture store for about three years, and that in April or May she had called Zeigler when she fell behind on some payments. The next day, she said, she had returned a call from Zeigler. He had told her that he was interested in buying some illegal guns, to circumvent a supposed new law that would prevent the sale of handguns.[1] At that time he had asked her about "Smitty"—her son-in-law, Frank Smith.

She also confirmed that Edward Williams had come to her home late on Christmas Eve, that he had been very upset, and that he had made several telephone calls. She did not remember when they had left her home to go to the sheriff's office.

Hadley tried to establish a motive for her unfavorable testimony against Zeigler, asking her about an incident in 1975 when Zeigler and Curtis Dunaway went to her home and tried to repossess some of her furniture; she told Hadley that Zeigler had tried to take pieces that she had bought elsewhere.

Hadley asked her about Christmas Eve, and she contradicted her deposition and her direct testimony of a few minutes earlier: Williams, she said, had not talked to anyone on the telephone while he was at her house that night.

---

1. No such law ever existed.

THIRTY-SIX

IT IS A MEASURE OF THE STATE'S PHYSICAL EVIDENCE THAT ROBERT Eagan's opening and closing statements referred mostly to untrained witnesses whose personal testimony tied Zeigler to the crime. Edward Williams and Felton Thomas directly incriminated Zeigler. Mattie Mays, Frank Smith, and Thomas Hale implicated him by easy deduction. The accuracy of their stories might be argued, but not their significance. The accounts they gave under oath were incompatible with any theory of Zeigler's innocence.

That could not be said of the forensic testimony. Much of it, including the FBI's blood work, was so sketchy as to allow almost any construction of the facts. Some, like the ballistic evidence, was thorough but meaningless: the results might show which gun had fired a given bullet, but gave no clue to who had pulled the trigger.

The fact that the crime scene was a public place complicated the fingerprint work and the hair-and-fiber analysis. Zeigler's fingerprints were to be expected in his own store. An FBI expert found a variety of Caucasian and Negroid hairs on the clothing of the victims, but these could have fallen from any of the dozens of people who walked through the store on Christmas Eve alone. (Similarly, hairs from the Zeiglers' cats were found embedded in the blood on Charlie Mays's sneakers. But Tommy was at the store every day; hairs from his cats could have been anywhere on the floor.)

Still, forensic testimony—some from defense witnesses, most called by the state—consumed many hours in the courtroom.

William Gavin, the FBI serological expert, followed Mary Ellen Stewart to the stand and used the entire afternoon session of June 21 to testify to the blood findings that had disappointed the prosecution when they were first released.

Gavin's testimony was most notable for his explanation of why he chose not to subtype the dry blood specimens. He explained that dry samples more than two weeks old are not suitable for subtyping because of the danger of false results. He said that he received most of the samples from Alton Evans and James Shannon on December 29, but that other examinations of the evidence (in ballistics, among others) had to be completed before he began his work. "The items of evidence were to be examined prior to my examinations for blood" was how he put it. He said that by the time he received the evidence back, the blood was too old to be sub-typed.

This did not resolve the controversy. OCSO technicians had collected much of the blood evidence on swabs and filter papers that required no other tests. Yet Gavin did not subgroup these important specimens, although they were received before they were a week old.[1]

Furthermore, none of the other tests was time-dependent. Ballistic evidence, for example, could be tested anytime. Even fingerprints tend to be far less fragile than dry blood samples. The only possible conflict was with hair-and-fiber testing of the clothes; but even this should have been no impediment, since gathering hair-and-fiber evidence consists simply of brushing each piece of clothing over a clean sheet of paper.

In effect, the decision to delay blood grouping until after all the other tests were finished meant the destruction of evidence that was potentially the most important in the case, certainly the most perishable.

Five more forensic specialists testified through most of Tuesday, June 22.

An FBI hair-and-fiber examiner said that he found on Zeigler's right shoe a head hair identical to that of Perry Edwards. But the value of this discovery was questionable, since Zeigler could innocently have picked up the hair at home, or even at the back of the store: another hair similar to that of Mr. Edwards was found on Mays's sweatshirt.

Two small fibers under the fingernails of Charlie Mays were

1. The specimens were from dry blood drops and smears around the showroom. If gathered and processed correctly, they represented a complete picture of where each of the victims was shot and where he or she went after being shot. They also could have proved, or virtually disproved, the existence of an unknown sixth bleeder at the scene.

similar to the fabric of Zeigler's shirt. Don Frye believed this demonstrated that Zeigler and Mays had struggled before Zeigler killed him. But the fibers equally supported Zeigler's version, since he claimed to have grappled with assailants in the back of the showroom.

The FBI's Robert Sibert testified to the major ballistics findings. The fatal bullets from the head wounds of Perry and Virginia Edwards were matched to the Securities Industries revolver, while the bullet that had killed Eunice shared class characteristics of both RG revolvers. The "grove bullet" and the Securities pistol shared an unusual rifling pattern that Sibert said he had never before encountered. However, Sibert could not positively match the bullet and that pistol.

Sibert also testified that he had examined the entrance hole at the front of Zeigler's outer shirt. He said that he found unburned powder grains, gunshot residue, and "blast discoloration" around the edges of the hole, and concluded that the shot had been fired at a distance of less than six inches.

Stephen Platt, a forensic chemist at the Sanford Crime Lab, testified about the few items of physical evidence that were sent to that facility. He said that he detected human blood, too little for typing, on the tissue from Curtis Dunaway's car.

Platt also testified to the results of the gunshot residue tests on the hands of Charlie Mays, Virginia Edwards, and Perry Edwards.[2] The residue on Mays's hands indicated that he had fired a gun. The residue on Mrs. Edwards's right hand could be explained by powder tattooing from a gunshot wound on her right hand. (Frye believed that she was holding her hands to her head when she was executed at close range.)

But the distribution patterns of the residue on Perry Edwards's hands strongly suggested that he had handled or fired a weapon. That, in turn, suggested that the sequence of the murders was far more complex that the reconstruction of Frye or Herbert MacDonell.

Thomas Gerald Ford, a dentist with forensic training (and a nephew of the incumbent U.S. President), examined the tooth found along the north wall at the rear of the showroom. He said the tooth was from the upper left of a human jaw, "middle weight,

---

2. Neither Edward Williams nor Felton Thomas was tested.

middle-aged, most probably a black individual." This described Charlie Mays, and it was consistent with the empty socket in Mays's jaw.

Hadley gave Ford a crime scene photograph of Mays's corpse. The photo showed a loose tooth on his blue hooded sweatshirt. Ford had studied enlargements of the photo. He told Hadley that the tooth in evidence, which he held in his hand, "is not the tooth on that parka."

Don Frye appeared for brief, mostly inconsequential testimony the morning of Wednesday, June 23. He testified about the handwritten consent form Zeigler signed on Christmas morning, and about driving the routes that Felton Thomas and Edward Williams described in their statements. This testimony was mostly for the purpose of introducing an aerial photo of Winter Garden with a plastic overlay that traced the routes in two colors.

This device would help to clear up the potentially confusing testimony about the various trips around town. Frye did not present his time-line study, with good reason: strong defense testimony would show that Williams did not appear at the Kentucky Fried Chicken until after 9:00, a time that was awkward for the state's reconstruction of the crime.

Eagan wrapped up his case shortly before the noon recess on the 23rd.

George Henry, the insurance agent who had sold Zeigler one of the two $250,000 policies on Eunice's life, had testified late Tuesday. Now the other agent, Russell Courtney, filled in details of the second large policy on Eunice's life. The two agents' testimony was that neither was aware of the other application, and that at one point the potential insurance on her was nearly double what Tommy carried.

Eagan rested after nine and a half days of testimony. That afternoon, Hadley moved for a judgment of acquittal. He argued that the state's own witnesses had suggested a hypothesis of innocence—he cited the missing .22 bullet, the bloody pants and shoes of Charlie Mays, the unexplained tooth in the photograph, and Zeigler's own emergency-room statement about a robbery.

A "moral certainty" of guilt had not been established, Hadley said: "The quantum of evidence required by Florida case law is simply not there."

It was a pro forma argument. Judge Paul denied the motion. On Thursday, 9:00 A.M., Hadley would begin to present his defense.

More than one news report had noted Tommy Zeigler's calmness and detachment as the state unfolded its evidence against him. Hadley believed that for much of the past three weeks Zeigler simply had tuned out what was going on around him, as if it were too much to deal with.

But he would have to confront it soon.

Hadley planned to put Zeigler on the stand as the climax of his defense. He believed that once the jury began to consider all the other contradictory evidence, the verdict would come down to a choice between Tommy Zeigler and Edward Williams. Zeigler's silence would be a surrender.

Hadley believed that his client would stand up under Eagan's cross-examination. Zeigler had managed to hold together under the questioning of his own lawyers, who were not bound by rules of order.

If anything, Hadley thought, Zeigler might handle himself too well. Some emotion, some passion, would not be out of place. The world had definite ideas about how people should act, and Zeigler was expected to act like a man who has lost almost everything. The jury would want to see an innocent man's grief.

They would have to settle for the truth, Hadley thought. Zeigler did not show his feelings easily, even at the best of times. His friends knew a funny and generous and self-effacing young man; the world saw a blank wall. Maybe it was pride, maybe an exaggerated sense of dignity. But Hadley believed that Tommy Zeigler would never publicly display the pain of his loss, much less manufacture it. Not even to save his own life.

THIRTY-SEVEN

EXACTLY SIX MONTHS FROM THE DAY OF THE MURDERS, ON THE MORN-
ing of Thursday, June 24, Terry Hadley opened his defense with a
quick succession of witnesses.

His first was Kenneth Walsh, a meteorologist, who fixed sunset on Christmas Eve at 5:35, with full darkness beginning at 6:02.

Boyd Holt, a Winter Garden barber at whose home Edward
Williams claimed to be working on Christmas Eve, testified that he
gave Williams $20 on the afternoon of the 24th. This agreed with
Williams's testimony, but Holt added that the money was a loan,
and that Williams did not tell him that he had worked that day. The
testimony was insignificant.

Mary Wallace, the manager of the Winter Garden Village
apartments, where Williams had rented a unit on December 23,
said that he stopped outside her office and spoke to her for five or
ten minutes on the evening of Christmas Eve, as he was leaving the
complex. (Williams had testified that he spoke to nobody when he
left the apartment.) She said that he was dressed in khaki trousers
and a light brown jacket; she placed the time at about 7:00, then
claimed that it was after sunset, but before full darkness, which
would be as much as an hour earlier. Eagan did not cross-examine.

Wallace was followed to the stand by Tommy Zeigler's cousin
Connie Crawford, who testified that she and Hadley had run a
time trial between the Winter Garden Village complex and Temple
Grove Drive. The time from Williams's apartment to the Zeigler
house was two minutes and forty seconds. The object of this testimony was to impeach Williams's statement that he had gone
straight from his apartment to Temple Grove Drive, where he

arrived at 7:28. Obviously this was impossible if Williams left the apartment before dark, as Mary Wallace testified. But Wallace's first statement, that she saw Williams around 7:00, confused the issue.

Lee Jones told of seeing two cars, including a dark automobile, parked in front of the store at 7:25 on Christmas Eve.

Patricia and Richard Smith repeated the story they had told under oath to Don Frye and Lawson Lamar in early January. Both agreed that at 7:57 they saw two cars, one very dark and smaller than the other, parked in front of the furniture store. Patricia Smith said specifically that neither car was the Dunaway Oldsmobile. Her husband said that the larger, lighter-colored car was possibly two-toned, darker on top than on the bottom—the reverse of the color scheme of Dunaway's car. Richard Smith also testified about the scene at the hospital on Christmas Day, when Zeigler wept after hearing that Eunice was dead.

Zeigler's neighbor Ed Reeves gave his testimony about the dark car in the driveway at 75 Temple Grove. He admitted under cross-examination that he could give no other description, but he told Eagan that it was certainly not a pickup truck.

None of these witnesses testified for more than a few minutes, and Eagan cross-examined them briefly or not at all. At one point Hadley needed a recess because he had used all the witnesses he had prepared for the morning session. The effect this rapid pace may have had on the jury can only be speculated; in transcript, though, the testimony seems perfunctory. And the quick tempo continued: Hadley now called his ninth and tenth witnesses, whose testimony was critical.

Madelyn Nolan was the sister-in-law of Ed Nolan, who had sworn in a deposition that he had opened the door for Williams at the Kentucky Fried Chicken. Ed Nolan by now was dead of cancer, and Hadley had decided against using his deposition. But Madelyn Nolan now testified about the same incident, and her words had disturbing implications for the state's case.

She said that on Christmas Eve she and her husband were at their home in Winter Garden until about 9:15, when they left to drive to her mother's house, where she was going to help prepare Christmas dinner.

They drove south on Dillard, she said. Her husband was at the wheel.

Q (HADLEY): Would you tell us what happened?

A (MADELYN NOLAN): A car pulled out in front of us and went up into the Zeigler Furniture Store. We turned into the tag place [a state auto licensing office] because we almost collided.

Q: Now, you described a tag place. That is the buildings in the area [the Tucker Buildings] that are located immediately next door to the Zeigler Furniture Store?

A: That's right.

Q: What did you do then?

A: Well, we saw it was a policeman. We didn't say anything.

Q: Was your husband a little mad because he had almost been hit?

A: That's right.

Q: Where did you pull up over here in the tag agency?

A: Facing Zeigler's Furniture Store.

She described seeing another car pull up at the store. Two men opened the door to the furniture store, and a third man came out and got in one of the cars: this was surely the moment that Don Ficke and Robert Thompson arrived at the store, and Thompson took the wounded Tommy Zeigler to his patrol car.

She testified that she and her husband watched one of the cars leave—Thompson taking Zeigler to the hospital. Then she and her husband noticed Ed Nolan in the front door of the Kentucky Fried Chicken, and they crossed the street to the restaurant.

Q: Okay. And what happened when you got over there?

A: We motioned for his brother. He was inside. We told him something—we motioned for him to come out.

Q: All right.

A: We told him something had happened at the Zeigler Furniture Store.

Q: Right. And what happened next?

A: A colored man come up and asked to use the phone to call the sheriff's office.

Q: That was after the police had arrived at the W. T. Zeigler Furniture Store and carried the man that you saw out the front door?

A: That was happening at about the same time.

Q: Okay. This happened and then after you saw this at the Zeigler Furniture Store, the police arrived and the man come out the door, then you went to the Kentucky Fried Chicken?

A: Yes.

Q: And it was then that this black gentleman you described came up and asked to use the telephone?

A: Yes.

Eagan had no questions.

Hadley now brought Madelyn's husband, J. D. Nolan, who described the near-broadside with Jimmy Yawn's unmarked police car as they approached Route 50 on Dillard. Nolan said that he made a U-turn and pulled into the front lot of the Tucker Buildings to see what was happening. He watched Thompson drive away with Zeigler. Then J.D. noticed his brother in the door of the restaurant. He crossed the street and spoke to him.

A (*J. D. NOLAN*): . . . I said, "There is some trouble going on over there. I don't know what it is," and I told him about the guy that liked to hit me and I went up there. About that time, I say it couldn't have been like four or five minutes, I say a short time, the colored guy come up and asked to use the telephone. I said, "I don't know because the place is closed."

Q (*HADLEY*): Now, could you describe this gentleman, build, age, and this kind of thing?

A: Well, I'd say probably he is around—I'd just rough guess like fifty or fifty-five years old, might be a little bit older or a little bit younger. I didn't pay that much attention, but he was kind of an old fellow. I would say probably about my age, but he must have been roughly, I'd say, weighed about a hundred and sixty-five pounds or it could have been more because he had a jacket or something or other on. You know, you could be a little lighter than you really are when you have got a lot of clothes on.

Eagan asked J. D. Nolan if he had seen "the boy with the long hair that works there in his teens or early twenties"—a description of the restaurant employee John Grimes, who had testified for the defense the week before.

Nolan said no.[1]

---

1. J. D. Nolan never entered the restaurant.

J. D. NOLAN: . . . I don't know who was working or what because
I didn't pay that much attention. I just told the guy that was
wanting to use the phone—

Q (EAGAN): Is that all you heard him ask?

A: Sir?

Q: Is that all you heard him ask?

A: He said, "I want to use the phone." I said, "You can't. This
place is closed." I said, "I'm sure they got one." He said, "I
need to use the phone to call the sheriff," and that's all I paid
any attention to.

Q: And since that time have you been shown any photographs of
black men?

A: I beg your pardon?

Q: Since that time had anyone come out to you and talked to you
and shown you photographs?

A: No, sir, no one at all. This is the first time I have even talked to
anybody like this about this.

Eagan's last question seemed to imply that J. D. Nolan was
mistaken in his description of Edward Williams. But on the whole,
his testimony was intact. His wife's testimony, virtually identical,
was unchallenged.

Hadley now put on Stoney Holon, a service station mechanic
who had worked on Edward Williams's pickup truck about a week
or ten days before Christmas Eve. Holon said that the truck had a
bad battery and a cracked carburetor float ball, which he had not
fixed before Christmas Eve.

Q (HADLEY): Describe what circumstances would cause him to
have difficulty.

A (HOLON): His most difficulty would become—I mean, would happen like after it's ran awhile, you know, and then shut down
and it was a constant fuel leakage into the ball which caused
it to hardly—you know, be kind of hard to start. . . . If it didn't
fire up the first time he was sunk. I mean, it would just flood
over.

Q: This was compounded with the battery, too, wasn't it?

A: The battery would be dead by this time.

Q: This occurred after the car had been running—I mean the truck
had been started and running for a long period of time?

A: Yes. He would have more problem when it was hot, had been
running.

Hadley now admitted to Judge Paul that he was out of witnesses. Paul recessed until noon. After lunch, Alton Evans, a sheriff's deputy, gave chain-of-custody testimony for several items that the defense introduced into evidence. Then Gene Annan and Ernest Crawford—the husband of Zeigler's cousin Connie—testified about a visibility test they performed in the store.

This experiment was similar to the one that Frye had tried with Denny Martin, testing whether Edward Williams could have seen a pistol in Zeigler's hand when he entered the showroom. But there were a couple of important differences. Annan, playing the part of Williams, did not allow his eyes to adjust to the darkness inside the building as Frye and Martin had. And Crawford, standing where Williams said Zeigler had clicked the pistol at him, held three different objects—a can of spray paint, a vacuum cleaner attachment, and a chrome-plated flashlight—as Annan came down the hallway three times.

Annan testified that parking-lot lamps at the Tri-City shopping center did throw some light into the store, but that the kitchen partition created a shadow where Williams claimed Zeigler was standing. Annan said that in three tries he could not make out what Crawford was holding in his hand.

Hadley was barely an hour into the afternoon session when he told the judge that he had no more witnesses for the day. The testimony had gone much more quickly than he had planned.

Judge Paul recessed until the morning.

It was a mixed bag of testimony for the defense: sixteen witnesses, some important and others almost trivial, all of them quickly on and off the stand. Among them were J. D. and Madelyn Nolan. Their testimony, by inference, directly refuted Edward Williams at the most critical point of his story—that is, his account of the events at the furniture store that supposedly caused him to run away and try to call the police. There was no innocent explanation for Williams's arriving at the restaurant after Zeigler had already left for the hospital.

Whether the jury understood that implication or whether the Nolans were simply lost in the fast shuffle of witnesses may never be known. Whether the defense team itself completely grasped the significance of the Nolans' testimony is arguable. But the fact is that the most important independent testimony in the trial, the potential centerpiece of the argument for Zeigler's inocence, had quickly come and gone within the first morning of the defense's case.

THIRTY-EIGHT

THE RAPID SUCCESSION OF DEFENSE WITNESSES CONTINUED THE NEXT morning, Friday the 25th.

Among them were:

- Cleo Anderson, who verified that Felton Thomas had come to his home late Christmas Eve while he cooked wild game for Christmas dinner but—in a direct contradiction to Thomas's testimony—stated that Thomas never mentioned anything strange occuring at the furniture store.
- Powell Walker, the superintendent of three citrus harvesting crews, including Charlie Mays's, who testified that he gave Mays $453 in salary and a loan on December 23, paid by check.
- Beulah Zeigler, who testified that at least $1,000, plus undetermined amounts of cash from the cigar box and the top of her son's desk, were unaccounted for after the crime.
- Rogenia Thomas, who repeated her testimony that Edward Williams never mentioned Tommy Zeigler by name after she met him in front of the Kentucky Fried Chicken and drove him to his car.
- Curtis Dunaway, who testified that he and Tommy Zeigler twice went to Mary Ellen Stewart's home in 1975, attempting to repossess furniture that was never paid for; also, that the roll-up cargo door at the back of the storeroom was usually left open during the day. (The defense theorized that someone might have entered the storeroom before closing, hidden, then opened the back door to let in other assailants.) Dunaway also said that he had bolted the swinging rear door at the back when he locked up on Christmas Eve. Under cross-examination, Dunaway told Eagan

that on Christmas Eve Zeigler had not turned on the large display lights that usually burned all night in the front windows.

• Felton Jones, an eyewitness who claimed that he saw only one car—the Edwardses' Ford—in front of the store when he left the Tri-City shopping center around 8:05. When Eagan cross-examined him, though, he said that no stores were open in the shopping center when he left, which would have meant that the time was after 9:00.

• Gene Annan, the defense investigator, who testified that he inspected the metal garage door at Zeigler's home around January and found that the door appeared to have been forced at the top.

• Claude Truby, the Sanford Crime Lab fingerprint expert, who had previously identified Zeigler's fingerprint on the tissue paper from Curtis Dunaway's car and now testified about the potential value of partial prints. Truby said that even with fewer than seven points of identification, it was sometimes possible to "eliminate" a partial print—that is, to show that it did not match the known sample print. A single characteristic, such as an S curve in the whorls, would be definitive if it did not appear in the same place on the sample print: "Even though there's only three or four or five characteristics, you could eliminate that print because that one characteristic is missing. It's obvious it couldn't be made by the same print. That one thing is missing, it doesn't correspond."

Hadley indirectly alluded to the testimony of Ruby Lee Ross, the FBI fingerprint expert who had destroyed the prints from the .357 magnum revolver because they had fewer than seven points.

Q: Now, Mr. Truby, have you ever, in working on a case, developed prints and then destroyed them if they had less than seven points?

A: No, sir. I keep them in my files.

Q: You keep all the prints you develop, don't you?

A: Until I eliminate them or identify them, yes.

Q: And even if you consider them of limited value you keep them, don't you?

A: Yes, sir.

Q: Such as the ones on the tissue in this case, is that not correct?

A: Yes, sir.

Q: The first photographs you developed were of limited value, weren't they?

A: Yes, sir.

Q: But you nonetheless kept those prints?

A: Yes, sir.

Q: Do you consider it good practice to destroy prints just because they merely are of limited value, sir?

A: I don't personally consider it good practice, sir, and I don't do it.

Again the pace of testimony was rapid. For the second straight day, Hadley ran out of witnesses early in the afternoon.

But the court had business out of the hearing of the jury. One juror, a black woman named Johnestine Young, had told Judge Paul in a note that her long-planned group vacation to Canada was now a week away; she would lose a $400 deposit if she didn't take the trip as scheduled. Eagan and Hadley conferred with the judge, and they all agreed that she should be excused if there was a chance that her attention might be elsewhere.

The first alternate juror, who would replace her, was a young white college student named James Roberts. In voir dire he had struck Hadley and the psychologist Stephen Robertson as something of a maverick. They thought he might be a slightly unconventional, antiestablishment voice on the jury.

Judge Paul released Mrs. Young and added Roberts to the panel.

Hadley then argued for the court to admit Zeigler's Sodium Brevital interview. It was a faint hope; in 1976, as now, narcotherapy interviews were accorded about the same legal status as lie detector tests, and were almost universally inadmissible as evidence. Judge Paul denied Hadley both the facts of the test and the videotape, and he recessed for the weekend.

The trial was now exactly one week away from a verdict.

THIRTY-NINE

THOUGH "REASONABLE DOUBT" IS THE LEGAL REQUIREMENT FOR AC-
quittal in a criminal trial, Hadley believed that he needed to show
the jury a convincing hypothesis of Zeigler's innocence. Bob
Eagan's closing statement would surely argue that the state's evidence foreclosed any possibility that Zeigler had not committed the
crime.

On one level, Zeigler's own testimony about Christmas Eve
would provide an alternative to the state's case: he drove to the
store with Edward Williams, he was beaten and shot as he walked
into the showroom. The footprint testimony of FBI expert Thomas
Delaney, though contradicted by Herbert MacDonell's findings,
nevertheless introduced the strong possibility of an unknown assailant. The "dark car" testimony of Ed Reeves and Richard and
Patricia Smith also suggested that someone else, unaccounted-for
by the state, had been a part of the crime.

But that evidence implied a deeper question. What was this
crime? Why had it happened? Eunice and her parents might have
walked unexpectedly into an ambush, but Zeigler—guilty or innocent—was there by appointment. If Zeigler was innocent, then he
was the victim of a plot. Who disliked him so greatly?

On Monday, June 28, Hadley called as a witness Andrew
James, the black bar owner whom Zeigler had befriended in the
fight to save his liquor license. Hadley hoped that this testimony
might help dispel the image of Zeigler as a man who contemptu-
ously manipulated his black acquaintances. But he also managed to
put on the record the possibility that Zeigler had made enemies of
powerful criminal elements in his hometown.

It was an extraordinary scene. Andrew James began to testify about preparations for the trial in which Judge Paul had been a prosecution witness. Surprisingly, Eagan did not object to the relevance of this exchange:

Q (*HADLEY*): Calling your attention to the summer months of 1975, who was your attorney at that time?

A (*JAMES*): You were, sir.

Q: And you and I had a case together?

A: Yes, sir.

Q: Did Thomas Zeigler at that time render any assistance to you?

A: Yes, sir, he did.

Q: Did he aid and assist in your case on obtaining any information?

A: Yes, sir.

Q: About whom was that information obtained?

A: Loan sharks.

Q: Did he obtain any information for you on that case about law enforcement officers as well?

A: Yes, sir, he did.

Q: And as a result of that was testimony presented on your behalf?

A: Yes, sir.

Q: Was that testimony about loan sharks and law enforcement officers that worked with them?

A: Yes, sir, it was.

Q: In fact, was it about law enforcement officers that protected loan sharks?

A: Yes, sir.

HADLEY: You may inquire, Mr. Eagan.

Q (*EAGAN*): Do you work in a bar?

A (*JAMES*): Yes, sir.

Q: An officer went there and bought some marijuana from you—

Hadley immediately objected that Eagan's question was irrelevant and immaterial. The jury was sent out, and Eagan argued for his question.

EAGAN: May it please the court, frankly, I think the whole of this witness's testimony is irrelevant and immaterial, but nevertheless it is here and now I am cross-examining him on it. . . . I propose to show that this man at that time was under prosecution for selling marijuana in that bar, that he was arrested by agents of the Florida Beverage Department for that offense, and that as part of his defense he was attempting to impeach the officers by this information, that the jury nevertheless found him guilty of the charge against him. I think that is the gist of it, Your Honor.

JUDGE PAUL: Let me ask a question. What is the relevancy and materiality of this testimony? I couldn't understand why we didn't have an objection.

EAGAN: I apologize to the court.

Hadley explained to Paul that he wanted to show a motive for revenge against Zeigler.

Paul asked Hadley: "Is it some of these loan sharks or law enforcement people who are seeking revenge? Is that what you are saying?"

Hadley said yes, that was the theory.

In any case, Paul was not being asked to rule on James's direct testimony—that was already on the record now—but on Hadley's objections to Eagan's line of questioning.

The judge said that Eagan could examine James.

"You brought it in," Paul told Hadley. "I can't limit the cross-examination once you bring it in if it's within the scope of cross, and it is."

The jury was seated again. Eagan, improbably, began a series of questions to identify the people who might have a grudge against Zeigler as a result of the James trial.

Q (EAGAN): You were arrested there in your bar by agents of the Florida State Beverage Department?

A (JAMES): Yes, sir.

Q: And it was against these agents that Mr. Zeigler was going to help you get information that they were protecting loan sharks, is that right?

A: Say that question over, sir.

Q: Who were the agents or law enforcement officers concerning whom this man brought you information? Who are they?

A: Officer Williams was one, on the Winter Garden Police Department.

Q: Of what police department?

A: Winter Garden Police.

Q: The Winter Garden Police Department. And who was the other one?

A: Agent Baker was one.
Q: Of the Florida Beverage Department?
A: Right.

Eagan elicited the fact that the jury in James's criminal trial returned a guilty verdict. Hadley, on redirect, established that the judge in the case had withheld adjudication, that James had kept his liquor license, and that the Winter Garden officer, Stoney Williams, had later been convicted of a crime.

The value of James's appearance may have been slight for the jury, since Hadley did not develop the revenge theory beyond a few questions. But for students of the record, it presents the remarkable tableau of the presiding judge, Maurice Paul, listening to testimony that one of "these loan sharks or law enforcement people who are seeking revenge" included the man for whose character he had vouched under oath just one year before.

During the rest of that Monday, Hadley brought on an assortment of witnesses who sniped at the state's case.

Rhonda Hull, the ex-wife of defense witness Thomas Hale, testified that Hale was a frequent liar who often exaggerated to make himself important.

Hadley got the same from Sonja Barker, who said that she had known Hale for eight years:

Q (HADLEY): Are you acquainted with the reputation of Mr. Thomas Hale for truth and veracity in the community?
A: (BARKER): Yes, sir.
Q: What is that reputation?
A: Well, he has a tendency to sometimes lie and exaggerate.
Q: On the tendency to exaggerate, do you know why he likes this to happen?
A: Yes, sir, he likes to have a lot of attention, to make himself look bigger, more important.
Q: Does he have a reputation for lying?
A: Yes, sir.

Philip Cross, one of Don Ficke's two volunteer deputies on Christmas Eve, testified that he saw one car—apparently the Edwardses' Ford—parked in front of the furniture store a couple of minutes after 8:00 P.M. He said that he placed the time exactly because he looked at his watch shortly before he drove past. (According to Don Frye's time line, this was when Zeigler was killing Charlie Mays, so the Dunaway car should have been parked out front.)

Cross also described entering the store with the original "search party" that went in looking for Mays.

Q (HADLEY): Were the lights on when you went in?
A (CROSS): No, sir, they were not.
Q: Did you have a flashlight?
A: No, sir, I did not.
Q: Describe how you proceeded into the store.
A: We proceeded—there was myself, Richard Sims, Officer Yawn, Chief Ficke, and Chief Thompson. Officer Yawn, Chief Ficke, and Chief Thompson were out to the front. Mr. Sims and myself were kind of to the rear of those three backing them up.
Q: Now, Mr. Cross, throughout the time you were in the store, were there periods where you were walking where you couldn't see where you were going?
A: Yes, sir.
Q: Is it possible, sir, that you may have in the darkness kicked or moved objects around without seeing them?
A: That would have been possible, yes, sir.

Hadley for the first time addressed the issue of the insurance when he called Ted Van Deventer, who testified that he had drawn wills for Tommy and Eunice. Each was the other's main beneficiary and executor; Tom and Beulah were the alternate beneficiaries of both wills.

Van Deventer said that he had advised Tommy and Eunice in April 1975 that the wills were not adequate for estate planning, and that they ought to consult with him and an insurance underwriter about life coverage. Then, he said, Tommy told him in the first or second week of December that he had purchased some insurance: "He indicated at that time that he had—I believe his terminology was 'beefed up' the insurance provisions, both for he and Eunice, in order to meet the estate tax requirements."

Eagan had hardly challenged most of the eyewitnesses. But he closely cross-examined Van Deventer, in a manner that the *Sentinel Star* described as "angered." Van Deventer admitted that

Eunice did not independently own a share of the family corporation, or any of the family's real estate properties; in case of her
death, the estate tax liabilities would have been limited.

Over Hadley's objection, Eagan asked Van Deventer about a
conversation he had had with insurance agent Russell Courtney at
the memorial service for Eunice on December 31.

Q (EAGAN): At that memorial service did Mr. Russell Courtney ask
you about this insurance and what your idea—
A (VAN DEVENTER): No, he didn't really ask me, he told me.
Q: What did he say to you?
A: He said that his company had furnished insurance to Mr. Zei-
gler, both for Mr. Zeigler and Mrs. Zeigler, in the amount of
$250,000.
Q: Did you tell him at that time, either in these words or words to
this effect, "Well, I don't know anything about it"?
A: My words to him were I did not know it was with his company
or the amount.
Q: Did you state to him—I want a yes or no on this, please, sir—
"Russell, I didn't know anything about it"?
A: Not in those words, no.

Alton Evans testified that the sheriff's property receipts did
not mention Eunice's two diamond rings and two $20 bills, which
the defense contended she had with her when she went to the store
on Christmas Eve.

Gene Annan presented the photo Thomas Hale had identified
as being of the car Zeigler was driving on Christmas Eve; Annan
denied Eagan's suggestion that he had hoodwinked Hale into identifying the wrong Oldsmobile.

Late in the afternoon, Hadley presented the defense's forensic expert. Roger Morrison, a former criminalist at the Sanford
Crime Lab, was now an owner of the private forensics laboratory
where the defense had sent its physical evidence for testing.

Morrison said that hair trapped in the dried blood on Charlie
Mays's shoes was consistent with hair from certain of the Zeiglers'
cats. More of the hair was embedded in an unidentified "gummy
sticky substance" that Morrison found on the soles of Mays's
sneakers. He said that pieces of gold glitter embedded in the
gummy substance—"gunk," Hadley termed it—was similar to
Christmas glitter from the Zeigler house, though generally smaller.

And he matched the shattered eyeglasses from the pocket of Perry Edwards to the glass fragments found in the bloody patch east of the counter: the spot where the defense believed that hidden assailants may have ambushed Eunice and her parents.

Hadley was unable to question Morrison about one piece of evidence—key evidence, as far as Hadley was concerned. In his cross-examination of Edward Williams, Hadley had pinned down Williams on the question of where he carried the Securities pistol when he went to the Kentucky Fried Chicken: in his right pants pocket, Williams said. Hadley saw this as a unique chance to scrutinize a specific point of Williams's testimony.

But that depended on results from Roger Morrison's laboratory. The laboratory's gunshot residue test of the right pocket of Williams's pants was still not complete, and the testimony phase of the trial was near an end.

The next morning, Tommy Zeigler would take the stand in his own defense.

FORTY

HADLEY OPENED TUESDAY, JUNE 29, WITH A REQUEST TO PUT THE defense's consulting psychiatrist, Allen Zimmer, on the stand. Hadley was about to attempt an unusual tack for a defense attorney: he wanted to present evidence that his client was too sane and well-adjusted to have committed the crimes.

With the jury out, Zimmer gave "proffer"—that is, a preview of his potential testimony, given with the jury out, so that the judge could rule on its value.

He said he had practiced his specialty for nine years, in Florida, Ohio, Missouri, and California, and that he had been "involved with approximately six to eight thousand personalities of antisocial behavior." He referred to his four-day psychiatric examination of Zeigler in the Orange County Jail.

Zimmer said that the murders in the furniture store were "a heinous crime in any standard and would require an individual who was completely irresponsible and who has no conscience and who has no compassion and who has no awareness of the consequences of his behavior for which he probably has rationalized." The crime appeared to be the work of a psychopath, he said.

Hadley asked whether Zeigler was a psychopath.

"Tommy Zeigler is not a psychopath. My diagnosis was that he had no mental disorder," Zimmer said.

Had he found any indication of antisocial traits?

"On the contrary. I found him to be just the opposite."

Eagan argued that the testimony was incompetent. Every man is presumed to be sane, he said, and no issue of insanity had been raised.

Hadley answered that by charging Zeigler with such crimes the state had, in effect, put his mental health in question.

Paul denied the proffer: Zimmer's testimony was irrelevant; he would not be allowed to testify that Tommy Zeigler was incapable of committing the crimes.

Alton Evans, on the stand for the ninth time, testified that no money or valuables were found on the bodies of Eunice Zeigler, Perry Edwards, or Virginia Edwards.

Hadley called Tommy Zeigler.

Zeigler's voice was quiet, perhaps slightly timid, as he answered some preliminary questions from Hadley about his position as president of the family corporations, and about duties at the furniture store.

Within the first several minutes, Hadley moved into critical territory.

Q (*HADLEY*): Did you see that gentleman that took the stand, Mr. Frank Smith?
A (*ZEIGLER*): Yes, I did.
Q: Have you ever met that man in your life?
A: No, I haven't.
Q: Before this case came up did you even know of his existence?
A: No, sir, I did not.
Q: In April of 1975 did you talk to Mary Stewart about any guns?
A: No, sir, I did not.

Q: Have you ever asked Mary Stewart to help you get some guns?
A: No sir, I have not.

Hadley next brought up the matter of the insurance policies. Zeigler said that in April 1975, Ted Van Deventer had suggested that he and Eunice should begin estate planning. This became more pressing, he said, after his father's stroke in July.

In August or September, he said, an insurance agent named Hardy Vaughn compiled an estate planning package that showed that the tax liability on his and Eunice's gross estate might run as high as $500,000.

Zeigler said: "Terry, everything the family had would go either to myself or to Eunice, depending on which one survived the other. This is the way that my family had it set up, and this is the way that Eunice and I set it up. . . . According to Judge Van Deventer when he was discussing this very briefly with both of us, we would have had to have sold off property in order to pay federal inheritance tax in the event that something had happened."

Zeigler said that he intended to buy an insurance package through Vaughn, who had served with him in the Army Reserve. But Tom and Beulah—"Papa" and "Mother," as he invariably referred to them—believed that any insurance should be carried through local agents; they wanted to keep their business in the community.

Zeigler said that two Winter Garden agents, Russ Courtney and George Henry, both frequently came into the store to try to sell him insurance. With each, separately, he applied for policies on Eunice. He did not apply for policies on himself, because he already had $250,000 in his own name and he still hoped to be able to take out one through Hardy Vaughn, if he could persuade his parents.

Q: Did you ever take out a policy with Mr. Vaughn on yourself?
A: No, sir, I did not.
Q: Why not?
A: Because Mr. Henry with Gulf Life told me that I would have to take out a like amount of insurance on myself with Gulf Life.
Q: That was part of the deal with getting a policy on your wife?
A: That's correct, sir.

Q: Now, Tommy, did either you or Eunice tell Mr. Courtney—or what was the gentleman's name from Gulf?

A: Mr. George Henry.

Q: —Mr. George Henry about the other?

A: No, sir, I don't believe so.

Q: Why not?

A: Number one, we weren't asked.

Q: There is a place on the application for it, isn't there?

A: That was never asked during the application, I'm sure, Terry.

Q: Did the gentleman fill out the application for you?

A: Yes, he did.

Q: Now was there any other reason you did not tell Mr. Courtney about Mr. Henry or Mr. Henry about Mr. Courtney?

A: Both of those men are very competitive and they would have wanted all the insurance. This is their bag. This is what they sell.

Q: You were trying to spread it around for community relations purposes?

A: This is correct. This is what we've always done.

Q: Take your business to as many different people as you can?

A: Yes, sir, and that way you get more customers in your business.

Hadley moved on.

Did Zeigler frequently handle the grocery bags around the house? He did.

And what of the white tissue found in the Dunaway car? The store used white tissue paper inside gift boxes, Zeigler said; he himself often wrapped gifts. On Christmas Eve, Curtis Dunaway had spread some of this wrapping tissue over the baked goods in the backseat of his car. These were the pies and cookies that he helped Dunaway to move when they switched cars.

Zeigler next admitted that he had bought pistols, including the chrome-plated Securities .38, from Ray's Bait and Tackle. But he denied ever having seen the empty gun boxes that deputies had found in the storeroom and that Ray Ussery had testified were given to Zeigler when he bought the pistols in October 1974.

Zeigler said that he kept the Securities .38 in the custom truck desk of his pickup.

Q: Did Edward Williams ever enter around your truck?

A: A lot of times.

Q: Now when is the last time you saw that weapon prior to Christmas?

A: Three, four, five weeks before.

Q: You had no knowledge as to whether or not it was still in your truck, then, at Christmas?

A: No, sir, I do not. I kept it covered with some rags and things.

Q: But Edward Williams frequently rode in your truck, did he not?

A: Edward Williams even drove my truck from time to time.

Q: By the way, was the lock broken on your truck door?

A: The lock on the right-hand side of the truck was broken.

Q: It could not be locked?

A: No, sir.

Zeigler said that he had bought the small Beretta automatic to carry as a personal weapon; he said that the larger Securities revolver, which he had carried in a shoulder holster, got uncomfortable under a jacket in the summer.

Q: Did you go out on your collections, sir, and collect cash?

A: I ran a collection route three nights a week.

Q: How much would you average on one of these collection routes?

A: Anywhere from fifteen hundred to two thousand dollars.

Q: How would most of the payments be made to you?

A: In cash.

Q: Now how about in the store itself? Did people come in and make payments on their bills and things like this at the store?

A: Yes, they did.

Q: How were these payments made? What form were they normally made in?

A: At the store you get a fair amount of checks and cash.

Q: Was there a considerable amount of cash normally on hand?

A: Yes, sir, we kept quite a bit for cashing checks.

Hadley and Zeigler began to cover the key points of the hours before the murders.

In the morning, Charlie Mays had asked about a used TV; Zeigler showed him one that he had on consignment, which he was selling for $350 cash. At no time during the day did he invite Mays back to the store after closing. He did not expect Mays to buy the TV, since Mays was already delinquent on an account. For that reason, the $50 down payment on the linoleum was larger than usual.

At closing time, he told Curtis Dunaway not to turn on the four sets of overhead lights in the front windows: "I really didn't think there would be too many people out doing any window-shopping over Christmas Eve and Christmas Day." A large Christmas wreath, two "chain lamps," and a pole lamp with three light fixtures were left on in the store.

That evening, after Curtis Dunaway drove off in Eunice's new Toronado, Eunice took some pots and pans off the stove and got ready to leave with her parents. They were going to the store, to pick out the recliner for Mr. Edwards, and then to church. He gave her a set of keys that was identical to the one he carried at his belt, except that it included the ignition key for his pickup truck. He showed her the key for the front door of the furniture store.

Q: Were the Edwardses visiting you for the holidays?
A: Yes, sir.
Q: Was this your mother- and father-in-law?
A: Yes, it is.
Q: How did you feel about them, Mr. Zeigler?
A: I liked them.
Q: Did you get along with them okay?
A: Yes, sir.

Zeigler said that after Eunice left with her mother and father, he called next door to his parents' house, but nobody answered.

He got ready to meet Edward Williams: their appointment was for 7:00. At about five or ten minutes after 7:00, he walked through the house turning off lights, then went out to see whether Williams had arrived.

But Williams was not there, Zeigler said. So he went to his pickup and wrote Williams a note at his truck desk. The note read, "Edward, I'll be back in ten minutes," and he signed it "TZ." Then he left in Curtis Dunaway's car. He started to drive to the local package store for two fifths of bourbon to take to the Van Deventers' party.

He was agitated, he said: "Everything was going wrong. Edward was late, it was going to make me late, I wasn't going to be ready when Eunice came back from the church to go over to the Van Deventer party."

He turned back before he got to the store. Getting the bourbon would only put him farther behind. He would have Williams stop by the liquor store when they finished delivering the three gifts: the gas grill for his father, the recliner, and the large potted plant for Rita Ficke.

He turned around near the end of Bay Street, which was the road that ran east, past Temple Grove, to the center of town. Anyone coming from the east side of Winter Garden would probably use Bay Street. He did not see Edward Williams coming the other way, yet when he got back to the house, Williams was there in the driveway, and his brake lights were on.

Zeigler said that he parked Dunaway's car in the garage and closed the garage door with the remote control in his pickup truck. He left the keys in the car. He did not wipe the car; he did not carry a bag into Williams's truck.

They drove to the store, taking Route 50, then north on Dillard Street. They did not stop in front, but drove straight down the north side of the building. He noticed the Edwardses' car, but was not alarmed to see that they were still at the store.

Q: Did you notice whether the lights were on or off?
A: No, sir, I didn't pay any attention to that.
Q: And you just went straight down the side?
A: Rather quickly.
Q: And you can't see the lights from this side of the store, can you?
A: No, sir.
Q: It is a solid wall. Did you come back here to the gate?
A: Yes, sir.
Q: What happened when you got back here?
A: Edward parked his truck there, or stopped his truck there. I got out of the truck and unlocked the gate and opened it.
Q: You opened the gate? Does this open in, the gate?
A: Yes, sir. It won't open out the other way.
Q: Is that the only way it opens, is in?
A: Yes, sir.
Q: Did Mr. Williams pull in?
A: Yes, he did.
Q: What did you do?
A: I locked the gate back.
Q: Why did you lock the gate back?
A: Sir?

Q: Why did you lock the gate?

A: Because we were going to unlock the back of the store.

Q: Just routine precaution? Did you do this all the time?

A: Yes, sir.

Q: Did Mr. Williams continue driving his truck in the parking lot area?

A: The last time I saw him he was pulling his truck over in an arc in front of the overhead doors.

Q: The overhead doors?

A: Yes, sir.

Q: Mr. Zeigler, did you at that time instruct Mr. Williams to come park at this door, the little door on the north side?

A: I didn't give Mr. Williams any instructions.

Zeigler testified that he opened the back door and flipped a light switch that was immediately inside the hall. The lights didn't come on, but he wasn't alarmed, because he knew that Curtis Dunaway often mistakenly turned off the breaker switch for that back area.

He walked up the hall and tried the next switch, just outside the hall door, before the showroom. Again the lights did not come on. He walked through the hall door and into the showroom, and he was hit on the right side of the head.

He fell to the floor. He lost his glasses, and presumably his keys, because he couldn't find his keys later.

Q: . . . What happened next?

A: As I was getting up I saw two blurs coming at me. I was carrying a .22 caliber Escort pistol, automatic pistol, on my side inside my trousers in a trousers holster. I drew that weapon, and I don't know whether I fired it or not. I know that it jammed because I had to eject a shell from it.

Q: And what happened?

A: It jammed again and I threw it.

Q: You say you might have fired it, you are just not sure?

A: I'm not sure.

Q: Do you know how long you were down after you got hit over the back of the head?

A: No, sir, I have no idea.

Q: What happened after you threw this .22?

A: I started flying through the air and bouncing off the walls and refrigerator and the shelves that are back in that area.

Q: Did you hear anything?

A: There was glass breaking and things falling.

Q: Now you said you saw blurs. Was that more than one?

A: There were two.

Q: Two blurs. Could you tell me about how big they were or anything about them?

A: One, I would presume, was as tall, if not taller, than I am, and the other one was a shorter individual.

Q: Could you tell whether they were black or white?

A: No, sir.

Q: Did you see anything about them?

A: Just dark blurs.

Q: Dark blurs?

A: Yes, sir.

Q: Was the store dark?

A: Yes, sir.

Q: You are fighting, being bounced off the north wall of the store. Were you afraid, Mr. Zeigler?

A: I was scared to death.

Q: What happened then?

A: I was thrown back into the hall through the door area. I hit some chairs and a desk.

Q: What desk did you hit?

A: The desk that was immediately inside the door.

Q: Was there anything inside that desk?

A: Yes, sir.

Q: What was in there?

A: There was a .357 magnum.

Q: Were you able to get to that gun?

A: I snatched that drawer open and took the gun out of the drawer.

Q: That gun wasn't in a box, was it?

A: No, sir, it was not. It was laying open in the desk drawer.

Q: What happened then?

A: I was bounced back out into the main part of the showroom area, and I believe I fired the weapon. I can't tell you whether I did or not.

Q: Did you try to fire it?

A: Yes, sir, I did.

Q: Could you have fired it several times?

A: I could have.

Q: What happened then?

A: I started swinging it with everything I had.

Q: Swinging what?
A: That magnum.
Q: Were you still frightened?
A: Yes, sir.
Q: Did you connect with that magnum?
A: I'm sure I did.
Q: Were you swinging at a part of the anatomy of your assailants?
A: Top and bottom and just as hard as I could.
Q: Were you swinging, for instance, at the side of the mouth?
A: Yes, sir.
Q: What happened then?
A: I was thrown against the linoleum racks, the twelve-foot racks up in the front, and from there I hit the floor.
Q: You hit the floor?
A: Yes, sir.
Q: Did you lose the gun somewhere along in there?
A: Yes, sir, I guess I did.
Q: What happened next?
A: As I was trying to get up off the floor I was shot.
Q: You were getting up and got shot?
A: Yes, sir.
Q: Do you know how far away the man was that shot you?
A: Terry, I don't have any idea. I know it was further away than any six inches, as the FBI has stated.
Q: You feel it was further away than what the FBI indicated?
A: Yes, I do.
Q: How did it feel when you were shot?
A: Like somebody slammed a hot poker all the way through you.
Q: Did it hurt?
A: Yes, it did.

Now events were disjointed, Zeigler said. He was "disoriented and fuzzy." As he lay on the floor he heard a voice say, "Mays has been hit. Kill him." He thought that the assailants left the store through the storeroom.

He lay on the floor at the back of the showroom—for how long, he couldn't say. He became conscious, and crawled around, trying to find his glasses. He crawled over a body, but did not know who it was. He kept picking up Christmas bows as he tried to find his glasses. Finally he got his gold-rimmed glasses from his desk in the front office. He went out to the front counter and used the phone there to call the Van Deventer home. Then he went to the front of the store and sat, or lay, in a lawn chair near the front door.

He said that when the police arrived, he went to the door and found keys in the lock: they were the keys he had given Eunice that evening. He didn't know how they had gotten there.

Hadley asked him to point out certain spots on the state's model of the store. Zeigler got up and pointed out the light switches, where he was first hit, and his office.

He took his seat. His voice remained steady and firm as Hadley began a final series of questions:

Q: Tommy, Christmas Eve 1975 how did you feel about your wife, Eunice Zeigler?

A: My wife and I were closer and more compatible then than we were when we got married.

Q: Did you love her?

A: Yes, I did.

Q: Mr. Zeigler, did you shoot to death Mrs. Virginia Edwards?

A: No, sir, I did not.

Q: Did you beat and shoot Mr. Perry Edwards?

A: No, sir, I did not.

Q: Did you beat Mr. Charles Mays to death?

A: No, sir, I did not.

Q: Did you harm one hair on your wife's head, Mr. Zeigler, on Christmas Eve?

A: No, sir, I did not.

Q: Did you shoot her?

A: No, sir, I did not.

Q: Did you love her?

A: Yes, I did.

LOVED WIFE, ZEIGLER SAYS IN DENIAL was the headline in the next day's editions of the *Sentinel Star*.

The story by reporter Diane Selditch began:

JACKSONVILLE—William Thomas Zeigler Jr. calmly told a packed and hushed courtroom Tuesday that he loved his wife and didn't kill her and three other persons Christmas Eve.

"My wife and I were closer and more compatible than when we got married," the 30-year-old defendant said in a controlled voice mirroring his emotionless demeanor during the trial of more than three weeks.

According to that account, Zeigler remained composed even through Eagan's cross-examination. The state's first chance to confront its accused began without preliminaries:

Q (EAGAN): When you got shot and went down on the floor did you lie on your back or did you lie on your stomach?

A (ZEIGLER): Mr. Eagan, I can't tell you how I was laying on the floor.

Q: You heard Mattie Mays say when you were at her house you had a conversation with Charles Mays. "Do you still want me to come down there tonight?" And you said, "Yes." Is Mattie Mays lying?

A: Mr. Eagan, the only thing that I said to them was, "Have a Merry Christmas."

Q: Mattie Mays was a liar?

A: I'm not calling Mattie Mays a liar, I'm just saying that that conversation did not take place between Charlie Mays and myself.

Q: Mary Stewart said you called her and told her some poppycock story about "We're all going to get our guns taken away from us," and you wanted to buy a couple to make sure that didn't happen, untraceable guns. Was she a liar?

A: Mr. Eagan, I never had that conversation with Mary Stewart.

Q: Frank Smith said that he was contacted by Edward. He talked to you on the telephone. He bought two guns for you and talked to you about them. Edward Williams brought the money to him and took the guns from him. Is he a liar?

A: Mr. Eagan, I never had a conversation with Frank Smith and never asked him to buy me any guns whatsoever.

. . .

Q: When [Williams] has testified that he walked into that dark store and you turned on him with a pistol and tried to kill him, to drop him there beside Charlie Mays, he is a liar?

A: I did not try to kill him, I did not pull a pistol on him, and I did not try to shoot him.

Q: Would you tell me again why you had Curtis Dunaway turn off all the lights in the store Christmas Eve?[1]

A: The only lights that I instructed Curtis Dunaway not to turn on

---

1. This was not in evidence.

were the four hanging displays, two on each side of the front door of the store.

Q: When Felton Thomas testified that you and he and Charlie Mays drove out to an orange grove and fired some pistols out the window of the car, is he a liar?

A: Mr. Eagan, I had never seen Felton Thomas before in my life until the preliminary hearing in Orlando on January the 16th.

Q: I want you to tell me, if you can, sir, how you got all the blood under the armpit of your clothing, Type A blood?

A: The only thing I can tell you is that during the fight I was grabbing everything I could grab ahold to and swinging with everything I had. That's the only thing that I can tell you.

Q: You can't tell me how you held Perry Edwards around the neck and clubbed him with your right hand as you held him with your left?

A: No, sir, because I did not do it.

Q: Why did you use Curtis Dunaway's car to go to the liquor store?

A: Curtis Dunaway's car was there and it had to be pulled from the dirt drive between the two houses and put in the garage anyway, and Eunice and I were going to use the car that night.

Q: Didn't you tell him it had carburetor trouble and you didn't want him driving it?

A: I didn't stipulate what was wrong with the car. It had a funny noise. Curtis doesn't know anything about cars and he was going out of town Christmas Day.

Eagan continued, relentless: *How did you get all this A Type blood under your left arm?* I have no idea, sir. *Did you ever get your hands on that derringer?* No, sir, not to my knowledge. *You did not snap it twice and reload it?* No, sir, I did not. *Put those cartridges with blood on them in your desk drawer?* No, sir, I did not. *Did you drive Curtis Dunaway's car to that orange grove with Felton Thomas?* No, sir, I did not. *You deny that?* I certainly do. *All you had was a little bump on the back of your head?*[2] Well, Mr. Eagan, I can't testify as to how big or how little it was.

Eagan took him through each of the eight pistols, sometimes asking virtually the same questions Hadley had asked on direct, and getting the same answers.

He ended this way:

2. This characterization of the injury was not in evidence.

Q: What was [Edward Williams] doing when you went into the
   store?
A: He was backing his truck up.
Q: He wasn't telling the truth when he said he put you out up here
   in front of the store?
A: No, sir. I did not get out in front of the store.
Q: You did lock the gate behind him, though?
A: Yes, I did.
Q: You never knew Felton Thomas?
A: I have never seen Felton Thomas before in my life.
Q: You know of no reason why he would want to tell such a story
   about you?
A: Not that I have any knowledge of, sir.

Zeigler was excused. It was now nearly noon; Judge Paul
recessed for lunch.

On Christmas Eve, the critical window—from the time Curtis
Dunaway left Temple Grove Drive until Thompson, Ficke, and
Yawn arrived at the store—was almost exactly two and a half
hours. Tommy Zeigler's explanation of his innocence, and the
state's questioning of it, had required less time than the crime
itself.

Zeigler was Hadley's last witness. The defense rested when court
came back in session that afternoon. Eagan could now present
rebuttal witnesses.

Rebuttal testimony is restricted to issues raised by the defense. Hadley believed that Eagan might call a witness to testify
that Eunice Zeigler was unhappy in her marriage. Eagan's likely
justification would be that a line of Zeigler's testimony—"We were
happier then than when we got married"—had introduced the
question of his wife's state of mind.

Eagan had told Hadley that he intended to call Eunice's hair-
dresser, who had disparaged Tommy in her statements to police
and who apparently was the source of a report that Eunice had
resisted moving next door to Beulah and Tom Zeigler's and that
Beulah had picked out all of the furniture for the young couple's
home.

But in a sidebar conference, Eagan said that he would not call
this woman. Apparently she had decided against repeating her

information under oath. "She didn't know what we expected her to know," Eagan told Hadley and Paul.

Instead, he would call Cheryl Clafler, whose incendiary statement to Don Frye not only accused Zeigler of threatening Eunice's life, but also tarred two of West Orange's important public figures.

Hadley asked that the proffer of her testimony be given in the judge's chambers: "It is just allegations that would do substantial damage to other people's reputation and things of this nature, and also it's just such gross hearsay I don't see any way it could be in."

Paul ruled that Clafler would give her proffer in open court, but out of the hearing of the jury, as with any proffer.

The proffer was brief, and Eagan was careful to restrict it: "Please listen to my questions and answer me directly," he instructed her on the stand. Clafler said that she had known Eunice for about a year, and that about a month before Christmas Eunice had told her about problems in her marriage. Two or three weeks later, she said, she and Eunice spoke again at Ronnie's Drive-In, when Eunice saw Clafler's car and pulled in beside her; at that time, Clafler said, Eunice told her that she was afraid and that Tommy had taken some insurance out on her.

Hadley brought out two aspects from her original statement: that Eunice had planned to meet her parents elsewhere on Christmas Eve, not at her home; and that she had not learned of the insurance until after the first week in December. Both of these allegations conflicted with the known facts of the case. The second was contradicted by Eunice's signatures on the applications, dated in September, and by the fact—as Hadley could easily establish— that in September she had undergone medical exams specifically to qualify for the coverage.

Hadley argued that Clafler's testimony was inadmissible: "It is irrelevant, it is immaterial, it is hearsay of the grossest and most offensive kind." Privately he felt that he could not lose on this issue; he believed that case law was so firmly in his favor as to represent an almost certain reversal on appeal if Judge Paul ruled against him.

Eagan told the judge that Clafler's story was offered "not to prove the truth of what was said but to evidence circumstantially the true state of mind of Eunice Zeigler in direct rebuttal of the defendant's testimony."

The two attorneys cited cases to support their arguments. Paul took a break to study the citations, and when he returned he sustained Hadley's objection. Clafler was not allowed to testify.

Beginning in April, Hadley had made at least six other motions or objections on important issues of evidence. He had moved to suppress the evidence seized during the warrantless search of the store; to suppress evidence seized at 75 Temple Grove; to suppress the footprint testimony of Professor MacDonell; to suppress the fingerprint on the tissue paper, which Hadley argued was surprise testimony; to admit Dr. Mackler's narcotherapy examination; to admit Dr. Zimmer's conclusions about the defendant's mental health.

Hadley had lost all six arguments. Judge Paul's ruling on Cheryl Clafler's proffered testimony was the defense's first—and last—victory of its kind.

Eagan still had a brief roster of rebuttal witnesses.

The custodian of records for the Orange County medical examiner testified that a ring with a clear stone was noted on Eunice Zeigler's left hand, and that "a white metal ring with two hearts, a white metal multi clear stone ring, earrings with a green leaf and red berries, and a bracelet and a Timex watch" were removed from Virginia Edwards.

But under cross-examination she told Hadley that she found no reference to two antique diamond rings on Eunice's right hand, and that no money was recovered from Eunice, Virginia, or Perry Edwards.

The insurance agent Russ Courtney testified about his conversation with Ted Van Deventer immediately after the memorial service, to which Eagan had referred in his cross-examination of Van Deventer. According to Courtney, he asked Van Deventer, "Ted, did you recommend all that insurance?" to which Van Deventer replied, "No, Doug, I didn't know anything about it."

Four witnesses, including Robert Thompson, testified to Charlie Mays's good character.

Eagan ended his rebuttal after little more than an hour. The defense had no surrebuttal, and Paul sent the jury home. That afternoon, the judge and the two attorneys decided the exact wording of the charge sheets that the juries would be given when they began deliberations.

Paul said that in a capital case he would not impose a time

limit on closing arguments, but he wanted to know how long each intended to speak.

Eagan said he had never argued for as long as an hour.

"I will make a bet with you now you will argue for more than an hour," Paul told Eagan.

"I probably will in this case," Eagan said.

"I am like Bob," Hadley said. "I have never argued in my life for an hour. I've had a couple that were thirty or forty minutes that seemed to be awfully long at the time, but there is a lot to this case."

Paul asked them: Did they think they would be finished by tomorrow afternoon?

They both said yes. Within a day, their case, and Zeigler's fate, belonged to the jury.

IV

VERDICT

FORTY-ONE

ATTORNEYS' CLOSING ARGUMENTS ARE NOT INTENDED PRIMARILY FOR the record. Reporters and spectators, even the judge, are almost beside the point. Eagan and Hadley were addressing an audience of twelve when they spoke on Wednesday morning.

Eagan spoke before and after Hadley. Early in his first argument he correlated the state's theory with the testimony of its two key independent eyewitnesses.

He recounted that Thomas Hale had seen the Zeiglers together at 7:05, rounding the intersection of Dillard and Route 50. The implication was that Eunice must have been killed within the next two to three minutes. At 7:25, he said, Barbara Tinsley heard the first of two volleys; these must have been the shots that stopped the clock and killed the Edwardses. Now, Eagan recalled, Zeigler had two 7:30 appointments, one with Mays at the store and another with Williams at his house. Eagan recapped Thomas's testimony about the trip to the grove and back to the store, turning off the electricity, and the fence-jumping, then the trip from the store to the house and back to the store.

He said: "At 7:45, estimated, Mrs. Tinsley hears another series of shots. I submit to you that that's when Tommy Zeigler walked into that dark store with Charles Mays."

The state had not presented a time line. This was Eagan's first and only attempt at trial to match his theory of the crime to Barbara Tinsley's testimony.

Hadley, sometimes referring to notes, told the jury that evidence showed a credible alternative to the state's case, a more than reasonable basis for doubt. He did not dwell on any single aspect of the case, but carefully reviewed all of the evidence and testimony that seemed to exculpate his client or contradict the state's theory, especially the indications of what he called "third-party involvement": the missing .22 slug, the tooth that did not come from any of the bodies in the store, the money that was missing from the office, Eunice's missing rings, the contested footprint.

He mentioned that J. D. and Madelyn Nolan had seen Edward Williams at the Kentucky Fried Chicken after Zeigler was taken to the hospital; the Nolans, he said, were "a fine lady and gentleman, nothing to gain in this case, they don't know anybody, they don't know anything about the case."

He said that the evidence for a conviction "must be consistent to a moral certainty of guilt . . . and if, even after the points I have made, you are still ninety percent convinced Tommy did it, you must acquit him, but I submit, ladies and gentlemen, that the evidence is not ninety percent. The evidence is not ten percent. The evidence is zero when you consider the credibility of Edward Williams and Felton Thomas and compare it to the known facts."

Eagan spoke briefly again after Hadley had finished. He attacked the testimony of J. D. and Madelyn Nolan: "There is no evidence at all that the black man seen trying to use the telephone after the Kentucky Fried Chicken was closed was Edward Williams. Edward Williams was there earlier. The place was open when he was there. There were other customers there. That's when he met the friend that took him to his next place, ultimately to Mary Stewart's."

Speaking of Mays, he said: "This was a deliberate planned act on this part of this man over here to lure that poor black man in there and kill him dead and make a murderer and a robber out of him."

He closed by repeating the dialogue that was supposed to have taken place between Williams and Zeigler in the rear compound: " 'Edward, I didn't know it was you.' 'Mr. Tommy, you knew it was me. You knew it was me.' 'No, Edward, I didn't know it was you.'

"Perry and Virginia Edwards are entitled to justice at your hands," Eagan said. "Charles Mays is entitled to have his good name cleared at your hands and this man deserves nothing more than your verdict of guilty because he has committed four of the most horrendous murders, the basest and foulest of murders you will ever hear of.

"For the State of Florida I ask you, don't turn your back on those men [Williams and Thomas] and their sworn testimony. Don't reject that evidence. Consider it, weigh it carefully, yes, but find it, as I am sure you will, to be convincing . . . and that guilt is the only true verdict that can be rendered on the evidence in this case. Thank you."

The jury began deliberations at 2:30 on Wednesday afternoon, having missed lunch to hear the closing arguments. During the next five hours, jurors requested the scale model of the store and a magnifying glass—apparently they were scrutinizing the controversial footprint.

In a largely circumstantial case, a verdict within the first few hours would almost certainly have meant an acquittal. But there was no verdict on Wednesday. Around 7:00 P.M., the foreman requested to retire, and Judge Paul recessed until the morning.

"At least they're thinking about it," Hadley told a reporter. "They're being very conscientious."

Maybe no jury deliberations can be called routine. These, however, were extraordinary. The first indication that something unusual was happening came shortly before jurors resumed deliberations at 9:00 on Thursday morning. One of the jurors, Irma Brickle, said she felt too ill to go on. This threatened a mistrial.

Brickle was a housewife, a white woman in her thirties. She rested for about two hours, recovering from what the *Sentinel Star* implied was some kind of stomach distress. In fact, it was much more serious.

Brickle's physician was called, and he sent in medication. By 11:00 A.M., she was ready to continue. Deliberations began again and went on for eight hours without a break—bailiffs sent in sandwiches. Then at 7:00 P.M. Thursday evening, the jurors retired once more.

FORTY-TWO

FRIDAY WAS A SULTRY SUMMER DAY IN JACKSONVILLE. MOST AMERI-
cans who are old enough to remember will recall something of that
day: if not specific details, then a memory of anticipation, of impatience to begin the biggest summer holiday of that year or many
other years. Friday, July 2, 1976, was the eve of the nation's Bicen-
tennial celebration.

Anyone who was involved with *Florida* v. *Zeigler* must remember it as a day of uncertainty and tension and turmoil, and
then decision. At 9:00 A.M., as the jury reconvened, Judge Paul
called Eagan and Hadley into his chambers. Irma Brickle had told
a bailiff that she wanted a private conference with the judge; if not
alone, then with the two attorneys present.

This request was problematic. The judge could not speak with
any juror apart from the others.

"I really don't want to bring her in," Paul said.

"Judge, I just don't know," Eagan said. "I've never had this
come up before. . . . I think the thing is fraught with peril in that
if we do bring her in we might have a mistrial right here."

They debated whether to send her a note asking her to explain.

"It might not be anything, you know, but it might be something," Paul said. "That is why I wanted to just sit down and talk
to you a minute. I don't want the press. That is why we came back
here. I don't want anything in the press about this."

"That's right," Eagan said.

Eagan speculated whether it could be misconduct by one of
the other jurors.

"It could very well be, but you never know," Paul said.
". . . Of course, it's all just speculation."

240

Hadley noted that Brickle and the juror who had been excused a week earlier, Johnestine Young, "seemed to carry the burden of being on the jury probably more heavily than anyone else, you know, just from the trial, watching their facial expressions and things like this."

"A lot of those people in there have never had to make decisions that anywhere approach the decision they are back there making today," Paul said.

Paul told the bailiff to take Brickle away from the rest of the jury, on the pretext that she was going to be examined by a nurse. Then the judge wrote a note to her, asking her to "advise, in writing, the nature of the subject matter you wish to discuss."

He told the bailiff: "Don't let anyone know what is in the note at all. We don't want anyone to know what is going on here but these lawyers, okay?"

The bailiff took the note to her, and brought back a written reply:

> Request concerns other jurors and decisions made before they permited [sic] to make them.

"I don't think I understand it," the judge said, and he showed it to the attorneys. They speculated what it meant:

PAUL: What she is talking about, I think, is when they were in there somebody was announcing a decision.
EAGAN: Apparently some of them have said how they stand. I don't think from that they have made a vote yet.
HADLEY: Or before it was submitted to them.
DAVIDS: That is what she is saying, they had discussions at some point before it was submitted to them for consideration.
EAGAN: Well, why did she wait this long to tell us?
PAUL: I don't think that is what it is.

Eagan recommended that the entire jury be brought in and instructed that their duty was to "discuss the thing, work together on it."

She was still alone in the bailiff's room. They decided to send a second note to her. Paul wrote:

"Do you mean decisions announced before or after the case was submitted to the jury on Wednesday afternoon?"

The reply came back:

Statement made immediately after foreman was elected and numerous other things this is just the main item.

And below that was written:

made befor [*sic*] Wed. afternoon.

A juror could announce an opinion at any time after the deliberations began. But any such statement made before then would be improper.

Paul and the attorneys examined the note.

PAUL: Not bad. "Statements made generally right after the foreman was elected."

HADLEY: Statements made before Wednesday afternoon.

PAUL: Well, I get the impression from that she is talking about since they were put in there Wednesday.

EAGAN: Some of them have obviously expressed their opinion regarding the weight of the evidence or something of this nature and she has heard it and it has got her disturbed. That is really what the jury is supposed to do.

PAUL: I really don't think we ought to go any further with this.

HADLEY: Your Honor, what does that portion "statements made before Wednesday afternoon" that she put in there narrow it down to? I don't know, I am just disturbed by that part of her response. . . .

EAGAN: She doesn't say that anyone has expressed prior to Wednesday an opinion as to guilt or innocence.

PAUL: She hasn't even said that. "Statements made immediately after foreman was elected and numerous other things. This is just the main item."

HADLEY: But then—

PAUL: It comes down and says "made before Wednesday afternoon," which is—

HADLEY: She has got down "made before Wednesday afternoon."

PAUL: Well—

HADLEY: How about just direct a question, "Were statements made prior to the case being submitted to the jury that would indicate someone had a preconceived notion?"

PAUL: I think we would be in bad shape if we started to do that.

HADLEY: What concerns me is the lady obviously thought it was serious enough to bring to our attention, so I am wondering if it is something that was said before Wednesday afternoon.

EAGAN: She is a nervous lady, though, and her view of that is not justified by the information that she has given us. I don't think there is anything here that would justify us now going into an inquiry to determine whether or not we are going to upset this jury's deliberations. . . .

Further contact with a sole juror jeopardized the integrity of the jury's work. But if another juror had announced a premature decision, then the trial was already compromised. And although Brickle hadn't hinted where she stood, both sides understood that she might be feeling the strain of being a sole holdout: the verdict could be imminent.

Hadley argued that Paul should ask her to be more specific: ". . . I think even the possibility of jury misconduct cannot be overlooked and must be inquired into. I don't know, I am in strange territory right now and I just don't know, but if there was jury misconduct I think we need to know about it."

At this point Brickle had already been out of the jury room for several minutes. The others, presumably, were still discussing the case: they had not been instructed otherwise. Paul said that he favored sending Brickle back into the room to resume deliberations, and Eagan agreed: "If she should come in here and say some other juror had done something, then we have got to talk to that juror, and immediately we are dividing this jury."

Paul ordered that Brickle be sent back to deliberate with the others. His third note seemed final: "After consideration, it appears that there is no present need to have a conference. Thank you for bringing the matter to our attention."

But that did not end it. At 12:15 the jury broke to go out for a meal; the judge noticed that Mrs. Brickle looked pale as she left the room. A few minutes later, she collapsed, unconscious. A bailiff revived her, and she fainted a second time. She had to be carried to a courthouse office, apart from the others.

"She is up there and has passed out twice on us in an hour," Paul told the attorneys. "She is tight as a tick."

They were looking at a possible mistrial again, with the question of Brickle's health thrown in.

"I can never recall being quite as wrung out from a case as I am right now from this one," Hadley said.

They considered the possibility of having Brickle examined either by a jailhouse doctor or by her own physician, who had sent in medication the day before.

Eagan, Hadley, and the judge went to the office where Brickle had been taken. But they did not see her; they sent a nurse to ask her whether she wanted a doctor.

Brickle answered, through the nurse, that she did not want to talk to a doctor. She wanted to talk to Paul. She felt that she was being pressured, the nurse said; one of the jurors had told her, "If you would make up your damn mind we could get out of here."

Paul instructed the nurse to tell her that he could not and would not talk to her, and the bailiffs sent her back with the others.

Now Hadley believed, almost to a certainty, that Brickle was a holdout against conviction. On the way back to the courtroom, he moved for a mistrial. Back in Paul's chambers, they put it on the record. Mrs. Brickle, he said, "is being pressured by other jurors to make a decision which she is either morally or conscientiously opposed to. . . . This pressure has been of sufficient magnitude to cause her these physical problems. . . . Therefore the defense feels that any verdict brought would be as a result of the emotional strain and trauma being placed upon this lady as opposed to being a true verdict based upon the evidence and the law. . . ."

Eagan argued against it.

". . . As I understand it she feels pressured to make a decision, not to change a decision already made," Eagan said. "It would seem to me that this is what a juror is expected to do, and it is one of the burdens they bear as jurors. In this case it is an extremely heavy burden on what apparently is an emotional lady, or at least a lady who has shown less strength in that regard to make heavy decisions than her fellow jurors, but I don't submit that it is grounds for a mistrial."

Apparently Eagan, too, believed that Brickle was a holdout. He suggested that the jury be called in and instructed to consider the views of their fellow jurors. This is a standard lecture designed to break a deadlock—the so-called Allen instruction, also known as "the dynamite charge."

Paul denied the motion for a mistrial, and he told Eagan that he was not ready to deliver dynamite. He sent the clerk of the court to take Irma Brickle back into the jury room.

It was 2:50 P.M.

Tommy Zeigler passed the afternoon in a jail cell. Wednesday afternoon and Thursday, bailiffs had allowed him to wait with the defense team in an unsecured room. This was contrary to procedure, but in Jacksonville, as in Orange County, Zeigler had won the trust of his jailers.

On Thursday afternoon, however, a reporter noticed the arrangement, and mentioned it in an article that Judge Paul read on Friday. Paul ordered Zeigler kept behind bars.

It didn't matter anyway, one of the bailiffs told Zeigler; an acquittal was in the works. Having attended hundreds of trials, he said, he was never wrong.

At 5:00 P.M., the jury announced that it had a verdict.

Zeigler was brought in from the cell, nervous and a little dazed. Another bailiff had told him that the clue to a verdict was in the jurors' demeanor when they came into the courtroom. If they looked directly at the defendant, it meant that they had acquitted. If they avoided looking at him, they had found him guilty.

Zeigler studied them as they filed in. Most of them averted their eyes. Irma Brickle looked at him, but she was crying, and the look in her eyes was pity.

The foreman was a black man named Charles Ashley. He handed the verdict forms to the clerk, who gave them to Paul, who gave them to the clerk to be read.

In the death of Eunice Zeigler, guilty of murder, first degree.

In the death of Charles Mays, guilty of murder, first degree.

In the death of Perry Edwards, guilty of murder, second degree.

In the death of Virginia Edwards, guilty of murder, second degree.

There were formalities. With the jury out, Paul adjudicated the verdicts, officially pronouncing Zeigler guilty four times. Law required that the convict be fingerprinted in open court; after the reading of each count, he was brought forward and his prints were affixed to the judgment forms. Then he was taken away, remanded to the sheriff.

Paul had kept the courtroom closed until the jury could leave. Now he recessed, and the doors opened. Mary Van Deventer, who had been seated behind the defense table, was distraught as she ran out. Leslie Gift followed her, to make sure that she didn't try driving home in that condition.

Terry Hadley was stunned and near tears as he walked out of the courthouse. Years later he told an interviewer that hearing one's client convicted of first-degree murder was an experience he would not wish on his worst enemy.

Outside, the sky was black and glowering. Thunder grumbled. The afternoon sultriness was resolving itself into a monstrous thunderstorm that rocked the city throughout the evening. It was a huge storm even by the standards of Florida's tropical atmosphere, so violent that it imprinted itself on the memories of many who were there. One more reason to remember July 2, 1976.

It might truly be said that thunder of another sort was grumbling on Tommy Zeigler's horizon. The lead story in the afternoon newspapers was datelined Washington, D.C.: earlier in the day, the U.S. Supreme Court had specifically declared that because of new sentencing guidelines, Florida's death penalty was now constitutionally acceptable.

FORTY-THREE

MUCH OF WHAT IS NOW KNOWN ABOUT THE DELIBERATIONS COMES from interviews that the psychologist Stephen Robertson conducted with Irma Brickle and another juror, Peggy Dollinger. He synopsized some of his information in an affidavit. Most of what follows is based on that document.

Immediately after the jurors went to the jury room on Wednesday afternoon, they elected the foreman, Charles Ashley. At that point Ashley told them that they could debate all they wanted, but he had already made up his mind; Zeigler was guilty, he said.

That was Dollinger's recollection. Brickle added that Ashley claimed to have made his decision two weeks before—even before the defense had finished its case.

Robertson learned that the first vote was an even split; voting for conviction were the five black jurors and James Roberts, the alternate who had been added to the panel. Gradually Zeigler's support eroded. By Thursday afternoon, Brickle was the last hold-out.

Both Brickle and Dollinger described an atmosphere of intimidation as the panel tried to change Brickle's mind. Both said that when Brickle would try to make a point, Roberts would step behind her seat, put one of the revolvers to her head, and pull the trigger.[1] Other jurors shouted at her and called her names. Dollinger confirmed that other jurors shouted at Brickle when she tried to discuss the case.

"I suppose it could even have come to actual violence," Robertson quoted Dollinger. "It was a very frightening situation."

Brickle was upset because other jurors refused to look at the evidence on the table beside her. She couldn't get them to study the photo of the tooth on Charlie Mays's sweatshirt. She blamed her illness on the intimidation and the tension in the room; she was unable to eat or sleep.

Brickle told Robertson that she didn't understand why the judge had failed to help her when she told him that she needed help.

The sentencing phase of the trial, held July 16, was literally moot for a number of reasons.

Testimony required less than an hour. Earlier, Judge Paul had ordered Hadley to limit his character witnesses—a decision that would become worth at least six years of life for Zeigler. Eagan called no witnesses. Hadley's one character witness was Zeigler's Baptist pastor, Fay De Sha, who said that he had known the family since 1966. He said that Tommy and Eunice attended services, belonged to church committees, and sang together in the choir, and that Tommy had often operated the sound mixer for the church's Sunday-morning radio broadcast.

Eunice always sat at Tommy's side while he ran the radio

1. The jury had all the evidence, including the weapons, but no live ammunition.

equipment, De Sha said. Eunice played the piano in the church, he said, and Tommy always came down and sat about two rows back, to listen to her.

The only other witness was the psychiatrist Allen Zimmer, who was now allowed to testify to his examination of Zeigler.

Zeigler, he said, was "raised in an environment where he had established tremendous self-control, where he had been able to develop within himself control over his behavior in such a way that he did not express outward emotion. What emotions were there were all kept within. . . .

"He was the type of individual who was extremely compassionate . . . he had tremendous feeling for people and peoples. One of the characteristics of Tommy Zeigler that was extremely impressive to me were his loyalties, loyalties to individuals who he became close to. This was manifested by the fact that he had respect for members of his family including his wife and in-laws and people close to him."

The jury deliberated less than twenty-five minutes before returning an advisory sentence of life in prison.

At Hadley's request, Paul now brought several members of the jury, individually, to be questioned in his chambers. He was inquiring about two minor allegations of misconduct: during the trial, Peggy Dollinger had brought a newspaper into the jury room, and Leatrice Williams was believed to have overheard a reporter's unflattering remark about Zeigler. But most important, Hadley wanted him to ask Irma Brickle about her claim that jury members had made up their minds prematurely.

Zeigler was barred from this proceeding.

Paul seemed hesitant as he asked Brickle to explain the notes she had sent during the deliberations.

Q (PAUL): . . . I was wondering if you wish to make any further elaboration about, you know, what you may have said or if you feel that—whatever. I don't want to put words in your mouth. We just want to make sure there was a good jury in the sense that everyone—

A (BRICKLE): If I could call back the Friday, I would have changed my mind. In fact, I almost did. I still feel he's innocent. My reasons don't seem to be important or they weren't.

Q: But you stated in open court that that was your verdict.

A: I know I did, but I just couldn't take any more.

Q: Well, we are not concerned—
A: I felt I couldn't take any more.

Paul refused to question any of the other jurors about Brickle's claims. He ruled that Dollinger and Williams had not violated the integrity of the trial. He dismissed the jurors with a strong recommendation that they not comment to reporters. Hadley complained that Paul's questions to Brickle hadn't adequately addressed the possibility of juror misconduct, but the judge overruled him. The matter was closed.[2]

Now the judge began to pronounce sentence, reading from a typed statement. Florida juries can only recommend a sentence; Paul's judgment here would be binding.

"This Court has considered the advisory sentence returned by the Jury this morning," the statement began, and Paul went on to say that he had also been considering the evidence.

"Why you, sir, wanted to kill your wife may never actually be known. However, the record does show one motive which is money, five hundred thousand dollars' worth of it."

At this moment Hadley realized that the judge was overruling the verdict. Under Florida law, murder for money is one of the aggravating circumstances that allow a sentence of death.

Paul continued: "The reason in the record for killing Charles Mays is more obvious: to cover up your involvement in the death of your wife. From the evidence it appears Mr. Mays was like a lamb being led to the slaughter, and slaughter it was.

"The killing of Mr. and Mrs. Edwards, from the verdict and I believe from the reasonable inferences of the evidence, apparently was not part of your original scheme but was the result of, unfortunate for them, happenstance; it appearing that they came to the store, they cannot be permitted to leave and, from the evidence, were executed.

"The evidence further shows the last step of your preconceived plan was to lure Edward Williams to the store and kill him to make it look like he too was part of a gang whose purpose was to commit robbery. Had this part of your plan succeeded, then we wouldn't be here today in this court of law.

"The law of this state permits a sentence of death for premeditated murder. The facts of this case require it."

2. Shortly thereafter, the judge barred Zeigler's attorneys from contacting the jurors.

For each of the first-degree convictions, Tommy Zeigler was to be committed to state prison, "and at a time to be fixed by the Governor of the State of Florida, you shall be put to death by means of electrocution as provided by Florida Statute 922.10. May God have mercy on your soul."

On September 8, Vernon Davids finally received the results of neutron activation tests to determine the presence of gunshot residue in the pockets of Edward Williams's green slacks. Williams had claimed that he had carried the gun in his right pocket. However, the left and right pockets showed equal, very low background levels of GSR metals; the examiner concluded that it was unlikely that any firearm had been carried in either pocket.

FORTY-FOUR

A FEW HOURS AFTER HE WAS SENTENCED, DUVAL COUNTY DEPUTIES delivered Zeigler to the Florida State Prison, in a rural area of north-central Florida. The town of Raiford is the closest community, but the prison's mailing address is a post office box in the town of Starke, about twelve miles distant. Inmates and staff usually refer to the prison as FSP.

Zeigler became the seventy-ninth and newest prisoner on Death Row, which at FSP is the name given to any wing or floor where prisoners under a death sentence are segregated. Through executions, reduced sentences, or (rarely) successful appeals, he gradually moved up in seniority. By the summer of 1992, he was a prison old-timer, tenth in a Death Row population of more than 150.

Death Row inmates are housed singly in six-foot-by-nine-foot cells and are permitted two hours of yard recreation per week.

They send and receive letters and may see visitors, but are allowed to use a telephone only under extraordinary circumstances; they are usually allowed to call their attorneys when they have been served a death warrant.

Death Row residence—as long as it lasts—is considered preferable to confinement elsewhere in the prison. The general population at FSP consists of the state's most violent and incorrigible criminals. While some Death Row inmates have a career of general brutality, many receive the ultimate penalty because of a single act of violence. Beatings and stabbings, though hardly unusual, are less common on the Row than in the general population. By the standards of a maximum-security prison, Death Row is a high-class neighborhood.

FSP's Death Row inmates are allowed to pass time with watercolor painting and crocheting, both of which Zeigler began to pursue single-mindedly. He sends hand-painted cards at Christmas and for birthdays. His mother supplies him with yarn, with which he crochets afghans and sweaters and comforters as gifts for his friends and supporters. At one point his output of these creations was so prodigious that prison authorities suspected him of pursuing a cottage industry for profit.

In sixteen years he has not been involved in a violent incident; his two disciplinary infractions have been for possession of a small tool for repairing his eyeglasses and of an electrical device with which prisoners heat cups of water for instant coffee.

After he had been in the prison for several years he obtained a copy of the trial transcript and depositions. He spent weeks picking through it, noting discrepancies in prosecution testimony.

That was when he read Don Frye's grand jury testimony for the first time—before the trial, Hadley and Davids had kept it from him. At the time he read it, he says, he had begun to despair; but the hope of disproving Frye's allegations has been a goad to keep him going.

He is circumspect about his religious beliefs and practices. But two devout Christians (not related to him) who have stayed close to him say that they take for granted the sincerity of his faith.

Florida's Death House is a ground-floor annex of the prison's Q wing. The annex consists of four cells, a shower and toilet, and a room containing the wood-framed electric chair in which more than two hundred men have died in the past eighty years. Once a week, usually on Wednesday afternoons, the lights dim in the prison for a few seconds, during the regular test of the apparatus.[1]

The death warrant is a black-bordered document that the governor signs and then transmits to FSP, where the superintendent or his assistant intones it to the prisoner in the presence of official witnesses. The condemned man—now said to be "under active warrant"—is moved immediately into the Death House. All of his belongings are placed outside the cell. If he wishes to brush his teeth, for example, he must request a toothbrush from one of the guards who keep him under constant observation. Usually warrants are valid for two to three weeks, and the actual executions are scheduled near the end of that window of time (although not so close to the end that they would expire before they could be rescheduled).

Zeigler has twice been under warrant, and walked out of the Death House both times. Once he came within about half a day of his execution.

But that story played out in the arcane arena of appellate law, far from the gritty reality of FSP.

---

1. The chair itself does not conduct electricity. The charge is conducted through the body by a metal skullcap and a metal ring that is placed on an ankle; the victim is strapped into the chair and usually dies of a broken neck, resulting from the violent spasm of his body in reaction to the current. Outsiders have christened the chair "Old Sparky," but the term is almost never used inside the prison.

FORTY-FIVE

TERRY HADLEY LEFT THE CASE SOON AFTER VERNON DAVIDS ARGUED Zeigler's first appeal, although he continued to represent Tom and Beulah in the civil suits that grew out of the crime. Davids had come to know Zeigler well during the month in Jacksonville and had become fond of him. More important, he believed that the verdict was unjust and that the evidence did not support Zeigler's guilt.

Typically for a first appeal, Zeigler's motion for a new trial was based on a wide variety of issues from the trial. But Davids believed that the key matter was Paul's decision to admit evidence seized during the search of the store. Paul had relied on a "crime scene exception" to the Fourth Amendment.

But in 1978, in a significant Fourth Amendment decision, the U.S. Supreme Court had found that the crime scene exception did not exist. In *Mincey* v. *Arizona*, the Court ruled that while the Fourth Amendment does not prohibit police from warrantless entry during an emergency, the police must obtain a warrant to remain on the premises once the emergency is ended.

Davids read *Mincey* with excitement, because it seemed to be completely "on point": the facts of that case seemed to apply directly to the search at the store. Police in Pima County, Arizona, went to the apartment of a suspected drug dealer named Rufus Mincey. An undercover officer, Barry Headricks, had been in the apartment earlier in the day and had arranged to buy some heroin. Officer Headricks left, ostensibly to get some money, and returned with nine other plainclothes policemen and a deputy prosecutor. Someone in the apartment opened the door for Headricks, then the others rushed in. Headricks and Mincey were critically wounded in an exchange of gunfire; Headricks later died. Police held the apartment for two days without a warrant and took over two hundred items of evidence that later were used to convict Mincey.

The Arizona supreme court ruled that the search of Mincey's apartment was legal under a crime scene exception to the Fourth Amendment. But the U.S. Supreme Court found unanimously that once the medical emergency had ended, the police should have obtained a search warrant to remain on the scene. They were entitled to any evidence that was in plain sight during the emergency, but anything else was inadmissible.

Justice Potter Stewart wrote: ". . . We hold that the 'murder scene exception' created by the Arizona Supreme Court is inconsistent with the Fourth and Fourteenth Amendments—that the warrantless search of Mincey's apartment was not constitutionally acceptable simply because a homicide had recently occurred there."

As Davids read it, that ruling applied precisely to the search at the furniture store. The issue seemed even more clearly in Zeigler's favor: no emergency existed once Ficke and Thompson and the others had found only dead bodies. The evidence in plain sight included the weapons and the holster and the bodies themselves. But the insurance policies, the storeroom bag, and the second .22 would all be inadmissible.

Further, Judge Paul had specifically cited the now-invalid crime scene exception: the police, he said, "were conducting a crime scene investigation which, due to its complexity, continued for more than a week."

Davids argued his case before the Florida supreme court on January 9, 1981.

The decision came down six months later; the court affirmed Zeigler's conviction and sentence and denied his motion for a retrial. It addressed these issues, among others:

• Judge Paul's refusal to grant continuance fell within the "sound discretion" of a trial judge.
• The "grove bullet" was admissible even though it could not be positively identified as from the Securities gun, and there was no way to know when it had been fired.
• The Sodium Brevital test and Dr. Zimmer's psychiatric examination were not admissible.
• The evidence from the Dunaway car was admissible, since

Thompson and Yawn had entered the home in the belief that an emergency existed.

• Frank Smith's hearsay testimony, about his telephone conversation with the man whom Edward Williams described as Zeigler, was not improper.

• Herbert MacDonell's footprint testimony may have been a breach of discovery, but Judge Paul had remedied it when he allowed Hadley and Davids to examine the evidence and to interview MacDonell. "Actually, there is very little contradiction between the testimony of [Thomas] Delaney and the testimony of McDonnell [*sic*]," said the opinion, by Chief Justice James C. Adkins.

• Judge Paul was justified in refusing to allow Hadley to question jurors about Irma Brickle's charges of misconduct.

• The judge had properly overruled the jury's advisory sentence.

• Most dismaying for Davids, the court ruled that *Mincey* did not apply to the warrantless search of the store, since Zeigler had invited the police when he asked Don Ficke for help.

Until 1978, Davids would have taken the search-and-seizure appeals to the federal system, beginning with the U.S. district court in Jacksonville; state courts have generally been less liberal than federal courts in upholding constitutional safeguards.

But *Stone* v. *Powell*, a 1976 decision by the U.S. Supreme Court, virtually ended the right of defendants to appeal Fourth Amendment rulings by state supreme courts. Defendants may still apply to the High Court, but the chances of review there are almost nil. In essence, clerks at the U.S. Supreme Court, who screen writs and submissions, are now the sole federal watchdogs of the states' compliance with Fourth Amendment rights.

Davids did file a writ of certiorari—a petition for review—which the U.S. Supreme Court denied in 1982, opening the way for the first of the death warrants against Tommy Zeigler.

"We have carefully examined the thirty-two volumes of record in this case and carefully considered the brief of the defendant," said the opinion by the Florida supreme court.

Actually, though, that opinion contains at least one serious misstatement of the facts. Justice Adkins described Thomas Delaney's footprint testimony this way (emphasis added):

> Although there were general characteristics of similarity, as an expert [Delaney] could not find any specific points of identification. He concluded that the prints in question *could have been made by defendant's shoes* but he could not positively state that the shoes in fact did make the print.

This is a gross error. Delaney positively testified that Zeigler's shoe could *not* have made the key footprint, strongly indicating the possibility of an unknown assailant. It was MacDonell, not Delaney, who refused to specify whether Zeigler's shoe had made the print. Given this misapprehension of a basic issue, it's not hard to understand how the chief justice could have found that there was "very little contradiction" between Delaney's testimony and MacDonell's.

The opinion also seemed to ignore the fact that the undercover policeman in the *Mincey* case was also on the scene by invitation, yet the U.S. Supreme Court found the search unreasonable.

The Florida opinion concluded: "In some instances defendant has been able to show some inconsistencies in the evidence. However, when one considers the magnitude of this case, all facts could not be expected to mesh perfectly."

FORTY-SIX

IN 1982, WILLIAM DUANE WAS A THIRTY-FOUR-YEAR-OLD TRIAL ATTORney in Orlando. He had recently tried two high-profile cases, including the defense of the "Pershing Plowshares" antiwar protesters, who had been charged with trespass during their demonstration at the Martin Marietta production plant in Orange County.

Duane found himself with some free time. He volunteered for a pro bono case and was asked to briefly represent a Death Row inmate whose Supreme Court writ had recently been denied and who was about to go on active warrant.

The job would last only a few days, Duane was told; he only had to fill in some forms and file a petition that would delay the execution and allow the inmate to start a second series of appeals.

The inmate was Tommy Zeigler. The cost of his trial defense had long ago exhausted Zeigler's own estate and had nearly crippled his mother's. Tom senior had died in 1980. Tom and Beulah had closed the furniture store in 1977, and sold it at a loss two years later. The apartments had gone to pay Hadley, Davids, and the investigators at trial; Davids had worked mostly without fee in preparing the first appeal.

As Duane remembers it, he nearly rejected the request to represent Zeigler, even for a few days. During 1976, Duane had worked for the U.S. attorney's office in Orlando. He had socialized with sheriff's officers and some of Robert Eagan's assistants, and he had heard the stories. Tommy Zeigler was a dog-mutilating homosexual who had ruined everybody's Christmas in 1975.

"Zeigler was guilty as hell, and everybody knew it, even before the trial," Duane said recently, recalling the early months of 1976. "You would hear these stories that weren't getting into the newspaper, testimony from the grand jury about what a vicious asshole Tommy Zeigler was. That was the scoop. All the insiders knew it. Everybody knew that Zeigler got what was coming to him."

In six years since then, Duane had heard nothing that had changed his mind. Zeigler was, literally, the last man Duane wanted to represent.

But he relented: it was for only a few days, and he would have advice from other attorneys who specialized in death penalty appeals. Vernon Davids and Leslie Gift, now married, agreed to help him with the brief.

Duane had no experience in death penalty issues. He remembers calling an assistant attorney general and naively requesting a few extra days to prepare his case. The man seemed almost amused as he denied the request: "It was the most chilling conversation I ever had. This guy basically told me, The system is in motion, if you don't file on time we are going to kill your client."

Duane drove to Starke and met Zeigler, expecting to meet a depraved, emotionless psychopath. Instead, Zeigler came across as polite, earnest, almost square . . . like John Boy Walton, Duane thought. Duane also scanned the trial testimony, looking for the "smoking gun" that had convicted Zeigler, and he didn't find it. He did find that the case was much more complex and ambiguous than he had been led to believe.

The brief was filed on time, and one day before the scheduled execution the Eleventh U.S. Circuit Court of Appeals granted a stay. Zeigler was returned from the Death House to wait out his appeals. Duane did not step out of the case. He read the transcripts again and looked at the evidence, and he became convinced that Zeigler had been unjustly convicted.

Not that Zeigler necessarily was innocent—guilt or innocence was another issue—but Duane believed that the crime had been badly investigated and wrongfully prosecuted, that the system had been ill-served.

The case captivated Duane. At the age of thirty, he thought, Zeigler had had everything. To Duane, the idea of Zeigler's guilt had implications about affluence and realized dreams. If he was guilty, he had deliberately thrown away a life that almost anyone would envy. Could success be so unsatisfying?

But if Zeigler was innocent, then he was the ultimate victim. He had lost his wife, his fortune, his reputation, his dreams, his liberty; and now Florida wanted to take his life as well.

Either alternative was disturbing.

By his own description, Duane became obsessed. He wrote letters to the editor and appeared on radio talk shows, declaring that Zeigler deserved a new trial. He found most minds closed on the subject. The *Sentinel Star*—now the *Orlando Sentinel*, and still the dominant media outlet in Orange County—seemed to have accepted the authorities' version from the beginning. The newspaper had always been one of the area's big boosters, and boosters are disinclined to question the local establishment.

In 1983, one of Orlando's television stations, WFTV Channel 9, aired a long piece by reporter Ken Kaltoff that summarized some of the lingering doubts in the case. It remains the only locally generated news report that has ever questioned the investigation or the prosecution of the case.

Duane also interviewed Frye and Eagan. Duane says that Frye told him that one of his confidential informants in the case was Robert Thompson, the Oakland chief of police. This seemed unusual to Duane: he had never heard of one policeman using another as a c.i., in effect shielding him from questioning while making his information the basis of an indictment.

Duane came to suspect that at least one major evidence find—the bags with cartridges, the blue towel, and the two empty gun boxes, said to have been discovered in a cabinet in the storage area—had been planted by police, either by the investigative crews themselves or by a local policeman directly involved in the actual crime, with access to the store. This cache of evidence was logged into evidence on January 2, nine days after the investigation began, and fully a week after the last item of evidence was seized from the store. Zeigler had been arrested four days earlier, and Duane believed that by then the OCSO had begun to realize how tenuous was the evidence against Zeigler.[1]

After several years of internal debate about the question of Zeigler's guilt, Duane took a new tack. It occurred to him that a gunshot wound in the abdomen was potentially lethal, even if self-inflicted with great care.[2]

Duane hypothesized how police would have investigated the case if Zeigler had died from his wound.

By living, Zeigler had offered only the sketchy story of an assault in the back of the store, plus the testimony that he loved his wife and had lived an upstanding life. The rest of the evidence would have been virtually the same, Duane thought. It would show that Charlie Mays had been found after hours in the furniture store, with cash and receipts in his pocket, his van parked in a position that suggested surreptitious purposes. It would show that

1. Don Frye has testified at least twice that the cache actually was found on December 27. But the evidence receipts are dated January 2, 1976. Alton Evans, who found the bags, testified that he made the discovery on January 2, and this is borne out by his official report. Evans was not even in the store on December 27: he was busy preparing the first shipment of evidence for the FBI Lab, which he brought to Washington on the 28th. If the evidence in the bags had been found earlier than the 27th, it would have been included in that original shipment. In fact, it became part of a later submission.

2. In May 1976, the National Institute of Law Enforcement and Criminal Justice published a study on the effectiveness of soft body armor. As part of the research, the authors canvassed surgeons to determine possible mortality rates from gunshots in unprotected torsos. The study quoted a mortality rate ranging from 5 percent to 20 percent for a shot from a .38 Special that does not strike any vital organs. A shot that struck the liver would have a mortality rate of 15 to 60 percent; one that passed through the spleen would have a mortality rate of 15 to 30 percent.

Edward Williams was in possession of the principal murder weapon, that ownership of the other two major weapons had been traced to Williams's friend, Frank Smith, and that Williams's truck had been found at the murder scene. The only difference would have been one more body. Would the police still have attempted to blame the murder on Zeigler?

The answer seemed obvious to Duane: Edward Williams would have been the immediate and obvious suspect. He could have been convicted with the same set of facts and findings that had been used to convict Tommy Zeigler.

If nothing else, Duane thought, this was a powerful argument against capital punishment. If Zeigler was guilty, then only his own luck and good aim had saved the state from convicting and executing an innocent man.

Guilty or innocent, Duane thought, Tommy Zeigler had been very close to keeping his good name on Christmas Eve. All he would have had to do was die.

FORTY-SEVEN

THE PRINCIPALS IN THE CASE WENT ABOUT THEIR LIVES.

Shortly after the trial, Don Frye became a state attorney's investigator. He is still with that office, where he holds an administrative job.

Robert Eagan left office in 1990, and now is a partner in a law firm in Orlando.

Terry Hadley accepted one more criminal defense and then quit the practice. He is a successful civil attorney in Orange County.

Edward Williams lives in Orlando. In 1986, when Zeigler's death was imminent, he told an interviewer from the *Sentinel*, "Zeigler messed himself up. He was a big man in Winter Garden.

Big man. I'd be working for him still. But he tried to move too fast. Wanted the whole world. His wife, she was a fine lady. Always good to me. He killed her. Killed her. Zeigler. That kid, he's all done now."

Jimmy Yawn became chief of police of Winter Garden, a position he held as of the spring of 1992.

Robert Thompson's resignation from the Oakland Police Department became effective during the trial. He and his family later left Orange County.

Felton Thomas's whereabouts are unknown.

Maurice Paul is now a U.S. district court judge in Jacksonville.

After the death of her husband, Beulah lived alone in her home on Temple Grove Drive. She twice underwent treatment for breast cancer.

Mattie Mays received an undisclosed sum in an out-of-court settlement of her lawsuit against the Zeiglers. The suit and countersuit involving the Zeiglers and the two insurance companies was also settled out of court, with Mrs. Zeigler receiving an undisclosed portion of the benefits.

Gene Annan was hospitalized with severe stomach ulcers shortly after the trial ended. He never investigated another case, and is now a computer programmer who specializes in custom billing software for physicians and attorneys. He considers the case an affront to logic and justice: "The prosecution put on two hundred–some pieces of physical evidence, and none of it proves that Tommy Zeigler was guilty. The jurors saw all these guns and all this bloody clothing, and they figured that it must mean something. They threw up their hands and voted to convict, and they gave him life so that somebody else could come along and figure it out."

In January 1986, Bill Duane joined a large law firm in Orlando and began phasing out his representation of Zeigler. A state-financed group of attorneys specializing in capital appeals was to take over the case. Zeigler's second appeal—known as a habeas corpus or "3.850" petition—was still working its way through the system. It was based on another set of collateral matters, including the argument that in restricting character witnesses during the penalty phase of the trial, Judge Paul had failed to consider possible mitigating circumstances.

That spring, a U.S. district judge, Susan Black, declared that

Zeigler and his attorneys had improperly filed his habeas petition. This cleared the way for an unexpected second warrant. Zeigler was scheduled to die on Tuesday morning, May 20, 1986.

This was grave. As far as Zeigler and his attorneys were aware, nobody had ever come back alive from the Death House after being found in procedural default.

Another condemned man was in the Death House at the same time. Ronald "Frog" Straight was a convicted murderer and a Death Row friend of Zeigler's who had run out of appeals. Both he and Zeigler knew that Straight's cause was lost, but neither admitted it.

Zeigler's time, too, got short. On Sunday, May 18, he wrote a series of good-byes and thank-you letters. He asked that his files and his collection of the official record be shipped out to his mother's home, along with all of his personal possessions; he didn't want her to have to deal with it after he was gone.

Vernon Davids had recently returned to work after multiple-bypass heart surgery. Although he had not been Zeigler's principal counsel since 1981, he had remained an attorney of record and had stayed current with the case. He knew that Zeigler still had favorable issues on his habeas petition.

With about thirty-six hours remaining before the execution, Davids finished a motion for a stay of execution, based on the last possible, and least desirable, grounds: Davids averred that his own representation of Zeigler had been incompetent and that Zeigler's newest attorneys had failed to file a timely appeal.

In the meantime, Leslie Gift and Tommy's cousin Connie Crawford made preliminary arrangements for a mortician to recover the body after the execution.

Insufficiency of counsel was the one issue that would earn a stay. After the U.S. district court denied the motion, a judge of the Eleventh Circuit Court of Appeals in Atlanta granted the stay. Zeigler learned of it when a guard summoned him to a telephone to take a call from Vernon Davids; at the time, Zeigler was in the visitor park with his mother, Connie Crawford, and Davids's ex-wife, Pat.

His visitors were joyful and relieved. Shortly afterward, they left the prison, happy—this wasn't going to be a last visit after all.

But Zeigler believed that he hadn't heard the last word. He suspected that the state would appeal the stay. And he was correct: he learned later that evening that Florida's attorney general,

James Smith, had flown to Washington to ask the U.S. Supreme Court to lift the stay.

Zeigler was moved out of the Death House to a cell on Q wing. At that time he knew that if the stay was lifted he would be brought downstairs and executed almost at once. He went to sleep knowing that he might be awakened by guards taking him to his death. By his own account, he read the Bible and prayed, as he did every night. He wrote a short, heartfelt poem about his wife, which he later gave to Leslie Gift.

In Zeigler's words, from a letter he wrote in January, 1992, responding to a series of questions:

> After I received my stay on May 19, all of my property was moved from the death house to Q-3-West-5. This cell is on the third floor of Q wing right above the death chamber.
>
> Ronald Straight was still in the death house in Q-1-East-3. I was not allowed to go back into the death house to communicate with him. I was taken to my cell and once I was secured there I called through the ventilation shaft to Frog and wished him good luck.
>
> After my visit that afternoon I had left word that I would see no one else. In other words if things went sour I wasn't going to have anyone here holding my hand. No man should have those memories to haunt him and especially not on my part. I was glad that everyone was home and out of the circus atmosphere.
>
> On Q wing the night before an execution it is so quiet you can actually hear your heart beat. The sounds of the officers opening/ closing the security gates and their footsteps making their rounds is deafening. This was not the first time I had been there prior to an execution so the chilling feeling was not new to me.
>
> Special thoughts? I wondered how my execution would affect my family and friends. This has always been my major concern. I don't want my death to haunt them or hurt them. My death should be a matter of rejoicing because all the pain and suffering will be over. I would be with Eunice, Papa, and Mom and Dad Edwards.
>
> My memories of times past all came flowing back and then the thoughts of the present and future pushed them out and I wondered what Frog was doing/thinking.
>
> Frog was executed at 5:00 P.M. on Tuesday. I was very aware of what was happening. I watched the vans bring the witnesses and media representatives to the death chamber. I could hear the generator running and smell the diesel fumes from it. At the same moment I could hear the switches clicking and the light bulb in my cell dimmed so I knew exactly what was happening!

A few moments later I heard the door to the death chamber open. I could hear voices outside, the vans cranked up, and I watched them drive the witnesses back down the little asphalt road from the death chamber. I then watched the hearse come in through the sally port gate, travel down the same little asphalt road to the death chamber. The doors opened and closed again and I watched the hearse retreat back down the road.

It's very accurate to say that had the United States Supreme Court lifted the stays I would have been taken back into the death house, prepped, and executed right after Frog.

The stays were not lifted. Zeigler's new lawyers, members of a New York law firm working pro bono, prepared a new petition for the Eleventh U.S. Circuit Court of Appeals.

Bill Duane's proselytizing paid off now. One of Duane's acquaintances in Orlando had been Dave Burgin, who became editor in chief of the *Sentinel* around the time that Duane took on Zeigler's case. Burgin, after many hours of hearing Duane expound on the case, had become convinced that Zeigler had been unjustly convicted.

Burgin had since left the *Sentinel* and was now a consultant to the *Atlanta Constitution*. Atlanta happens to be the seat of the Eleventh U.S. Circuit. Burgin commissioned the *Constitution*'s Florida correspondent to do a series of articles on the crime, incorporating details that the media in Orange County had largely overlooked.

The articles appeared on the three days immediately preceeding Zeigler's hearing in Atlanta. Zeigler and his supporters believed that they may have been responsible for saving his life, for shortly afterward the three judges of the Eleventh Circuit accepted Zeigler's argument that Judge Paul should have heard testimony about possible mitigating circumstances before overriding the jury's recommendation.

The two death sentences were thrown out, and Zeigler was awarded a new sentencing hearing.

Shortly before that hearing took place—in Orlando, in 1989—a *Sentinel* article claimed that a former Death Row inmate named Eddie Odom[1] was going to testify that in 1979, Zeigler

---

1. Odom is a career criminal who received the death sentence for a 1976 murder conviction; the sentence was later reduced to life.

persuaded his mother to pay $50,000 to Odom's wife, so that Odom could arrange to have Tom Zeigler, Sr., murdered; the motive was that Tommy's father supposedly opposed spending any more money on his son's behalf. According to the *Sentinel,* the state attorney's office also had a witness who would testify that Zeigler tortured small animals when he was a teenager.

But Odom never testified about the supposed murder plot. And the witness to Zeigler's alleged brutality toward animals never took the stand; according to the prosecutor, he had gone to Costa Rica.

Two psychiatrists and a psychologist did testify that Zeigler was unlikely to be violent.

"Had I not met Mr. Zeigler at Florida State Prison, I would have come away having met just another man," said Orlando psychiatrist J. Lloyd Wilder.

Assistant State Attorney Jeff Ashton cross-examined psychologist Brad Fisher, who said that Zeigler was unlikely to be violent:

ASHTON: In early December 1975, could you have predicted he would murder four people?
FISHER: My best prediction would have been that he wasn't likely to become violent.
ASHTON: Wouldn't you have been less likely then than now to predict that he would commit murder?
FISHER: That's correct.

Ashton intended to discredit the psychologist's ability to predict Zeigler's future behavior, since Zeigler had been convicted of a violent crime. However, another conclusion was possible. In 1976, virtually the same testimony—that he was unlikely to be a murderer—could have been used to defend Zeigler.

Nevertheless, Circuit Judge Gary Formet did find that Zeigler deserved the death penalty, and restored the sentences. In 1991 the Florida supreme court again affirmed the sentences, and Zeigler's attorneys began the appeal process once more, basing their latest habeas petition on new evidence that had been revealed during the past fifteen years.

Zeigler admits that in 1979 he tried to persuade a Death Row inmate who had run out of appeals—a onetime member of the so-called Ski Mask Bandits—to confess to the Christmas Eve killings. As for the alleged murder plot, he and his mother claim that she was a victim of extortion, that she and Tom were pressured into paying protection money to save their son's life. Apparently the Zeiglers were sent prison photographs showing a murdered inmate: the implication was that this could happen to Tommy.

The sole source of the information about the murder plot was Eddie Odom and his wife. In 1991, two FSP inmates wrote remarkable letters denying that Zeigler was involved in any such plot. The letters were remarkable, in part, because they violated the unwritten prison rule against snitching.

One was from Robert Lewis, who participated with Odom in several violent armed robberies during the 1970s and who in 1979 escaped from Death Row by walking out, wearing a guard's uniform. (He was arrested three weeks later.)

Lewis sent an affidavit that alleged, among other things, that "most stories about [Zeigler] were created by my crime partner Eddie Odom for personal gain."

Convicted murderer Jimmy Lee Smith said that he met Odom in 1979, shortly after arriving on Death Row, and that Odom offered to have him moved to a more desirable cell on the ground floor of the wing.[2]

Smith was one of several inmates willing to repudiate Odom at Zeigler's resentencing hearing. He writes: "Eddie welded [sic] a little power around death row because he had money and he was the biggest dope connection in the prison. He tells me that he can get me moved to One-North, but, for doing so, he wants me to keep tabs on someone for him. . . . He says that someone on that floor has information he needs and if I would help him get it he would have me moved. . . . It turns out that Eddie wants me to spy on William Thomas Zeigler Jr.—everybody calls him Tommy. I was moved into the cell right next to him. . . . Eddie wanted any sort of information about Tommy, especially about his Mother and Father."

According to Smith, Odom told him that he had arranged to have photos of a murdered inmate sent to Zeigler's parents, and that Odom boasted of having repeated the threat to Tom senior in the visiting room. According to Smith, Robert Lewis's escape was

2. The upper floors at FSP are said to be stifling hot in summer.

part of a larger escape plan that would be financed by the money extorted from the Zeiglers. But the plan failed when Lewis was caught three weeks later.

"I asked Eddie what he did with all that money since the grand escape attempt failed," Smith wrote. "He says that he paid for a boob job and a new Cadillac for his old lady. I laughed as tho I tho't that was the slickest con in the world."

FORTY-EIGHT

IN 1991, ROBERT EAGAN COMPLAINED TO AN INTERVIEWER THAT SUCCES-sive defense attorneys for Zeigler had so distorted the evidence that he could hardly recognize the case he had tried in 1976. He compared them to Communist revisionists, rewriting history to serve their own ends.[1]

If the debate about the case has been somewhat transfigured with time, it may be because the body of evidence—some direct, some peripheral—has grown over the years. Successive revelations of new information have kept the case controversial, and in some instances have prolonged Zeigler's appeals. Some of that new evidence actually dates from the original investigation and remained in the files of the state attorney for more than ten years, literally undiscovered.

---

1. In that same conversation, Eagan also stated that the grove bullet "was positively identified as having been fired from one of Tommy's guns." In fact, FBI ballistics experts could not positively match the grove bullet to the Securities .38, although they shared general rifling characteristics.

THE ROACH STATEMENTS

In 1979, a husband and wife, Ken and Linda Roach, gave the most detailed eyewitness accounts of events at the store at the time of the murders. If their affidavits are at all accurate, they leave no possibility except that Zeigler is innocent.

The couple lived outside Orange County, but said that they were driving through the town on Christmas Eve in 1975, and that they passed the furniture store that evening as they drove south on Dillard Street. Ken Roach said that the time was about 7:20 P.M. as they approached Route 50.

Both swore that as they passed the store, they heard a single loud noise that sounded like a tire blowout. It was followed quickly by a series of firecracker-like reports, some louder than others. Ken Roach said it was like "a pack of firecrackers being ignited all at the same time . . . a series of at least ten or more shots or explosions, some at different levels of sound."

Both looked to the right, toward the source of the noise: the furniture store. The lights inside were low.

Each saw *four* vehicles parked in front.

Linda Roach described two of the cars. One was large, white or cream. The other, also large, was dark metallic blue-green, which is consistent with the Edwardses' sedan. She could not remember the others.

Ken Roach said that one of the four cars appeared to be a new white Cadillac. He also saw a dark-skinned man calmly walking along the front of the store, toward a pickup truck which was backed in along the north side of the building. Ken Roach described the man as of medium build, 150–170 pounds, average height, thirty to fifty years old, wearing dark work clothes or everyday clothes, a dark jacket, and a cap or a hat. (This was compatible with Charlie Mays's height, weight, and age; also, Mays on Christmas Eve wore a dark sweatshirt with a hood).

The Roaches said that after Zeigler was indicted they realized that they had been near the scene of the murders. They discussed several times what they ought to do, and Ken Roach finally called the OCSO. According to him, he gave this same information to a woman who answered the phone, who told him that his statement wasn't needed and refused to give him the name of Zeigler's attorney.

They said that they didn't pursue the matter, but that it continued to bother them, so they looked up Tom Zeigler in the Winter Garden phone directory, to finally give the information. They claimed that they did not know Tommy Zeigler or the rest of the family.

According to Vernon Davids, who took the statement, the Roaches were credible witnesses: a middle-class couple with children, active in state politics.

Besides the rest of their information, the Roaches' statements are notable for the appearance of the light-colored Cadillac from Felton Thomas's account.[2] Their recollection of the lighting in the store resembles Zeigler's description of the lights he claims to have left burning that evening, and the timing is consistent with the first shots heard by Barbara Tinsley, although she did not hear as many as ten reports.

Of course, the Roaches' observations are utterly incompatible with the state's case. Among other details, the prosecution's theory cannot accommodate four cars, a pickup, and a dark-skinned man walking in front of the store at 7:20; and even with a revolver in each hand, one man alone could not fire off ten shots so rapidly as to produce a sound "like a pack of firecrackers being ignited all at the same time."

THE MCEACHERN CHARGE

In 1981, former OCSO officer Leigh McEachern claimed that he was present at a pretrial conference at which Judge Paul discussed the evidence in the Zeigler case with Robert Eagan, Don Frye, and a third party whom McEachern could not recall.

McEachern had been the chief deputy to Sheriff Mel Colman in 1976. He made this charge from a prison camp in northern Florida, where he was serving a sentence after being convicted of embezzling from his department's investigative funds.

According to McEachern, the ex parte meeting[3] took place in

---

2. Vernon Davids, among others, believes that Felton Thomas's statement could be substantially true, except for the identification of Zeigler; that is, that Thomas and Mays actually did meet a stranger—not Zeigler—in a Cadillac, that they did test pistols in the orange grove, that Thomas pulled the switch on the breaker box, and that he actually did run away because he was frightened by something that he witnessed at the store.

3. That is, a meeting away from the courtroom.

a conference room of the offices of the state attorney. He said that Eagan outlined for Paul the major points in the state's case, including the expected testimony of Professor MacDonell.

McEachern claimed that as the meeting broke up, Paul told Eagan: "Bob, get me one first-degree [conviction] and I'll fry the son of a bitch." McEachern said that he later mentioned the meeting to Colman, but did nothing else. He said that he decided to come forward after the Florida supreme court affirmed Zeigler's conviction and sentence.

Such a conference would have been completely improper. Eagan, Frye, and Paul all denied that the meeting had taken place; Zeigler was awarded a hearing on the matter. That occurred in August 1984; Duane examined Frye, Judge Paul, Eagan, and the former beverage agent Herbert Baker, attempting to establish a judicial conspiracy against Zeigler based on ill will from the Andrew James matter. Circuit Judge James Stroker, who heard the testimony, ruled that the charge was without substance, although he admitted that he could find no obvious motive for McEachern to have lied.

LATE DISCOVERY

In 1987, after Florida passed its Public Records Act, Zeigler's appellate attorneys were granted access to the state attorney's files of the case. Leslie Gift, who had catalogued the original discovery evidence in 1976, went along to examine the documents in the file.

Gift found at least three potentially relevant items that prosecutors had not turned over to the defense.

One was a thirteen-page report by Robert Thompson, in which he described the blood around Zeigler's wound as being "dry." In his sworn statement Thompson had said it was "dry and damp," a crucial difference. The significance was that the state claimed that Zeigler had shot himself after calling the Van Deventer home, when he was sure that help was on the way. But Thompson arrived on the scene within a minute after that call; the blood around a wound that fresh could not possibly be dry.

Gift also found a long twenty-nine page interim report written by Don Frye, the existence of which which Frye had denied.

She also came across an audiotape, which she copied. The tape was remarkable. It recorded an interview between Jack Bachman, Eagan's investigator, and a young man named Jon Jellison.

On Christmas Eve the Jellison family—Jon, his parents, and his teenage sister, from Minnesota—had been registered in the back wing of the Winter Garden Inn. Their room overlooked the rear compound of the furniture store. In April, Eagan sent letters to motel guests, asking whether they could substantiate some of the specifics of the statements of Edward Williams and Felton Thomas.

Apparently, only the Jellisons had any information. And it was not what the prosecution hoped. This is a partial transcript of the tape that Leslie Gift found, and that apparently was never turned over during discovery:

Q (BACHMAN): What is your name—Jon?

A (JELLISON): Jon, right. Really, we didn't observe very much or we can't really add much more than, you know, what you've got there already. We ate supper—my mom told Mr. Eagan all about this—ate supper at the motel, came back to our room at, I suppose, between 8:15 and 8:30, and we sat around awhile looking at postcards and I, uh, I was going to go over to the office there at the motel and mail them back home there—

Q: Right.

A: —so I went to the door, I cracked the door and I was just going to walk out and there was a policeman out in the parking lot aiming his pistol over the hood of his police car at the back of the building—

Q: Right.

A: —at the furniture store. That was the first time that we had known, you know, anything funny was going on at all. And then, so rather than go to the post office at the office there we just stayed inside our room there and looked out through the window and through the door.

Q: Were you on the back side of the motel?

A: Right. Let's see. We just stood there and watched for quite some time and then we heard what we figured were probably shots, maybe 9:00 or so, it said in the letter—that would be about the right time. We didn't notice particularly what time it was but as close as we can figure that must be about what time it was.

Q: Now, when you heard the shots, was this after you saw the police cars?

A: Right, right, it was. We saw the police car and that was the first time we knew anything was going on at all.

Q: But you didn't hear any shots—in other words, as you were leaving the restaurant or something you didn't hear any shots.

A: Nothing at all, no, uh-uh. We knew nothing was going on whatsoever.

Q: So then you didn't hear the shots then until after the police had arrived.

A: Right, right. So I am sure they have already filled you in on all that.

. . .

Q: Well, I was almost on my way up to talk to you—but if you heard the shots after you saw the police cars—

A: Yeah, yeah.

Q: It was all over with at that point.

A: Yeah. What—is there any new leads or anything—do you have any information on what—

Q: Well, I mean, we got a man charged. In fact, we have got the owner of the furniture store charged.

A: You do?

Q: Oh, yeah.

A: Oh, I see. I didn't know that.

Q: See, he had his wife insured for $500,000.

A: Oh, I see.

Q: And the policies were only about thirty days old when he killed her.

A: Oh.

Q: He killed her, his mother-in-law, his father-in-law, and a customer in the store.

A: Oh, I see. You have *him* charged then. Oh, I see.

. . .

Q: . . . What we are really trying to find is somebody that saw them [Zeigler and Mays] jumping that fence back there.

A: Oh, yeah, right.

Q: But, nope, as long as you heard the gunshots after, you know, you say you saw the police car then that wouldn't help us a bit. . . . Okay, you might tell your mother I called.

A: Okay. You won't need to talk to her or anything will you?

Q: Not unless, you know, you all get together and decide you heard those gunshots—

A: No.

Q: —before you saw the police car and in that case we'd give you a free trip back to Florida.

A: (Laughs) No, we've, uh, ever since we got the letter here, about last Thursday I guess it was, we've been talking it over and that's as close as we can come. . . .

The tape is startling. The Jellisons were clearly in a position to corroborate key points in the testimony of Edward Williams and Felton Thomas. But they did not. Rather, they stated unequivocally that they heard shots *after* a policeman drove up to the back of the store.

This was powerful material, considering that Zeigler had always charged that he had made enemies of local policemen because of his interest in Andrew James and the alleged loan-sharking racket. Years before the existence of the Jellison tape became known, Zeigler claimed that a Winter Garden patrolman had threatened his life.

The defense deposed every officer who was on the scene during the first half hour after police arrived. None of them described an action like the one related on the Jellison tape. No police car should have been in the rear compound at any time on Christmas Eve. What the Jellisons claimed to see, if accurate, is a corroboration of Tommy Zeigler's long-held theory that he was set up by police.

In 1988, the murders were the subject of a syndicated TV documentary. Researchers for the independent production company interviewed juror Irma Brickle, who told them that on the afternoon of the last day of jury deliberations she was given Valium to calm her nerves; shortly afterward, she said, she gave in to pressure from other jurors and voted to convict.

The documentary left unclear the questions of who gave her the drug, and by what authority. Zeigler's latest motion for a new trial states that Judge Paul persuaded Mrs. Brickle's physician to prescribe her the drug over the telephone.

Shortly after the documentary was broadcast, Vernon Davids received a letter from a certain John Bulled, whom Davids later verified as one of the prison trusties on the work crew that dug up the grove bullet.

According to Bulled, crews searched the grove for two days and found nothing. On the afternoon of the second day, Bulled said, a sheriff's deputy told the crew supervisor, "We will just have to produce one anyway."

Bulled said he believed that the evidence had been fabricated, because inmates were told to say that they had found a slug, when actually they had found none.

Two of Zeigler's present attorneys, from the New York City law firm that has represented him since 1986, have sworn that they contacted a second member of the work crew who confirmed Bulled's story and reluctantly agreed to testify.

And in 1982, Ed Rowe, the manager of a West Orange grocery, signed an affidavit regarding conversations that he had had with Charlie Mays's son seven years after the murders. According to Rowe, he had discussed the crime with Ernie Mays, who was one of his employees. (Ernie Mays denied that the conversations took place.)

Rowe claimed that Ernie had told him that his father had taken a gun along the last time he left his house, and that before he left had told his family that there would be money for Christmas.

"My father wasn't supposed to die that night," is how Rowe quotes Ernie Mays. "Tommy Zeigler was supposed to die."

V

ALMOST
TRUE

FORTY-NINE

A CRIMINAL TRIAL IS NOT A SEARCH FOR TRUTH. IT IS MUCH TOO circumscribed for that. Rather, a trial is a formalized contest for the hearts and minds of a panel of twelve. It is a quest for a verdict, in which information is selected and screened (we can almost say "processed") before it is allowed to reach jurors.

A trial jury sees two competing products that each side has gathered and arranged and artfully presented. The verdict goes to the more convincing product. We hope that any verdict is correct—which is to say, that it is grounded in truth and reality. But a verdict can only be as true and real as the evidence-product that the jury receives. An incompetent investigation cannot produce a competent verdict. A bad-faith prosecution precludes a good-faith judgment.

In the shorthand of computer hackers: garbage in, garbage out.

The extensive documentation of *Florida* v. *Zeigler* allows us to trace the investigation and follow the work of those who brought the case to trial. It is disturbing. It suggests that the means by which the crime was investigated and the case was prosecuted—the entire process by which Tommy Zeigler was convicted—are so flawed as to render the verdict invalid by any reasonable measure of fairness or justice, if not under the law.

This is an important distinction. As individuals, and as a society, we often stake out moral boundaries that are much more stringent than what statutes allow. To be legal is not necessarily to be right; otherwise attorneys would be the ultimate arbiters of morality.

What happened to Tommy Zeigler is wrong, by the standards

that most of us accept. The public officials whose duty it was to bring the case to justice, and to bring justice to the case, long ago failed their trust. I include police, prosecutor, and judiciary. They failed Zeigler, they failed the victims and the victims' families, they failed the system, they failed their state. *Florida v. Zeigler* began to go wrong within the first few hours after sheriff's deputies took control of the crime scene, and it never got back on course. To this day, it has not been put right.

THE CRIME SCENE

Beginning on Christmas Eve and continuing for as long as they held the store, the crime scene investigation by the Orange County deputies was fundamentally marred by a series of errors and omissions, many of which violate accepted police procedure. It is a compendium of awkward thinking, poor judgment, and questionable methods:

• Don Frye never inspected the soles of Thomas's shoes, even though the detective believed that bloody footprints on the terrazzo floor might identify the killer. When Thomas left police custody after giving his statement early Christmas morning, his clothes and his shoes went with him.

Thomas's own statement put him at the front door of the furniture store within a minute of Mays's death, and at the back of the store within five to ten minutes after the first three killings. Sound practice and common sense dictate that anyone who admits being at the threshold of a murder scene, nearly at the moment when the crime was committed, deserves a certain amount of skepticism and close examination. Yet no OCSO officer ever examined Thomas's clothes. He was never tested for gunshot residue, which could have verified or disproved his story of the orange grove.

• At 3:00 A.M. on Christmas Eve, Alton Evans found a key ring with three keys in one of Charlie Mays's pockets. According to Evans in his deposition, the keys were released to Mattie Mays, at Frye's request. Evans said that the keys were not processed for fingerprints and were never tried in any of the store's locks. Apparently they were never photographed.

Releasing untested evidence from a crime scene is such an

egregious breach of investigative protocol that it needs no further comment.

• OCSO deputies violated a basic rule of procedure when they began smoking at the crime scene before all the evidence had been collected and processed. Beginning on Christmas Eve they smoked in at least two areas, at the front of the store and in the office that Zeigler and his mother shared.

This became a issue when one of the state's photographs showed a burned matchstick atop a .22 cartridge on the floor of the office. Since neither Tommy nor Beulah smoked, this seemed to show that someone else had been in the room during or after the crime. But the OCSO claimed that the match had been dropped by one of its deputies, and the defense could not prove otherwise.

The question would have been much clearer if sheriff's personnel had observed the prohibition against smoking at a crime scene, not to mention the universal rule that a scene should be disturbed as little as possible until technicians have finished their jobs.

Except perhaps in this instance, smoking at the scene may not have directly influenced the evidence. But it does reveal a certain attitude, an approach to the work: that in the first few hours of the biggest investigation of their careers, the OCSO investigators did not observe a basic principal of their profession—they could not be bothered to step outside when they wanted a cigarette.

• Faulty work by OCSO technicians apparently was responsible for the FBI's inability to identify some of the dry blood specimens. After the FBI released the disappointing serology results, Robert Eagan wrote a biting letter to the chief of the OCSO Technical Services Division, criticizing the technicians' crime scene work. Eagan implied that some specimens had been improperly collected, resulting in insufficient quantities for typing.

Insufficient samples may have accounted for the FBI's decision to withhold testing of most of the dry samples for more than two weeks, after which subtyping would no longer be reliable. If the samples were good, then the decision to delay testing was the equivalent of destroying valuable—probably crucial—evidence.

The FBI serologist William Gavin was the chief examiner on the case, responsible for distributing the evidence to other departments in the lab. Gavin said that he made a judgment call to delay his own testing until all the other examinations had been made, even though that would greatly diminish the potential value of the blood evidence.

However, this doesn't explain why Gavin didn't attempt to subtype the sample swabs and filter papers that contained the dry blood specimens from around the store. These items were gathered specifically for blood typing.

The sheriff's transmittal letter to the FBI asked that blood specimens be subtyped as far as possible. But we also know that the test of Tommy Zeigler's trousers was done under an informal verbal agreement, and that the results were never committed to paper.

The defense was prepared to do its own tests. But while the evidentiary potential of the police's blood specimens ebbed away in the FBI Lab, the OCSO and the state attorney retained control of the crime scene, preventing Gene Annan and Pete Ragsdale from gathering their own samples. Sheriff's deputies did not relinquish the store until after fifteen days—after the two-week limit for collecting and subtyping dry blood evidence.

The ultimate upshot was that probably the most valuable potential evidence in the case was lost forever, for reasons which were within the control of the sheriff and the prosecutor and the crime lab of their choice.

• The Winter Garden Inn, adjacent to the crime scene, represented a potential trove of witnesses. Anyone at the motel might have heard shots. Furthermore, both Felton Thomas and Edward Williams described specific incidents that were supposed to have taken place in and around the fenced rear compound, within open view of more than twenty rooms in the north wing.

Knocking on doors and asking questions is one of the basic techniques of police investigation. Incredibly, no OCSO detective or patrolman ever canvassed the staff and guests of the motel.[1] Investigators did not begin door-to-door interviews in the neighborhood until after the preliminary hearing, which was on January 16. (Judge Kaney's low opinion of the state's case, as manifested in the paltry $40,000 bail figure, must have been a shock to the system.)

---

1. The Oakland chief of police, Robert Thompson, interviewed some motel guests on the evening of December 27, seventy-two hours after the murders. By that time most of the Christmas Eve guests had checked out. Nobody has ever explained why a local officer out of his jurisdiction was doing the work of county deputies.

This is not just a failure to observe formalities. Don Frye appears to have been completely satisfied with the reliability of Edward Williams and Felton Thomas, but the fact is that their accounts were mostly uncorroborated. The guests in the motel's north wing were in a unique position to confirm or deny the veracity of two witnesses without whom a guilty verdict, even an indictment, would never have been possible.

Eagan did send a letter to the registered guests, asking their help. The only concrete product of that mailing was the Jellison interview, which the prosecution apparently ignored. Eagan's request was dated April 12, 1976: three and a half months after the murders. Furthermore, letters and even telephone interviews are no substitute for face-to-face questioning. The time for that was Christmas Eve, when memories were freshest and potential witnesses were still available, just a brief stroll away from the crime scene.

Sheriff's deputies should have knocked on doors at the motel immediately. That they did not do so—that Frye and ranking OCSO officers on the scene did not order them to do so—is inexcusable. It represents the loss of unique testimony that could have settled the case, one way or the other.

In fact, it is such a stunning oversight that we must wonder whether someone did not actually interview north wing guests on Christmas Eve and come back with damaging information that investigators decided to disregard. Ordinarily we would accept the word of the police on this matter. But in this case the question cannot be so easily dismissed, given the Jellison tape and how the prosecution handled it.

• The OCSO investigators chose to bring Felton Thomas into the furniture store when they questioned him during the early hours of Christmas morning, at a time when evidence technicians had just begun collecting their specimens. (James Jenkins questioned Thomas, with Frye present.) There was no reason for Thomas to be in the building; he could add nothing to the investigation there.

But good reasons did exist for Thomas to be kept out. One of the axioms of forensics is that any visitor potentially alters a crime scene either by removing traces of evidence or leaving some behind—hair, fabric fibers, dirt, fingerprints, footprints—or by disturbing the arrangement of what is already there. Strict procedure dictates that the scene should have been off limits to all but those whose job required them to be there.

Thomas, in particular, should have been kept far from the scene. His claim that he had never gone into the store with Mays was one of the key points of his account. But that was still an open question until all the evidence was collected and analyzed. His story would be badly compromised if a hair from his head, for example, was found at the scene. But the fact that he had been at the store after the crime—even if confined to a part of the showroom—could muddle what otherwise would be damning evidence.

• In their most glaring offense against basic procedure, Frye and Jenkins apparently failed to obtain from Felton Thomas even the barest description of the stranger who approached him and Charlie Mays when they were parked in the motel lot. The transcript of their interview of Thomas early Christmas morning shows that the detectives did not challenge his identification of Zeigler, whom Thomas had never met before that night.

Thomas was a key witness in a capital crime. He should have been required to give a head-to-toes description of the man he was implicating. A proper interrogation might include the following line of questioning: "How did he wear his hair? Was it long or short? What color was it? What was the shade of his skin? Did he wear glasses? Were they wire-rimmed or did they have plastic frames? Did he have a mustache? Sideburns? Any scars? What color was his shirt? Did it have buttons up the front? Long sleeves or short?" And so on down to his shoes. At the very minimum, Frye and Jenkins should have asked Thomas about the stranger's age, height, weight, and general physique.

According to Thomas's account, the stranger in the Cadillac must have been with him and Mays for at least twenty minutes. During much of that time Thomas sat beside the stranger in the front seat of the car. Thomas observed him standing, walking, jumping fences. Thomas's story is worthless if he could not describe in detail the man whom he accused of having murdered Charlie Mays.

When he did get the chance to describe the man he met, Thomas was wrong on the two most obvious details: what he wore and what he drove. Zeigler's clothes on Christmas Eve were not light-colored, and he did not drive a light-colored Cadillac. Even allowing for an unlikely misidentification of the make of the automobile, Thomas at least should have known the obvious fact that

Dunaway's Oldsmobile was two-toned—distinctly, unmistakably dark and light. Above all, as we'll see in the next chapter, Thomas failed to note the single most striking detail about Zeigler that night, a detail he could not have failed to mention if he had seen Zeigler that evening.

Thomas also should have been asked to pick Zeigler out of a photo spread—that is, a collection of several head-and-shoulders photographs, including one of the suspect. This is a standard test of an eyewitness identification. (Some detectives also like to test a witness's reliability by using a photo spread that does not include the suspect.)

Frye probably didn't have a photo of Zeigler that night. But he could have gotten one a few hours later, when he searched 75 Temple Grove. The fact that Frye didn't seize any photos from the home indicates that he never intended to subject Felton Thomas's statement to this simple test.[2] As it happened, Thomas was not available for photo spreads anyway: immediately after Frye and Jenkins released him, he went missing for four days. But Frye didn't know that until later.

(Since the transcript of the original interrogation probably doesn't record the entire conversation between Thomas and the two detectives, we can't know for certain that Frye and Jenkins didn't ask the right questions. But we *can* be sure that Thomas didn't accurately describe Zeigler that night. If he had, that description would have fortified Thomas's credibility and surely would have become a part of Frye's official report. Frye had no reason to withhold an accurate identification.)

• The recognition experiment that Frye and Denny Martin conducted in the back of the showroom was poorly conceived, and proved nothing.

Frye was testing whether Edward Williams could have identified a gun wrapped in a towel in Zeigler's hand. Under actual conditions, Williams would have been coming from relative brightness (exterior lights at the motel shone on the rear compound) into the darkness of the showroom. Also, Williams would not expect to find a gun in Zeigler's hand.

---

2. Zeigler and members of his family confirm that the house contained photo albums as well as framed pictures on display. One of those photos is reproduced in the photo section of this book.

But in Frye's experiment, he and Martin stood inside the store so that their eyes could adjust to the darkness. (Frye himself admitted this.) Then each took turns walking up the hallway while the other held an unloaded service revolver. Frye said that Martin went outside and then came in, but Martin denied it. He said that he simply went to the end of the dark hallway and then walked back into the showroom.

Frye devalued the experiment when he used a known object. He did not wrap a cloth around the pistol. Above all, he undercut the premise of the test by allowing his eyes to adjust. Under the circumstances, it is not surprising that he found that the test confirmed Williams's story.

Even so, Martin remembered it with less confidence. From his deposition of April 29, 1976:

Q (VERNON DAVIDS): What did you see?

A (MARTIN): Well, I could recognize Detective Frye.

Q: You could recognize him?

A: Yes, sir. But it was very close. I can't say whether or not it was part of my imagination, knowing it was Detective Frye there or not. But I could make out Detective Frye.

Q: What about in his hand?

A: Yes, sir, I could see something in his hand.

Q: Could you tell if it was a gun? If you had not known it was a gun?

A: That's a question I can't answer.

The defense's version of the same experiment was more realistic. Gene Annan and his assistant used unknown objects wrapped in a towel, and Annan walked directly from outside into the showroom. Annan testified that he could not identify what his assistant was holding.

A MATTER OF LOGIC

How, and when, did Tommy Zeigler become a suspect?

Terry Hadley says that Frye claimed to have deduced Zeigler's guilt within minutes after he first inspected the crime scene. Frye denied this, but did admit in his first deposition that his original observations of the blood spatters did lead him to consider

Zeigler "the main suspect." This would have been within an hour after he arrived on the scene, and at least an hour before Edward Williams first told his story to Denny Martin.

In particular, Frye was aroused by:

1. Zeigler's apparent blood trail from the counter to the front door.
2. The holster on top of blood spatters from the fatal beating of Charlie Mays.
3. The fact that those spatters fell on dry swipes of blood apparently left by Perry Edwards, indicating that Mays had been killed at least a quarter of an hour after the struggle in which Edwards died.
4. The apparent fact that the kitchen door had been closed after Eunice Zeigler was shot.
5. The bloody footprints.

Frye believed that these observations contradicted Zeigler's story about a robbery attempt involving Mays.

But what was the basis for his suspicions?

Frye had not interviewed Zeigler. The only information from Zeigler was Thompson's brief interrogation at the hospital, when Zeigler was barely coherent. That entire conversation, as Thompson reported it, was that Zeigler had shot Charlie Mays, that Mays had shot him, and that Zeigler believed Mays was trying to rob him.

Frye could not have known any more that night. He could only have *assumed* what Zeigler's explanation of events would be.

To put it another way, *Zeigler became suspected of lying (and therefore of murder) before he ever had a chance to make a statement.*

Much of Orange County's law enforcement establishment, including Robert Eagan, converged on the store before midnight. No doubt, most of them believed that the crime had been a single event: a robbery that got out of hand, a shootout. (Who could imagine what a tangled web it would become?) Frye alone, through his training at Professor MacDonnell's workshop, understood that it was more complicated. He was the first to grasp this, and he was absolutely correct. We know that he told others of his findings. We can imagine his satisfaction when he informed his colleagues and his superiors that this was not the conventional crime they believed it to be.

He had reason to be proud. He had just uncovered the first essential truth about what had happened in the store that night.

But now he jumped to an unwarranted conclusion: he reasoned that since it was not a conventional crime, not simply a robbery gone bad, Tommy Zeigler must be guilty.

He remembered it in a deposition: "Primary thing was the thing that he was alleged to have been shot when the killing of Mays occurred. It was at that point I think I said to myself, we don't have what would be total; more or less is what I thought to myself. So that was, I would say, an hour from my entering the store."

We can also understand Frye's impatience to interview Zeigler, and his confidence of being able to extract a confession: *Give me half an hour with him. . . .* As soon as Zeigler described a conventional crime, a simple shootout, then Frye had him, because Frye knew it hadn't happened that way, and he knew how to prove it.

But Zeigler never told that story. When he was conscious and coherent on Christmas—before he ever could have known about Frye's observations and assumptions—Zeigler told Terry Hadley a story that is compatible with the blood spatter evidence, and that has remained consistent for nearly seventeen years.

All of the observations Frye made that night can be explained within the context of Zeigler's story and the evidence that later developed:

1. *The blood trail to the front door.* That trail was not Zeigler's blood type.
2. *The holster on top of Mays's spattered blood.* Jimmy Yawn testified that the holster had been moved, a suggestion that is easily believed, considering the foot traffic through the crime scene.
3. *The appearance of Mays's blood spatters on top of Perry Edwards's dry blood swipes.* Zeigler's testimony is compatible with the theory that Mays was killed some time after Perry Edwards. In that sense, the blood spatters actually corroborate Zeigler's testimony.
4. *The closing of the kitchen door after Eunice was shot.* The door could have been closed anytime after Eunice's death, but before Zeigler arrived on the scene.

5. *The bloody footprints.* The issue of the footprints is in
   doubt. Even Professor MacDonnell was unwilling to identify the prints as having been made by Zeigler.

And it may not matter. An innocent man could have made
those prints. When Frye finds conflicts between Zeigler's story and
the evidence in blood, he assumes that Zeigler was aware of his
actions. Frye's argument goes like this: Zeigler says he crawled
around the store, and the footprints show that he walked; therefore Zeigler is lying and must be guilty.

But we cannot assume that Zeigler was lucid. Actually, we
should assume the opposite. Traumatic stress amnesia is a legitimate phenomenon. Anyone who has ever been involved in a serious auto accident knows that abrupt violence can alter memory
and distort perceptions. If Zeigler is innocent, he was the victim not
only of a sudden violent assault, but of the psychological shock of
finding his world turned upside down. He may very well have
stumbled around the store. He may have come across the body of
his father-in-law, and discovered the body of his wife, and have no
memory of it. The assumption that Zeigler is capable of rendering
a rational account of his actions is convenient, but it is not war-
ranted. Rather, if Zeigler is innocent we should not be surprised to
find that his recollection is incomplete.

Frye made another observation on Christmas Eve. He noticed
that there were no straight-down blood spots on or around the
body of Charlie Mays. (These are the uniform low-velocity droplets that would drip from a wound.) To Frye, the absence of these
droplets around Mays proved that Zeigler was lying.

Frye's words; the emphasis is added:

"Tommy Zeigler claims that when he entered the store and
was pushed up against the wall, he was shot. He in turn attempts
to fire at Charlie Mays and shoots him. He never did admit he shot
him. Okay. Mays was laying there alledgedly shot after Zeigler
received his injuries. Okay. I mention again the bloodstain school.
If Tommy Zeigler had been injured before this man died, there
would be his blood somewhere on the body or somewhere around
it. The test results showed no blood dripping or anything that
indicated anything. *So, Tommy Zeigler was not injured when he
killed this man.*"

Frye set forth this theory for the grand jury, his logical argument for an indictment. He brought it out again in a deposition. It
was one of the foundations of Zeigler's arrest.

It is a classic error in reasoning. Frye assumes as fact the very hypothesis he is trying to prove: that Tommy Zeigler stood over Mays and beat him to death.

This is the masterpiece of deduction that helped to set Florida's legal machinery in motion against Tommy Zeigler.[3]

FULL AND FREE INQUIRY

The four murders were a confusing crime that deserved a thorough, careful, and far-reaching investigation. Jack Bachman, a veteran homicide detective, called it the largest crime scene he had ever encountered. From his deposition:

"You know, there was four different areas where there were four bodies and then in between there were a lot of furniture knocked over. There was a lot of blood splattered about. There were a lot of bullet holes, there were a lot of weapons. You know, it's not one of those deals where we used to knock them out like petit larceny, where you're in and out and you're gone to the next one. I mean, this was a highly complex crime scene."

It was not only logistically complex, but mentally challenging. The forensic evidence is ambiguous, and most of the witness accounts are full of variables. In all, the case presents a very few unquestioned facts within a fluid matrix of great uncertainty. It will assume almost any shape, depending on one's willingness to make assumptions and stretch probabilities. You see what you are ready to see.

Such a problem needed an investigator who was ready to see everything, and nothing: someone who could comprehend all the possibilities without committing himself to any one of them.

Don Frye appears to have committed himself almost at once. A careful review of the record gives no hint that he ever considered, much less investigated, any other possibility besides Zeigler's guilt. He must have banished all doubt before he arrested Zeigler on the 29th. By then he also had to be certain that Edward Williams—whose truck was found at the crime scene, and who showed

---

3. Would Frye have considered Zeigler innocent if he *had* found Zeigler's blood droplets around Mays? It is an argument that Zeigler cannot win and Frye cannot lose. Actually, the absence of droplets only indicates that whoever stood there wasn't dripping blood.

up at the police station several hours after the murders with a bizarre, mostly uncorroborated story and a murder weapon—was unquestionably telling the truth.

Once Zeigler was arrested, any chance of an open-minded inquiry was lost. The work of Frye and the rest of the OCSO seems to have been directed toward confirming the correctness of the arrest. Frye and Bob Eagan have often claimed that Zeigler received a full and fair investigation, and that they carefully examined every possibility of Zeigler's innocence. But once the police and the prosecutor had committed themselves to convicting Zeigler, their motives for demonstrating his innocence were slight indeed.

In at least one instance, Frye attempted to debunk important, credible evidence that he should have investigated if he truly was conducting a full and fair inquiry. This is the matter of the dark, Mustang-like car that appears in several witnesses' statements.

Two of those witnesses were Richard and Patricia Smith, who answered questions from Frye and Lawson Lamar under oath on January 12. Each of the Smiths said that at 7:57 P.M. on Christmas Eve, they saw two cars parked in front of the furniture store. One car was a full-size sedan, they said, the other a smaller, dark-colored automobile. Richard Smith thought that the dark car was "boxy," which would describe an early-model Mustang. Patricia Smith said that she thought the smaller car was "an early-model Ford."

This was key testimony. According to Frye's theory, relying on Felton Thomas's testimony, the only two cars that should have been parked in front of the store at that time were Perry Edwards's full-sized sedan and Curtis Dunaway's full-sized two-tone Oldsmobile.

Frye pressed the point hard; his questioning of the Smiths was far more aggressive than any recorded interview with Edward Williams or Felton Thomas. But both Smiths insisted that the smaller car they saw was not two-toned. Patricia Smith, who knew Dunaway's car, repeatedly told Frye that Dunaway's Oldsmobile was not the car she saw in front of the store. Frye tried to convince her otherwise:

Q (FRYE): But, the car you saw parked on the curb, do you think it could have been Curtis Dunaway's car?

A (PATRICIA SMITH): No, sir.

Q: Think hard on it.
A: The car I saw was dark.
Q: I don't deny that. I'm not saying that.[4]
A: It was not two-toned. It was a totally dark car.

Frye disregarded the Smiths' description of the dark car. In May, he claimed that the Smiths actually confirmed his theory of the crime. This was how he remembered their testimony:

Q (DAVIDS): You said you correlated the time (when Zeigler led Mays into the store) by the statements of the witnesses that Dunaway's car was back there by 7:58?
A (FRYE): I said cars; two cars were seen in front of the store at 7:58, I believe is what the Smiths say. That correlated with the time trial run that I conducted with Mr. Felton. . . .
Q: Don't those statements say it was not Curtis Dunaway's car?
A: Didn't say it wasn't either. If you will read the deposition we took by the Smiths, they are stating in there they did not pay that much attention to the vehicle, that most of their attention was directed from the dark store.

Seeing what we want to see, remembering what we want to remember, is a human failing. That's why open-mindedness is crucial in an investigation. Belief is the enemy of skepticism; when we start believing, we stop asking questions. Belief (unlike faith) requires constant affirmation, and does not tolerate contradiction.

No doubt, Frye really was sure that Patricia Smith had left open the question of whether the dark car was the Dunaway Olds. Moreover, Frye—who was not there at the time—was ready to substitute his own belief for the sworn, specific testimony of the Smiths. He *knew* that the dark car was actually the Dunaway car. It was true because it had to be true, regardless of what Patricia Smith or anyone else said.

But the Smiths were emphatic about what they had seen. If their observations had supported the state's case, we can be sure that Frye and Eagan would have regarded them as highly credible witnesses, which indeed they were. They maintained their stories during the questioning by Frye and Lawson Lamar, and their

---

4. Frye accepted Felton Thomas's description of that car as a "light" car.

description of the smaller dark car went unchallenged at trial. The only problem with their testimony was that it denied, rather than supported, the state's case.

This is not an isolated example. We'll see in the next chapter that the state disregarded two reliable independent witnesses whose unassailable testimony convincingly discredited Edward Williams and the heart of the prosecution's case.

But let's return to the dark Mustang-like car.

In a legitimate investigation, Frye would have used motor vehicle records to compile a list of dark-colored Mustangs in the West Orange area. He might have checked ownership records against a list of persons who Zeigler believed were involved in the loan-sharking operation. This might have provided a lead: successful investigations have begun with much less.

In fact, how did the OCSO treat this question?

During Frye's first deposition, Terry Hadley asked him about the Christmas Eve incident when two black men in a dark Mustang drove into the Gulf station on the corner of Dillard and Route 50 and talked about a shooting at the furniture store before the police were on the scene.

HADLEY: Did you make any subsequent effort to ascertain the identity of those individuals driving that Mustang?

FRYE: No; other than verbally to people who ride that area out there to be on the lookout for that vehicle.

And there the matter ended.

Frye wasn't required to believe that suspected murderers had driven a dark Mustang on Christmas Eve. He wasn't required to subscribe to Zeigler's version of the crime; he just had to make a good-faith effort to investigate the possibilities, and be prepared to follow the answers where they might lead.

But he did not. The record belies any claim of a full and fair investigation. The state's investigators seem to have assiduously avoided any area of inquiry that might have tended to exculpate the defendant.

CUSTODIAN OF JUSTICE

Few public officials hold positions of such power as a chief prosecuting attorney, through whose office the state administers the law and attempts to punish the offenses of its citizens, sometimes by death. A defense lawyer represents a single client; a chief prosecutor is the custodian of justice in his jurisdiction.

It is an enormous trust, requiring probity and even-handedness. Vincent Bugliosi, who successfully prosecuted the Manson Family murder convictions, has written of the prosecutor's duty to be fair. The prosecutor, he says, "represents 'the people,' and in more than a theoretical sense, one of those people is the defendant. So while he can justifiably seek a conviction in cases he believes in, he has the concomitant duty to help insure that the person he is prosecuting receives a fair trial. . . . [I]t is as much a prosecutor's duty to refrain from using improper methods to secure a wrongful conviction as it is to use every legitimate measure to bring about a just one."[5]

That is the ideal.

The reality of *Florida* v. *Zeigler* was far different. A March 12, 1976, letter over Eagan's signature reflects the prosecution's methods. Eagan addressed a sergeant in the OCSO's Crimes Against Persons section:

> I was disturbed to learn at our conference yesterday that T. Zeigler had been interviewed by sheriff's deputies reference loan sharking or other matters.
>
> I specifically recommended to Deputy Jim Harris, when he asked me about it, that no interview be had until Zeigler was ready to talk about his gunshot wound. I further suggested that any information he might give could wait until after the trial, since in my opinion he is creating a spurious defense which now is supported by the very fact of the interview.
>
> It therefore becomes necessary that I be furnished forthwith a complete report of this matter with the names of all persons participating.
>
> In addition I hereby request an immediate and complete investigation, with detailed reports furnished to me, of each and every allegation made by Mr. Zeigler, and that each officer participating

5. *And the Sea Will Tell*, Vincent Bugliosi with Bruce B. Henderson, 1991.

be ready to testify at the murder trial as to what his participation revealed. This is absolutely necessary.

(Zeigler, Hadley, and Vernon Davids all deny that any OCSO deputy, or any prosecution investigator, ever tried to interview him about his loan-sharking claims.)

Additionally, Vernon Davids swore in a 1987 affidavit that Eagan and his assistants deliberately misled him about the location of evidence items, including Charlie Mays's shoes and Edward Williams's pants. It is also clear that, by design or error, the prosecution failed to turn over potentially exculpatory evidence, including the Jellison tape. As this is written, the courts are considering Zeigler's motion for a new trial, based in part on the suppressed evidence.

The use of the FBI Lab, rather than the Sanford facility, had great ramifications for the conduct of the trial.

The decision to use the FBI erected a wall between the defense and the evidence that went to Washington. And FBI examiners are not subject to state subpoena; the state's control of the evidence and the experts allowed Eagan to arrange the footprint testimony of Herbert MacDonell in a perfect counterpoint to the FBI's Thomas Delaney. MacDonell's testimony, regardless of its substance, would not have had such a maximum impact if Delaney had testified in turn. Most damaging, Delaney could not be recalled to argue the validity of his work; a state employee would have responded instantly to subpoena.

We cannot assume that police and prosecutors chose the FBI in order to frustrate the defense; at the time, it was a sound, legitimate decision. But the decision to exploit that advantage was Eagan's.

The slow pace of results from the FBI forced the prosecution to postpone its grand jury presentation until two and a half months after Zeigler's arrest. This delayed the defense's ability to invoke discovery, while time was tolling on the six-month speedy-trial deadline. Eagan might have begun at least informal discovery during February and March, but he did not. His office finally released discovery material on the last hours of the last possible day—and then it was incomplete. This may be an indication of the precariousness of the state's evidence. A well-founded case, based on a competent investigation, need not be protected from scrutiny.

It is preposterous that a major criminal trial should begin while forensic results are still pending. Yet that is what happened. In effect, Zeigler was caught in a bind between his right to discovery and his right to a speedy trial.

Eagan applied the bind and tightened it in a way that seems almost punitive. He opposed all of Terry Hadley's motions for a continuance, even though Hadley, his former assistant, declared in court that he was running out of time to prepare adequately. A short continuance would have cost the state nothing at trial, except for the obvious advantage of contending with an opponent who was not fully prepared.

Eagan must also take some responsibility for the shoddy investigation; he was at the scene on Christmas Eve, and the OCSO consulted closely with him and his office.

Lastly, Eagan's attempt to interject gutter gossip into the process cannot pass without mention. Cheryl Clafler's statement was so inconsistent with the known facts that it ought to have been put aside, not brought to trial. Don Frye's grand jury allegations about Zeigler's character would have been slanderous in another forum.

Frye defended his testimony on the grounds that hearsay is legally admissible before the grand jury. Furthermore, he said, he was not claiming it to be true, only laying it out for the panel to consider. But mere legality is a poor shelter in this instance; some minimal standards of justness and fairness and rectitude must apply to the work of public officials. How many of us might become indictable, upon the innocent but mysterious death of a spouse, if gossip from our neighbors and casual acquaintances received the official imprimatur of the authorities? How many of us might appear guilty if the police were allowed full access to our homes and offices and files, to search for scraps of evidence with which they could selectively cobble together a theory of motive?[6]

---

6. Records and personal files to which the police had full access in the house and the store demonstrated that Tommy Zeigler had no debts he could not easily service. The grand jury was never exposed to this evidence.

JUDGE PAUL

Of all the setbacks the defense took from the bench, the most disquieting are the denied motions for a continuance. Judge Paul disregarded Hadley's pleas that he needed an additional two to three weeks, all within the speedy-trial limit, in order to prepare his case.

Hadley didn't stand to gain any tactical advantage from such a delay, especially after his client finally waived speedy trial. He seems to have truly needed the time to prepare.

The defense's work is open to question in several areas. Hadley and Davids reacted poorly to the MacDonell surprise; they needed days, not minutes, to prepare adequately to question the professor, and even if they had no chance of getting that time, they ought to have demanded it in order to create an appeals issue on the record. During the discovery phase of the case, some important questions remained unanswered in the depositions of Felton Thomas and Edward Williams: we do not know who accompanied Thomas on his aborted trip to Orlando, to report to the sheriff; we do not know specifically where Edward Williams went when he visited the Winter Garden Inn after leaving the store, or what he did at the motel.

Also, the defense seems to have failed to grasp fully the significance of the Nolans' testimony, and the decision not to put the Fickes on the stand probably was a miscalculation. In Hadley's closing argument he introduced several threads of an alternative theory of the crime, but he never fully developed it.

But all these observations occur only after months of leisurely examination of the record in this most complex case. As Hadley approached trial, he and the rest of the defense team were under constant pressure of time. Today they remember it almost as a frenzy. The prosecution did not turn over its discovery material until barely six weeks before the trial began. Any criticism of Hadley's work must be made in the light of Paul's repeated refusal to grant even a two-week continuance.

Simple fairness alone dictates that the defendant in a capital trial should get the benefit of the doubt on such a relatively minor matter. (And, if not fairness, the people's interest in ensuring fair trials.) The reaction of the defense psychologist, Stephen Robertson, is probably typical of most laymen: *A man's life is at stake, what's the rush?*

We have to take on faith, or leave aside, the question of whether Judge Paul was hostile to the defense, as Hadley alleged. A trial transcript is unsuited for displaying such nuances. Adverse rulings, even a consistent pattern of adverse rulings, are not proof of prejudice.

The judge's defenders would probably point out that appeals courts upheld the judge on all matters, save one: the admission of character witnesses in the penalty phase.

That Paul's rulings have stood is no surprise. Appeals courts grant judges wide latitude in their conduct of a trial. One of the reasons trial judges have such discretion is that they traditionally have avoided the appearance of conflict of interest. Generations of judges have excused themselves from cases that involved far more tenuous connections than the one that existed here.

But Judge Paul insisted on trying the case. He declared that he was not prejudiced. In refusing to step down, however, he allowed an almost unique situation in which rulings from the bench might plausibly be examined for personal motive.

Ordinarily we would reject out of hand Leigh McEachern's story of the ex parte conference. Such things do not happen in our system. But given the extraordinary background of this extraordinary case, McEachern's charges acquired a credibility that otherwise would have been impossible. They created reasonable doubts that persist even to this day.

I set out at the beginning of this project to understand and to explain the verdict of *Florida* v. *Zeigler*. I became convinced that the verdict was unjust because the system that delivered the case to the jury was so faulty and skewed that a just result was impossible.

That is almost self-evident. The actions of the police and the prosecutor are stark in the record.

There is another issue, though: the reality of the crime itself, the questions about what really happened in the store on Christmas Eve. The jury's decision in 1976 settled most of the legal issues, but it did not end the questions.

Every day the actuality of the crime becomes more distant, and recollections more suspect; memory fades more slowly than the Rh factors of a bloodstain, but just as surely. We are left with the documentation, which is unchanging. It has been studied and discussed and argued for more than sixteen years. After all that scrutiny, can the extended record possibly hold new answers— not just speculation or assumption, but real answers based in fact?

I found that it does.

Table Six

TIME SEQUENCE (PARTIAL): DILLARD STREET

Incorporating testimony of Ed Nolan and J. D. and Madelyn Nolan, as well as other depositions. Controversial elements from the state's case are emphasized.

7:05 P.M.	*Thomas Hale sees Eunice and Tommy.*
7:10	*Tommy kills Eunice.*
7:20–7:25	Barbara Tinsley hears first volley; Ken and Linda Roach hear multiple shots; clock stopped by bullet; *Zeigler kills Edwardses.*
7:30–7:35	*Charlie Mays and Felton Thomas arrive at store, Zeigler is gone.*
7:35	*Zeigler meets Mays and Thomas in motel parking lot, drives to orange grove.*
7:40	*Mays and Zeigler climb back fence.*
7:45	Tinsley hears second volley.
7:45	(Eagan): *Zeigler kills Mays.*
7:45	(Frye): *Zeigler, Mays, and Thomas drive to 75 Temple Grove.*
7:55–8:00	(Frye): *Zeigler kills Mays.*
8:30	Yawn and Thompson out of service at Kentucky Fried Chicken.
8:35–8:40	*Zeigler and Edward Williams arrive at furniture store.*

8:40–8:50   *Zeigler attempts to kill Williams, who climbs fence and runs to Winter Garden Inn, then to Kentucky Fried Chicken.*

8:50   Yawn and Thompson leave restaurant; Thompson to Oakland.

9:20   Zeigler calls Van Deventer home, talks to Ficke, *shoots self.*

9:21   Thompson makes radio call en route from Van Deventer home; Yawn takes call at Winter Garden Inn, nearly broadsides J. D. Nolan car southbound on Dillard; Thompson and Ficke arrive.

9:22   J. D. and Madelyn Nolan make a U-turn, park, and watch Zeigler stumble into Thompson's arms at furniture store. Thompson and Zeigler to hospital, Yawn to back gate.

9:25   Edward Williams and J. D. and Madelyn Nolan arrive at Kentucky Fried Chicken simultaneously. J. D. and Ed Nolan speak to Williams.

9:27   Williams leaves Kentucky Fried Chicken, meets Rogenia Thomas.

FIFTY

ON THE MORNING OF CHRISTMAS EVE IN 1975, TOMMY ZEIGLER WAS A successful and prosperous young man who had showed no tendency to violence. By all evidence, he enjoyed the loyalty of friends and the love of family. His life was full of good things, both material and intangible.

We are told that this person brutally murdered four people, including his wife.

The state's theory of the crime is a bridge that spans the chasm between the Tommy Zeigler whom the world knew before Christmas Eve of 1975 and the Tommy Zeigler who was convicted of these ghastly acts. It is a bridge we must cross entirely if we are to believe him guilty. The state's theory is the only way to get there from here.

That theory, as expressed by Don Frye before the grand jury and by Robert Eagan in his arguments at trial, relies on speculation and improbable testimony.

It is largely uncorroborated, and ignores strong contrary evidence.

It fails to address strong indications that Charlie Mays was in the store to commit a crime.

And it is finally, irretrievably, undermined by J. D., Ed, and Madelyn Nolan: disinterested witnesses whose observations on Christmas Eve discredited the heart of the state's case, and who—as we'll see—could not have been mistaken in their testimony.

Science and the rules of logic tell us that a hypothesis must, at the least, not be contradicted by the pertinent evidence. To accept Zeigler's guilt we must embrace every important aspect of testimony by four witnesses who convinced the authorities that he plotted and executed the murders. Those four are Edward Williams, Felton Thomas, Frank Smith, and Mary Ellen Stewart, without whom the case against Zeigler does not exist.

This seems to be an impressive array: Williams, Thomas, Smith, and Stewart, each adding to the mosaic of guilt. Yet they are mainly uncorroborated, except by each other. Furthermore, Williams, Thomas, and Smith all had a supreme stake in the outcome: Williams's truck was found at the crime scene and he was in possession of the primary murder weapon; Thomas fled the scene; and Smith was the owner of record of two other significant weapons. Mary Ellen Stewart had a personal relationship with Williams and Smith and had argued with Zeigler over a disputed loan.

The state's theory presumes that Williams, Thomas, Smith, and Stewart were innocent and unwitting. Therefore we must completely accept their testimony on all important points, since the guiltless would have nothing to conceal. If any one of them is unconvincing, they are all unconvincing. If any one of them can be impeached on any important matter, the entire case against Zeigler withers.

What does this mean, in terms of the testimony of these four witnesses?

If we are to believe that Tommy Zeigler is guilty, we must accept that he told at least three people—Williams, Smith, and Stewart—that he was in the market for untraceable guns. Yet to do so was to guarantee that he would come under suspicion. Even if he managed to kill Williams, both Smith and Stewart could implicate him.

The state's theory is almost schizophrenic in the assumptions that it makes about Zeigler's behavior. Here, and at several other points, Zeigler appears to be almost oafish in his planning of the crime. Yet at other times, he is claimed to be highly clever and obsessed with details. For example, Frye speculated (without evidence) that Zeigler arranged for Charlie Mays to park his van behind the store, on the wrong side of the six-foot fence, a position far more suited for burglary than for picking up a television.

If we are to believe that Zeigler is guilty, we must accept that Frank Smith used his own money to buy two pistols for a stranger whom he knew only as a voice on the telephone. According to Smith's testimony, he bought the guns after a single telephone conversation with a man he believed was Zeigler. He paid between $100 and $150 of his own money (Smith's testimony varies on the exact amount), although he was not even sure that Zeigler would want the weapons, since Zeigler was said to have requested name-brand weapons.

After the murders, Smith did not immediately go to the police with the story of the transaction. His first statement was dated January 21, which apparently was the date that police discovered the sales records of the two RG pistols. Yet Zeigler's name and the story of the murders were extremely prominent in the local news. As early as December 27, the *Sentinel Star* reported that police did not know who owned some of the weapons.

Both Williams and Stewart claimed to have been aware that Zeigler was interested in untraceable guns, yet neither included this important allegation in their original statements to police. Williams did not mention it when he testified at the preliminary hearing on January 16. The first recorded mention of it from Stewart is a signed statement dated May 28, only a few days before trial.

If we are to believe that Zeigler is guilty, we must believe that he gambled everything on Charlie Mays's arriving no sooner than 7:30. According to the state's theory, Zeigler had planned the murders almost to the minute, and must have known that he would be killing Eunice and her parents shortly before 7:30. Mays was supposed to be eager to receive his bargain-priced TV. If he had driven up while shots were being fired inside the store—Eagan claimed that Zeigler was killing Perry and Virginia Edwards at 7:24—then Zeigler's elaborate plot would have been ended hardly before it began.

If we are to believe that Zeigler is guilty, we must believe that Edward Williams was terrified for hours by three clicks in the darkness. Williams said that when he heard the gun snapping, he knew immediately that Zeigler was trying to kill him.

Williams's reaction, as he described it, might have been appropriate at the climax of a tense, uncertain situation. But this was not the case on Christmas Eve. He knew Zeigler well, and trusted him. As far as Williams knew, their errand was routine. He had no reason to be anything but relaxed as he walked up the hallway toward the showroom. Moreover, visibility was marginal at best, and Zeigler was supposed to have wrapped a towel around the object that he carried in his right hand. Yet Williams claimed that he knew at once that the clicking was from a gun, and was instantly terrified, certain that Zeigler was trying to kill him. Moreover, his terror did not ebb when he got away from Zeigler. In fact, by his testimony, it grew greater. He managed to drive his Camaro from Winter Garden to Mary Ellen Stewart's home in Orlando, yet claimed that two hours or more after the incident, he was so shaken that he could not drive the few blocks to the sheriff's station.

If we are to believe that Zeigler is guilty, we must accept that he allowed the two principal witnesses against him to escape without a struggle. First, according to Felton Thomas, Zeigler left him sitting in the Oldsmobile while he took Charlie Mays into the store and killed him. Thomas said that Zeigler tried to coax him inside, then gave up and told him to stay in the car when he refused to follow Zeigler into the dark building.

But Zeigler did not have to coax Thomas. According to Thomas himself, Zeigler had a bag of loaded pistols; he could have forced Thomas into the store at gunpoint, or at least tried to do so.

Later, according to Edward Williams, Zeigler tried to coax him back into the store after Williams ran out. Williams represented Zeigler's last chance to stage the burglary successfully. According to the state's case, Williams's escape was so disastrous that Zeigler was forced to shoot himself in order to deflect suspicion. But Zeigler never physically tried to bring Williams into the store.

The two men weighed about the same, and Zeigler was more than twenty years younger than Williams. Yet Zeigler never tried to fight or wrestle the man whose knowledge could wreck him forever, who had to be killed if the plan was to succeed.

If we are to believe that Zeigler is guilty, we must believe that Charlie Mays, Felton Thomas, and Edward Williams all ignored the heavy stains and smears of blood on Zeigler's face and clothes. Zeigler's upper torso was slathered with blood when he stumbled into Robert Thompson and Don Ficke at the door of the store. Blood was splattered on his face, and was so thick around his torso and his arms that it looked to Thompson "as if it had been uniformly painted on."

And it was dry. Thompson carried Zeigler over his shoulder, and got only a negligible spot of blood on his white uniform shirt.

The blood on Zeigler was so copious that it was recognizable even on Zeigler's shirt, which was near-vermilion color. Thompson noticed the blood at once. It was the most obvious feature of Zeigler's appearance that night.

According to the state's theory, Zeigler met Mays and Thomas in the motel parking lot within minutes after having fought and killed Perry Edwards, who bled heavily from his wounded ear during the struggle. Yet Thomas never mentioned seeing blood on Zeigler, although according to the state's theory he was with Zeigler for twenty minutes or more. For at least ten minutes, if Thomas's testimony is correct, he sat beside Zeigler in the front seat of Curtis Dunaway's Oldsmobile but never noticed the blood.

Williams twice saw Zeigler in the well-lit garage at 75 Temple Grove, and sat beside him as they drove to the store. By this time Zeigler had bloodily beaten Mays to death, according to the state's theory. But Williams did not see the blood.

At one point in the relatively well-lit back compound, Zeigler was supposed to have put his arm around Williams. Williams finally claimed to notice "spots of blood" speckled on Zeigler's face and clothes as Zeigler pleaded with him. But Williams never mentioned the heavy bloodstains that would be so obvious to Robert Thompson.[1]

In short, the testimony by the four principal witnesses against Zeigler requires us to accept improbabilities compounding improbabilities, all of which must be credible if Zeigler is culpable. But the implicit difficulties in believing Zeigler's guilt don't end there. Let's look at some of the broader issues that the state's theory addresses only with great awkwardness.

THE MOTIVE

Why would Tommy Zeigler want to kill his wife? The insurance policies were a classic motive for murder that any jury could comprehend: half a million dollars is a lot of money.

Yet it was money that Tommy Zeigler didn't need.[2] In all of their investigation, including the extraordinary opportunity to examine Zeigler's financial records, police investigators were unable

---

1. This observation is by Vernon Davids, who says that he realized it only after ten years of studying the record.

2. The magnitude of Zeigler's defense is proof of this. The family hired multiple lawyers, two of them full-time, and multiple investigators, two of whom worked overtime for more than five months, and multiple experts. Neither Tommy and Beulah, nor the attorneys, dispute the estimate that the defense cost well over $500,000.

to show that his finances were anything but solid. His material well-being was assured. The furniture store was a thriving enterprise, Tommy's pet project and the solid foundation of the family's wealth: yet, if the state is to be believed, this was the place that Zeigler chose to stigmatize forever with a quadruple murder—the ultimate example of fouling one's own nest.

Two elements of the state's own evidence suggest that the insurance could have been no more than an afterthought.

First, Frank Smith and Mary Ellen Stewart claimed that Zeigler was attempting to buy guns as early as the spring of 1975. Yet Zeigler didn't apply for the first insurance policy on Eunice until September. The OCSO's investigation showed that one of the insurance agents had tried to sell Zeigler a life policy as early as April 1975, and Zeigler put him off.

But perhaps Zeigler had another motive, and at some point added the insurance to benefit from a murder that he intended to commit anyway. If so, he was working at cross purposes. The state's theory is that Zeigler hoped the investigation would be a low-key affair under the jurisdiction of his friend Don Ficke, whom he might be able to manipulate. But the huge insurance policies virtually guaranteed that other agencies would enter the picture. Zeigler could not hope to keep the fact of the policies hidden; the companies themselves would demand a thorough investigation.

Second, if Zeigler intended to murder his wife for money, why should he commit the crime at such a time, and in such a way, that he would be forced to kill his in-laws? For if he is guilty, then the evidence is clear: Perry and Virginia Edwards did not walk into the store by chance. Zeigler knew that they were only a few minutes behind. He must have arranged for them to be there.

This is the most glaring drawback to the purported insurance motive that Robert Eagan carefully laid out at trial: *It does not explain the murders of Mr. and Mrs. Edwards.*

Don Frye's answer is what might be called Version B of the motive, based on Cheryl Clafler's statement. This theory is that a great rift had opened between Tommy and Eunice because she had discovered his homosexual affair, that she had told her parents of her unhappiness and her fears, and that she intended to leave with them after Christmas; therefore Tommy was forced to act quickly. He also had to kill the Edwardses. Knowing what they knew, they would have instantly accused him of Eunice's murder.

This idea has a number of drawbacks, not the least of which

is that by all the evidence, the Edwardses' visit was cordial and normal. Perry Edwards, Jr., who lived near his parents in Moultrie, gave no indication that they had planned anything but a routine visit. Rita Ficke spent some time with Eunice on Christmas Eve, and saw nothing amiss. Also, Tommy invited Curtis Dunaway into his home a little before 7:00 P.M. on Christmas Eve—an odd gesture for someone who knows that within half an hour he is going to kill everyone in the house—and the scene Dunaway later described was peaceful, domestic, ordinary.

Furthermore, if Eunice truly feared for her life and wanted to leave Winter Garden, as Cheryl Clafler claimed, she had had opportunity to do so. She had gone alone to Moultrie in October, when her father took ill, and could have stayed. (This forced her to postpone one of the medical exams for her insurance.)

If Eunice really did know some awful secret that threatened Tommy's reputation in Winter Garden, then his interests would be best served by getting her out of town, out of the state, as quickly as possible—thereby, incidentally, clearing the field for him to continue his homosexual affair without interference.

But let's assume that this wasn't good enough for him, that for reasons of greed and depravity he couldn't allow Eunice to leave. Let's assume, against all evidence, that Cheryl Clafler's accusations are actually true, that his wife had caught him *in flagrante* with another man, that she had told her parents, that Zeigler knew she had told her parents, and that he decided to kill all three in order to preserve his secret.

Unlikely as it may be, this is the only scenario that addresses Zeigler's motives for killing Perry and Virginia Edwards. It answers all the questions but one: if all this is actually true, what were Eunice and the Edwardses doing in the furniture store with Tommy, whom they must have despised? The state's theory depends on the proposition that Zeigler was able to manipulate his wife and his in-laws into leaving the house almost to the minute on Christmas Eve; and not only that he was able to do so, but that he *knew* he could do so. Otherwise his elaborate preparations with Edward Williams and Charlie Mays would be useless.

Under the circumstances, Tommy would have no influence on Eunice and the Edwardses. If the state's theory is to be believed, Eunice willingly went to the store, alone, with the husband whom she was going to leave in less than a day, and who she feared was planning to kill her. And the Edwardses willingly, compliantly, gave them a head start of five to ten minutes before they, too, drove to the store to pick out this La-Z-Boy chair, which they must have desperately desired.

THE PLOT

But let's assume that Tommy Zeigler was so persuasive as to make all this happen exactly the way it had to happen. How did this plot take shape? When did it turn from vague musing to concrete preparations?

Zeigler must have settled on his course of action no later than Monday, December 22. According to Edward Williams, that was when Zeigler first made the Christmas Eve appointment. *Then, for the next two days, Zeigler apparently did nothing to further his complicated plans.* He must have known that if his plot was to succeed, he would need at least one more credible "robber," yet there is no evidence that he approached anyone else until he saw Charlie Mays at the store, less than ten hours before the murders.

Apparently Zeigler decided on the spur of the moment that Mays would be a victim that night. In spite of extensive publicity, no other people ever came forward and claimed that Zeigler tried to involve them at the store on Christmas Eve; nor is there any indication that Zeigler spoke to Charlie Mays about it until the 24th.

Why did Zeigler let these preparations go until the last few hours? What would he have done if Mays hadn't walked into the store on Christmas Eve? This is decidedly slipshod behavior for someone who is otherwise cunning and thorough.

It might be suggested that Williams wasn't part of the original plot, that the plot didn't exist until Christmas Eve, when Eunice said or did something that forced Zeigler's hand. But this, too, is most unlikely. If that were the case, Zeigler would have had to break the appointment with Williams. He couldn't allow Williams just to sit in his driveway all evening, witness to the fact that Zeigler was elsewhere at 7:30. Furthermore, Zeigler had a chance to break his appointment with Williams, when Williams came by the store around noon on Christmas Eve. But Zeigler didn't break the appointment—he confirmed it. So he must have known as early as Monday the 22nd that he was going to kill Eunice, the Edwardses, and Williams, and he must have known exactly how he was going to do it.

In light of that, Zeigler's actions on the afternoon of Christmas Eve are truly inexplicable. Having gone to such lengths to set up Williams as a robber, Zeigler destroys all his preparations when he informs Curtis Dunaway that he's planning to meet Williams at 7:30. (Before they leave the store at closing, Zeigler further draws attention to himself by specifically telling Dunaway to turn off the display lights, which he could just as easily have done himself, by waiting a minute or two until Dunaway drove away.)

According to Eagan's first closing argument, Zeigler intended to show up at the Van Deventer party after he had murdered five people: "If he had killed Edward Williams, he would have been back at that party asking the Chief [Ficke], 'Gee, I wonder where Eunice is. Maybe you better go down to the store and check around and let's see if we can find her.' "

This is absurd. Such a plan could be feasible only if Tommy could claim that he had been nowhere near the store between 7:00 and 8:00. But at least three people—his mother, Dunaway, and Ficke himself—knew that Tommy was supposed to be at the store that evening to pick up the gas grill and Ficke's potted plant. They knew because Zeigler himself had told them. By the state's own evidence, Zeigler deliberately sabotaged his own careful arrangements.

Let's assume that, as Eagan argued, Zeigler planned to show up at the party acting as if nothing were wrong. Having killed Williams, he would have faced a stunning problem: *He had no way to get home from the murder scene.* The Dunaway Oldsmobile was in his garage, where he had left it. Walking would be out of the question: he would almost certainly be spotted during the twenty to thirty minutes he would need to cover the distance at a brisk walk. He couldn't very well drive the Edwardses' sedan. He might conceivably drive Edward Williams's truck, but he couldn't take it all the way home, because that would connect him to Williams, who would now be dead. At some point he would have to park the truck and walk the rest of the way home.

If Zeigler was actually guilty, he had an easy solution to the problem. He could have followed Williams to the store in the Dunaway car, so as to have a getaway. He could have accomplished this with one line to Williams: "I think I'll drive to the store, Edward—you follow me." This would have been an easy feat for a man to whom the state ascribes powers of persuasion so great as to cloud the minds of men.

The simplest, most credible explanation for why he didn't do so is that he saw no need to do so: that he planned no murders, that he went to the store that night for no other reason than to deliver Christmas gifts, that he expected Edward Williams to drive him home after they had finished the job.

Zeigler's actions during the day on Christmas Eve, and later that night, do not fit the image of a predator planning to murder and trying to cover his tracks. Just the opposite: the evidence shows that throughout that day and evening, Tommy Zeigler behaved like a man with nothing to hide.

THE GUNS

The weapons seized in the store seem to damn Zeigler by their very number.

"That's quite an arsenal for a furniture dealer," Robert Eagan said in his summation, voicing an impression that surely some of the jurors already entertained.

But what is the true significance of those guns? Ownership of several pistols is not prima facie proof of evil intent. Four of the five guns Zeigler kept in the store had been there for a year and a half or more, and they were no secret. Indeed, choosing to commit murder in a place where one is known to have kept weapons is yet another instance in which Zeigler, according to the state's theory, seems to have deliberately chosen to create suspicion.

Let's examine some of the implications of the state's theory about the handguns.

Assume that Zeigler did ask Frank Smith to buy hot guns, and that he believed the two RG revolvers were untraceable, and that he wanted to commit murder. Those two weapons, the RG revolvers, were most useful to him if he used them to kill his first three victims: Eunice, Perry Edwards, and Virginia Edwards. Ballistics tests would show that the "robbers" had used these two unknown guns. This would be even more credible if he disposed of the two guns. (He must have had the chance to do so, according to the state, since he apparently got rid of the rubber gloves and the Dunaway raincoat.) The absence of those guns would strongly suggest that one or more of the robbers had escaped with the murder weapons. In fact, if Zeigler did dispose of those two weapons, they wouldn't even have to be untraceable.

In any case, it would be crucial that he kill his first three victims with the two RG revolvers, not with any of the six weapons that could be traced directly to him.

The ballistics results do show that one of the RG revolvers killed Eunice, and that one or both inflicted the original gunshot wounds in the Edwardses. But then, in spite of the fact that one of the "unknown" guns was still perfectly functional, Zeigler must have decided to use a third weapon to inflict the shots that killed each of the Edwardses. He decided to use a gun of his own: not even one of the store guns, but one that at some point he must have brought in from the truck—the Securities .38. That gun couldn't have been in the store by accident. Someone had to have brought it there.

Thus, according to the state's theory, Zeigler deliberately introduced to the murder scene a weapon that could be traced directly to him, the presence of which could not be explained. Then he must have deliberately chosen it to commit two murders. And he must have done so after days of forethought and planning.

Furthermore, since at least eight empty cartridges from that gun were found, it must have been fired until empty, and reloaded, then fired at least twice more, and then emptied again. (There were no spent cartridges in the gun when Edward Williams turned it over to the police.)

Why should Zeigler use one of his own guns to kill? And of all the guns he owned, why that one, the one he would least be able to explain? If he insisted on killing his in-laws with one of his own weapons, why not one of the five that were already in the store? Why bring in one more? How many weapons did he expect to need?

Zeigler faced two more choices on Christmas Eve, according to the state's theory. He had to decide where to shoot himself, and he had to decide which gun he would use. Even granting the prosecution's contention that he acquired some specialized knowledge in the Army (a charge for which no supporting evidence was ever offered), the decision to shoot himself in the abdomen was an act of extraordinary bravado, if it happened.

This is especially true in light of the fact that, if guilty, he chose to shoot himself with a .38 Special when two .22 pistols, much less powerful, were available. The Beretta automatic in his desk drawer was loaded with .22 Short bullets, the least lethal of any common ammunition. The .22 Short is the bullet used in carnival shooting galleries, and at close ranges is ballistically comparable to a slug from an air pellet rifle. Zeigler might have shot himself several times with the Beretta without risking serious damage.

THE TIMING

Oddly, it was some of the state's own evidence, with Bob Eagan's closing arguments, that first led me to doubt the state's case (and, by extension, the verdict and Zeigler's guilt).

The evidence was the "earwitness" testimony of Barbara Tinsley, who said she heard two distinct volleys of shots from the direction of the furniture store around the time of the murders.

Her testimony was this: three or four shots between 7:20 and 7:25, then six or seven more shots that came fifteen or twenty minutes after the first set, which is to say between 7:35 and 7:45.

The time she claimed to hear the shots is critical. Precision is a rare commodity in this case, and Tinsley specified a narrow range of time in which these shots occurred. Furthermore, she was able to place these times with some credibility, since she claimed to be watching the clock, waiting for her brother at their parents' home.

This testimony seems to have become part of the prosecution's case for two reasons. It ties in nicely with the clock-stopping bullet at 7:24, and it strengthens the state's basic contention that the crime consisted of at least two separate acts of violence, separated by fifteen minutes or more.

But Mrs. Tinsley's testimony contained a huge defect as far as the prosecution was concerned. By the state's theory, *Tommy Zeigler could not have fired any shots in the store between 7:35 and 7:45.* During that entire period he had to be with Felton Thomas and Charlie Mays, and Thomas accounted for all of Zeigler's movements and actions. According to Don Frye's grand jury testimony, Zeigler didn't leave Thomas's presence until 7:55, when Zeigler brought Mays into the store and Thomas fled the scene.

What is the basis of Frye's estimate?

He believed that Zeigler had fired several shots inside the store at 7:25, probably in killing Mr. and Mrs. Edwards. Since Felton Thomas didn't mention hearing any shots when he and Mays were parked out back, Frye deduced that Thomas and Mays must have arrived at the scene after 7:30. At that time, according to Thomas, only one car was parked out front when he and Mays pulled up outside. That had to be the Edwards sedan. Therefore Zeigler must have been gone from the store, for some murky purpose, and then returned and met Thomas and Mays in the motel parking lot at 7:35.[3]

The problem for Frye and Eagan was that the actions and movements that Thomas then described—the trip to the orange grove, pulling the breaker switch, the fence-hopping, the drive to Temple Grove, and so on—couldn't possibly have occurred in less than fifteen minutes, and probably consumed twenty minutes or more. This would mean that Mays, Thomas, and Zeigler didn't arrive at the store before 7:55, with Mays being killed shortly afterward.

Eagan told the jury in his first closing argument: "At 7:45, estimated, Mrs. Tinsley hears another series of shots. I submit to you that that's when Tommy Zeigler walked into that dark store with Charles Mays."

But Eagan had to know that Mays wasn't killed at 7:45.

We could almost say that ten minutes isn't much of a gap, that Tinsley was in the ballpark. Unfortunately for Eagan, Tinsley specifically testified that she heard the second volley *no later* than 7:45. If she is correct, she heard a volley of shots from the store while (according to the state's theory) Zeigler, Mays, and Thomas were pulling into Zeigler's driveway at 75 Temple Grove.

Eagan had to choose between Tinsley on one hand, and, on the other, Thomas and Williams, whose accounts are both very vague about time. If Thomas and Williams were correct, then Tinsley had to be inaccurate (though Eagan did not say so to the jury). Yet Tinsley was much more specific, and much more credible, given her awareness of the time. Furthermore, the disrupted clock in the store seemed to demonstrate her accuracy in placing the time of the first volley.

---

3. Why Zeigler should want to leave the murder scene and drive around for five or ten minutes, further risking identification, is not explained. It is another of those peculiar circumstances that must be true if the state's theory is to accepted.

THE LIGHTS AND THE GATE

The state's theory does not adequately address some of the physical circumstances that police found when they arrived at the store.

The OCSO uniformed deputy, Frank Hair, discovered that a prong of the back gate latch had been bent in such a way that the gate could be opened in one direction, but the damage was not obvious. The front prong of the yoke had been bent back, so that the gate could be swung back into the compound.

Yet Edward Williams testified that when he ran out of the dark store after hearing the three clicks, he went to the gate, tried it, and found that it was locked. If this is true, then the only possible conclusion is that after Williams ran away, Zeigler must have unlocked the gate, bent the front prong, then locked it again. This is the only possibility that accounts for both Williams's testimony and the condition of the gate when Hair found it.

That is improbable, to say the least. Zeigler surely would have been close to panic at Williams's escape—with Williams and Felton Thomas at large, there would now be two living witnesses to his treachery. He would have had to expect that Williams, in his terror, would call the police at once—who could have imagined that Williams would give up after a single wrong number at the restaurant?

Zeigler would now have had an overriding concern: to shoot himself and call Don Ficke before Williams got to a telephone. Yet, according to the state's theory, Zeigler not only took the time to move Williams's pickup truck to the bay door and wipe it clean, but also bent the prong for no apparent reason before he went into the store and performed .38-caliber surgery on his own abdomen.[4]

Improbable as that seems, another circumstance is even more unlikely under the state's hypothesis. That is the position of the light switches when Yawn and Thompson and the others first entered the store.

Yawn and Thompson both testified that they found some of the wall switches in the up, or on, position when they first tried to turn on the lights. The lights did not come on, of course: the main

4. Williams said that he left the truck beside the small hallway door near the corner of the building, but it was found beside the large bay door at the back of the store room. The implication is that Zeigler must have moved the truck, but no fingerprints were found.

switch had been turned off at the outside breaker box. When sheriff's deputies pushed that arm up, the lights came on inside.

That is straightforward enough, and it jibes with Zeigler's testimony that several lights had been left on inside the store at closing time.

But consider the testimony of Felton Thomas. He said that the store was completely dark when he and Mays drove up. He also said that a few minutes later, following Zeigler's instruction, he went to the breaker box and pulled the arm down. In other words, when Thomas and Mays arrived at the store after 7:30, the arm was up, the power was on, but the store was dark.

Only one possibility accounts for Thomas's testimony and the position of the inside switches when Yawn and Thompson tried to turn on the lights. It goes like this:

Zeigler must have turned off all the wall switches before Mays and Thomas drove up and found the store dark. Then Thomas pulled down the breaker box switch, cutting off all power inside. Then, after killing Mays, Zeigler went through the store putting some of the wall switches into the on position (but not turning on the lights, since the breaker box was now turned off). Thus Yawn discovered some of the switches turned up, but the lights would not come on.

Why Zeigler should engage in such a pointless exercise in the midst of a quadruple homicide is not apparent. Yet by the state's theory, this is the only explanation for the conditions that police found.

A much simpler explanation exists for both the gate and the lights.

First, the perpetrators—not Tommy Zeigler—bent the prong because they had to get a vehicle in or out of the gate. However, this directly contradicts Williams, who claimed that he found the gate locked after Zeigler tried to kill him.

As for the switches, the simple explanation is that some of the lights were on inside when the perpetrators—not Tommy Zeigler—pulled down the breaker box arm, so that they could enter the store in darkness. It accounts for what police found after the crime: breaker box turned off, lights switches inside turned on.

But this compels us to discount Thomas, who said that the store was dark but the breaker switch was up.

BLOODY SOLES, BLOODY CUFFS

Charlie Mays's blood-smeared sneakers and blood-soaked trouser bottoms are inexplicable by the state's hypothesis. Mays could have collected that amount of blood in only two places: the pool around Mr. Edwards and the pool around Eunice. These are not places where Mays would have innocently walked. Furthermore, even if he did happen somehow to stumble into Perry Edwards's blood at the back of the store, his sneakers certainly would have left some traces on the terrazzo—some print or bloody scuff. But there is none. In fact, the evidence photo of Mays, sprawled on the terrazzo, is almost eerie. Here are two obviously bloody sneakers, with no bloody footprints. It's as if Mays has been carried there and put down.

But the blood splatters from his beating showed that Mays was killed on the spot. And there are also the bloody cuffs, which do not appear to have left a trace on the white floor, even though Mays's legs must have been jostled as the killer squatted astride his chest and violently beat in his skull.

How does Frye explain these phenomena?

Frye said in his second deposition that he believed that Mays was shot about five feet from where he was killed, in an area of smeared blood and half a dozen blood droplets, which appear in a photograph reproduced in the photo section of this book. (The caked blood on the soles of the shoes is unclear, but the soaked dark areas of the cuffs are apparent.)

Frye theorized that the blood droplets fell from Mays's gunshot wounds, that Mays put his feet down into his own fresh blood and thereby smeared the soles of his sneakers. As for the heavy soaked-in stains of the cuffs, particularly the left cuff, this blood was soaked up from the same spot "as he is pushing back [pushing away from Zeigler as he lay on the floor]."

But this is clearly absurd. The amount of blood on the floor near Mays's feet is not even close to the quantity that was found on his shoes and cuffs. The blood on the floor appears to be no more than a few smeared drops. Frye seems to believe that Mays stood in place and pumped out blood from his wounds, yet if Zeigler killed Mays the way he was accused of doing, the two must have struggled immediately after Zeigler shot him. Also, Mays was wearing two shirts under a bulky sweatshirt; even if he had managed to stay on his feet after being shot twice, even if Zeigler for some reason had allowed him to stay standing, even if all that was true, he would be unlikely to have dripped much blood onto the floor; his shirts would have soaked it up.

Furthermore, the bloody marks on the floor are part of a pattern that continues past Mays's right arm, where it seems to join the major "swipe trail" that runs along the back wall. And finally, where is the smeared blood that would have transferred from the cuffs to the white floor "as he is pushing back"? There are no marks anywhere near the body that were identified as "transfer stains" from bloody fabric.

Frye's explanation is no explanation at all.

"That is my theory only," he qualified it during his deposition. "Can't say that positively."

But some explanation is necessary. If the state's hypothesis is to have any validity, it must credibly address the question of the blood on Mays's shoes and cuffs. It does not.

However, a credible, feasible explanation exists. In the police photo of Charlie Mays's body, the contrast between the bloody cuffs and the pristine white floor immediately around them is striking. And there is only one way for this to have happened.

Dry blood would not have left any marks on the floor. Dry blood on the soles of Mays's shoes would have left no prints.

But that blood would have needed at least fifteen to twenty minutes to dry. In that case Charlie Mays would certainly not be an innocent victim.

Could it have happened? Professor MacDonell admitted that the "swipe trail" that led to (or from) Mr. Edwards's body could actually be wiped-up footprints. Let's assume that Mays crouched beside Perry Edwards's body and tracked his blood along the back wall, and then decided to wipe up the prints with Curtis Dunaway's raincoat. (Somebody obviously used the coat for some purpose, and then disposed of it.) He wouldn't have wanted to track back across the floor; it is reasonable to believe that he removed his sneakers and walked in stocking feet, wiping up the tracks. Meanwhile the blood dried on Mays's cuffs and sneakers.

However it occurred, the hypothesis that that blood was dry when Mays died is the most likely explanation for the absence of bloody footprints and transferred blood under Mays's cuffs. It is also a hypothesis that leaves no room for Tommy Zeigler's guilt.

THE NOLANS

In one way, in its obvious appearance, this is an extremely complex and confusing case. The evidence is massive, complex, ambiguous.

In another sense, though, it is actually quite simple. The case is a choice between Tommy Zeigler and Edward Williams. Their accounts of Christmas Eve begin at a common point—Williams and Zeigler driving to the store in Williams's truck—and then diverge so drastically that they cannot both be telling the truth. If Williams's story is true, then he is an innocent near-victim, and Zeigler is certainly a murderer. If Zeigler's story is true, then he himself is the innocent victim.[5]

With that in mind, I looked for evidence that clearly, unambiguously reflects on the truth or falsity of their stories.

In that respect, the primary evidence against Zeigler is the testimony of Thomas Hale and the accounts given by Felton Thomas and Williams himself.

The primary evidence against Williams is the testimony of the eyewitnesses who placed him at the Kentucky Fried Chicken after 9:00 P.M. Williams himself didn't specify what time he went to the restaurant, only that he went there immediately after Zeigler tried to kill him. But according to the observations of Don and Rita Ficke, Williams had left the driveway before 8:45; Don Frye told the grand jury that Zeigler picked up Williams between 8:20 and 8:30; if so, the attempt on Williams's life would have taken place between 8:35 and 8:50. Williams's testimony was that he jumped the fence of the rear compound, ran into the Winter Garden, and then walked across the street to the restaurant. This would have required less than a minute.

If Williams's account is essentially accurate, he should have walked into the restaurant before closing time at 9:00. Yet nearly everyone in the restaurant who testified or gave a statement said that he showed up after the door was locked, and had to be let in. Only the clerk, John Grimes, failed to specify whether Williams showed up before or after closing.

The trial testimony of J. D. Nolan and Madelyn Nolan is especially compelling. Both of them swore that they watched Rob-

---

5. In nearly half a year of intensive investigation, the police and prosecutor never turned up any evidence that both Zeigler and Williams were guilty.

ert Thompson drive off with Zeigler to the hospital. The Nolans continued to watch the store, then crossed the street to speak with J.D.'s brother, whom they saw in the door of the restaurant. At this time, according to J. D. Nolan, the black man who resembled Edward Williams walked up and said that he wanted to use the telephone. By now Zeigler must have been on the gurney at the hospital, probably lying in the emergency room.

This is devastating testimony. There is no innocent explanation for Williams's arrival at the restaurant at this late moment. By Williams's own testimony, Zeigler was whole and healthy when Williams jumped the fence and ran away. His trip across the street, via the motel, could have consumed no more than a minute. In that time, according to the state's theory, Zeigler would have had to move Williams's truck and wipe off his fingerprints, bend the fork of the gate, go into the store and speak to Ted Van Deventer and Don Ficke, shoot himself, wait for the police to show up, be carried into the back of the squad car and examined by Thompson, and be driven to the hospital.

It is not possible that all of this took place while Williams was traveling from the store to the restaurant. It is not possible even if Williams *crawled* from the store to the motel and across the street.

To put it another way: the Nolans' testimony implies that Tommy Zeigler must already have been shot when Williams left the furniture store. Not only was Zeigler already shot, but Robert Thompson and the emergency room nurse both found that the blood had dried around his wound.

If the Nolans saw what they claimed to see, Williams's story is fatally flawed, and so is the state's hypothesis of guilt.

If the Nolans saw what they claimed to see—what they swore they saw—then really nothing else matters. Tommy Zeigler could have had $10 million in insurance on his wife; it doesn't matter anymore, as far as Zeigler's guilt or innocence is concerned. Zeigler could have made fifty footprints in blood; it doesn't matter. He could have owned a hundred pistols, he could have told Curtis Dunaway to turn off every light in the store; it doesn't matter. If Edward Williams was at the restaurant when the Nolans said he was there, then Tommy Zeigler is not a guilty man.

So why didn't the Nolans create at least reasonable doubt?

I believe that neither the prosecution nor the defense saw the true significance of the Nolans' testimony. The reason is simple: the Nolans were eyewitnesses, and lawyers and cops know that eyewitnesses are unreliable. Even Terry Hadley doesn't appear to have regarded the Nolans' testimony as a "smoking gun."

Yet that is exactly what it is, in its implications and its clarity and its credibility, because the Nolans were almost unique as eyewitnesses. *They could not have been mistaken about what they saw. They could not have been mistaken about when they saw it.*

The time of the events is perfectly fixed by the radio call that sent Jimmy Yawn rolling out onto Dillard Street, where the Nolans nearly collided with him. That was at 9:21. The Nolans could not have been there at 8:50 or 9:15 or at any other moment. The clock starts ticking on their observations at 9:21. Both agree that they watched the police at the store for several minutes. So, it is 9:24, give or take a minute, when the black man tells Ed and J. D. Nolan that he wants to use the phone; by now Thompson and Zeigler are already at the hospital.

Who is the black man? The Nolans cannot be mistaken on this point, either. That man has to be Edward Williams.

Here again the Nolans' testimony is unique. Descriptions of strangers are the great failing of eyewitnesses. Somehow the details are never quite right.

But the Nolans didn't have to know what clothes Edward Williams was wearing. They didn't have to specify how tall he was, or how old (although J. D. and Ed Nolan got both of those details right). On Christmas Eve, Edward Williams was one of a kind. He was the only black man that night who asked to use the telephone at the Kentucky Fried Chicken, so that he could call the police. He was as identifiable as a unicorn.

Eagan tried to refute the Nolans' testimony in his final closing argument at trial. He told the jury: "There is no evidence at all that the black man seen trying to use the telephone after the Kentucky Fried Chicken was closed was Edward Williams."

Eagan was incorrect. J. D. Nolan did accurately, if briefly, describe Williams at trial. In his direct testimony, Nolan said that the man who asked to use the phone was a black man age fifty to fifty-five, weighing about 160 pounds. Ed Nolan, in his deposition, said that he was a "squatty man, not too tall, about 160 pounds."

Eagan continued during his closing argument: "Edward Williams was there earlier. The place was open when he was there. There were other customers there. That's when he met the friend that took him to his next place, ultimately to Mary Stewart's."

No evidence was ever produced, at the trial or in deposition, that showed that the restaurant was open when Edward Williams appeared there. Two of the state's witnesses—Williams and the clerk John Grimes—could have testified on that point at trial, but Eagan never asked them.

More important, no evidence ever suggested that two different black men tried to use the restaurant telephone to call the police on Christmas Eve.

John Grimes, who was there all day, described only one such incident. Ed Nolan, who was there all evening, saw only one such man. Furthermore, Ed Nolan saw the same man meet a young woman outside, which describes the meeting between Williams and Rogenia Thomas. The waitress who stayed past 9:00 P.M. told Gene Annan that only one man asked to use the telephone, and that was after closing. The waitress who left at 9:00 P.M. told Annan that she never witnessed any such incident.

The fact is, if the Nolans saw a man asking to use the telephone at the Kentucky Fried Chicken, that man could only have been Edward Williams.

So the Nolans could not have been mistaken about what they saw. They could not have been mistaken about when they saw it. The only possible rebuttal is that they were lying, and the state never attempted to show that they were anything but independent, disinterested, and truthful.

I cannot find another piece of important evidence in this case which is as clear, as unequivocal, as indisputable as the Nolans' testimony. It is not colored by personal interest, nor is it subject to debate. Its implications are so great, and its significance is so obvious, that it goes straight to the heart of the argument about what happened on Christmas Eve.

It cannot be dismissed. It cannot be ignored. It may have been unrecognized at trial, but that does not diminish its ultimate value.

This is what it means:

If the Nolans saw what they swore to have seen, then Tommy Zeigler was wrongfully convicted.

Anyone who believes that Tommy Zeigler deserves to spend another day in prison—much less be killed—has the ethical obligation to demonstrate that J. D. and Madelyn Nolan lied.

Because if they did not lie, then Tommy Zeigler is an innocent man.

HYPOTHESIS OF INNOCENCE

I believe that two or more assailants waited for Tommy Zeigler to arrive at the store on Christmas Eve. Possibly one of them hid in the storeroom during business hours, having climbed the back fence and come in through the bay door, which was open most of that day. They may also have entered using a key. They turned off the lights at the breaker box.

This was not a casual break-in. Seven-thirty in the evening is a poor time for a burglary. The perpetrators were there because they knew that Tommy Zeigler was going to be there. As a bonus, they probably intended to rob the store of the cash that they knew the Zeiglers kept in the building, and they may have intended to steal the several pistols they knew were available. But they were there mainly to do harm to Tommy Zeigler.

They expected Zeigler to arrive around 7:30. They did not expect Eunice Zeigler and her parents to let themselves in at the front door about fifteen minutes before Tommy arrived.

These unexpected arrivals had to be dealt with. They were probably ambushed between the counter and the front door. They may have had some slight warning. Perry Edwards may have had a chance to grab one of the guns from under the counter and exchange shots with the assailants. The GSR test results from his right hand are consistent with this possibility.

Eunice probably was running away when she was shot in the kitchen. The theory that she was surprised by the shot that killed her is unconvincing. The bloodstains on the inside of her lapel strongly suggest that someone tampered with her coat after she was dead. If so, then the fact that her hand was found in her pocket is meaningless.

Virginia Edwards was most likely shot at this same time.

Several bullets struck Perry Edwards, wounding him but not killing him. The blood-soaked area of carpet between the counter and the front door marked where he fell. The glasses case in his breast pocket stopped a bullet that would have hit his heart. Instead, the slug probably put him down and incapacitated him for a time, but did not kill him. He lay there long enough to lose a significant amount of blood from his wounds, especially the ear that a bullet clipped.

The blood trail to the front door probably originated at that spot. Most likely that blood was his. If he found the front door locked he may have started for the back and encountered his assailants again. He fought, was beaten, and was shot to death with the Securities revolver.

If Tommy Zeigler is innocent—and after months of resisting the notion I have gradually become convinced that he is—then at some point he was the victim of a frame-up: a deliberate attempt to make him appear guilty. It is possible that someone among the killers conceived that plan after they ambushed Eunice and her parents, but before Zeigler arrived. This would have required a cool head and considerable intelligence, but it would also have been the solution to an impending disaster, since the original plan now was out of control.

At least one of Zeigler's former attorneys believes that just such a cool head was involved in the crime. Bill Duane is convinced that one or two local policemen took part in the crime, if not in the store then overseeing it from nearby. Duane points out that a cop's experience and knowledge would have allowed him to think the thing through in the moments of panic that must have followed the original shoot-out.

Evidence does suggest that a frame-up was already under way the moment Zeigler walked into the store. If he is innocent, Zeigler's account of the assault at the back of the showroom is probably reliable: that his assailants first tried to subdue him without shooting him, and that they finally shot him only after he had fired several times. This would be consistent with a plan to frame him. A scheme to set him up him for the murders would also explain why his killers did not execute him. Placing the derringer misfires in his desk drawers would be pointless if Zeigler was trying to cover up his guilt; as a detail in a setup, however, they are logical. Likewise, the Securities .38 at the murder scene is calculated to cast instant suspicion on Zeigler. For Zeigler himself to have put it there would have been virtually suicidal. Executing Perry and Virginia Edwards with that pistol, the most damning weapon of all for Zeigler, may have been the killers' deliberate choice.

Nothing in the forensic evidence forecloses this theory. However, any hypothesis of the crime must deal with two other areas of physical evidence: the Dunaway Oldsmobile, with the Smith & Wesson .38, and the cache from the storeroom cabinet that included the spent cartridges and ammunition, the towel and gun boxes, and the paper bags.

Bill Duane, among many of Zeigler's supporters and defenders, charges that that collection of evidence was planted by someone who had access to the store while the OCSO held it. Duane says that the evidence is highly suspect because it was not logged until January 2, more than a week after the last other piece of evidence was collected—that is, apparently a week after the OCSO technicians had completed their search. (The property receipts, and Alton Evans's testimony from his notes, are unequivocal on the date of the find.)

Property receipts also show that early Christmas morning, investigators impounded a can of furniture wax and a rag, which were kept on or around that cabinet, beside the large bay door. This indicates that the storeroom, specifically the immediate area around the cabinet, was searched long before January 2. Why was this sizable cache not discovered in this original sweep?

The only evidence connecting Zeigler to the gun boxes in the bags was the testimony of Ray Ussery, owner of the bait and tackle shop where Zeigler bought three pistols in 1974. Ussery testified that the boxes came from a pile that accumulated when customers bought pistols but did not take the boxes that came with them; those boxes would then be thrown into the pile, and given to other customers who wanted them. Ussery was testifying nearly two years after Zeigler bought the pistols, a transaction he himself did not handle. Yet he was certain that the two boxes in that cache were the very same boxes that his clerk had given Zeigler.

The dates are significant. Gun boxes carry the serial number of the gun they originally contained, and thus can be traced just as the weapons are. One of the two boxes found in the storeroom cache belonged to a pistol that Ussery sold in December 1974—two months after Zeigler's purchase. According to Ussery's own testimony about his procedures, the box he attributed to Zeigler could not have been in the pile of leftovers when Zeigler bought his three pistols in October.

It should be noted that Ussery swore that Zeigler's transaction took place on January 9, 1975, although the paperwork was dated October 31, 1974. Ussery attributed the discrepancy to "a clerical error."

Does any of the other evidence from the cache preclude its having been planted?

The empty shells were from the Securities revolver, which was in police custody. The towel came from the Dunaway Oldsmobile, also in custody. One of the paper bags was found to have Zeigler's palm print, which seems to be damning. However, the record shows that police removed a similar paper bag from the home at 75 Temple Grove; yet that item was never logged into evidence.

That still leaves Curtis Dunaway's Oldsmobile, with the Smith & Wesson revolver, the traces of blood on the headrest, and the signs that it had been wiped down.

Several of Zeigler's attorneys believe that the killers drove Dunaway's car to the store that evening. Terry Hadley claimed in his closing argument at the trial that the killers' original plan was for Edward Williams to drive away from the scene in his pickup truck, and that the gate had been forced open for this reason. The implication is that the Dunaway car had to be brought to the store in order to establish how Zeigler arrived on the scene.

But then, according to Hadley, Williams discovered that his truck would not start because of the carburetor problem. "Imagine Edward Williams's panic," Hadley told the jurors. "He's sitting there trying to get this truck started. It wouldn't make it. He's got to sit for a second with a murder weapon in his pocket. He thinks Tommy Zeigler is dead and everything is fine, nobody knows anything. The crime has been committed. There isn't a soul inside that store alive. . . . He finds out that Tommy Zeigler is alive and he knows, number one, Mr. Zeigler knows who brought him to that store and, number two, more important, his truck, it can be traced to him and he's in a panic."

Hadley believed that this explained Williams's ostensibly voluntary appearance at the police station: "[He's] in a panic and he's got to make up a story."

Bill Duane recently enlarged on this theory: "Zeigler locked Williams's truck in when he got to the store. Now they've got a real problem—the truck won't start. They have to take the Oldsmobile back, because if the truck is there they've got one too many vehicles at the store.

"This would explain all the evidence in the car: the pistol, the small bloodstains, the fact that somebody wiped it down. It would also explain the cat hairs on Charlie Mays's shoes. Tommy and Eunice kept their cats in the garage—the floor was full of cat hairs. Charlie Mays probably walked around in Zeigler's garage. That's how he got those hairs on his sneakers. Felton Thomas was probably telling the truth when he said he rode in the Oldsmobile, and that he and Charlie Mays were at Zeigler's house. I think all that really happened. I just don't believe that Zeigler was with them at the time.

"This took a lot of quick thinking, but it's something that a cop could have done, somebody who was used to thinking on his feet."

Who would have done such a thing?

According to Terry Hadley, Zeigler told of friction between him and the alleged loan sharks, and about the threat on his life, months before Christmas Eve.

The existence of some kind of loan-sharking organization in Oakland and Winter Garden seems very likely. Several black witnesses in the Zeigler case, including Edward Williams and Mattie Mays, referred to it in their depositions as if it were fact. And within a year after Zeigler's trial, Hadley successfully instigated a prosecution for loan-sharking against the owner of a "country store" in the area.

I found Hadley to be a credible source for several reasons. He is careful and objective. He has lived most of his life in Orange County and has practiced law there for twenty years. His involvement with the Zeigler case ended soon after the trial; Eagan and Don Frye speak respectfully of him.

Hadley told me in 1991 that he believed the information he received from Zeigler during the Andrew James episode. It was consistent with what he knew about practices in the fields and camps.

Hadley said that Zeigler was in a position to know what he claimed to know. "Tommy had amazing contacts in the black neighborhoods," he said. "I could not have made that defense [of Andrew James] without him. He knew a lot of good people and a lot of low-lifes. Tommy went to Atlanta four times a year, on [furniture] buying trips. If he really wanted his wife dead, he could have had it done while he was hundreds of miles away. He knew plenty of low-lifes who would have done it for him as a favor."

Clearly the state had a case. It stood up to cursory examination. At trial, Robert Eagan's obvious skills and the great mass of mostly ambiguous evidence helped to disguise its shortcomings.

The state's case was almost true. It was a case good enough to win. But even a winnable case is not necessarily *the* case.

During my research and writing I discussed this story with a friend who is experienced in investigations, and who also is a committed rationalist. He believes that our tendency to jump to conclusions, to seek answers on the basis of incomplete evidence, is one of the great human failings.

At some point he sent me an epigram that he felt captured the essence of *Florida* v. *Zeigler*. The quotation is attributed to the nineteenth-century clergyman Henry Ward Beecher:

"Whatever is almost true is most certainly false, and is among the most grievous of errors."

EPILOGUE

IN MARCH 1992, ZEIGLER'S ATTORNEYS SUBMITTED A NEW HABEAS PETI-
tion to state circuit judge Gary Formet. This was the beginning of
what almost certainly would be Zeigler's last series of appeals.
Formet, who had reinstituted the death sentence against Zeigler in
the 1989 penalty hearing, refused to consider arguments about
Irma Brickle's possible use of Valium during jury deliberations, and
about the unreleased material, including the Jellison tape, which
Leslie Gift had discovered in the state attorney's files.

Formet did grant a hearing on the allegation by John Bulled,
the Orange County jail trusty, that sheriff's officers had fabricated
the "orange grove" bullet. That bullet, which shared the class
characteristics of the Securities revolver, was supposed to have
been discovered by a four-man crew of jail trusties digging through
the grove. If true, that would invalidate Zeigler's trial and conviction.

During the hearing, on May 27, 1992, Bulled repeated his
charge that sheriff's officers had fabricated the bullet in the grove.
Zeigler's attorneys had persuaded a second member of the crew to
testify. That man, John Beverly, testified that he saw a sheriff's
deputy toss a slug down on the ground, then reach down and claim
that he had discovered it.

The hearing lasted less than one day. Formet found that
Bulled and Beverly were not credible, and he denied Zeigler's
motion for a new trial.

As of this writing, Zeigler's hopes for a new trial rest with the
state's supreme court, which has never ruled favorably on any of
his appeals issues, and with federal courts, which in recent years
have become increasingly reluctant to consider appeals on matters
that have already received "full and fair review" in state courts.

"I know the chances are good that I will be executed," he wrote in a letter a few days before Formet's decision. "I will not fight another death warrant. I have seen what this does to my family and friends, and I will never put them through this again.

"I am not afraid to die. I know where I will be going. I will be with Eunice and Papa and Mom Edwards and Pop Edwards. I know I am innocent of these crimes, and God knows it, too."

The murders on Christmas Eve, 1975, exacted a horrible toll. The list of victims only begins with the dead. It includes their families and friends, who continue to suffer. The execution of Tommy Zeigler, while the killers remain unpunished, would mean that the final victim is justice itself.

ABOUT THE AUTHOR

PHILLIP FINCH is the author of more than ten books, including *Sugarland,* which *The New York Times* named one of the notable thrillers of 1991. He is a former newspaper reporter and was consultant to the President's Commission on Organized Crime.

Date Due

MAR 4 '97	FEB 8 2003		
MAR 15 '97	JUN 2 3 03		
MAR 29 '97	MAY 0 6 04		
	JUL 1 2 05		
APR 19 '97	DEC 19 05		
MAY 2 '97	MAY 2 2 2007		
MAY 7 '97	SEP 1 7 2008		
MAY 8 '97	JUN 2 9 2009		
APR 1 7 1998	JUN 2 9 2015		
DEC 5 1998	OCT 1 - 2015		
DEC 1 4 1999	JUL 2 7 2016		
FEB 2 2000	AUG 1 7 2018		
OCT 2 4 2000	DEC 2 7 2018		
NOV 1 3 2000	JUL 1 5 2019		
JUL 03 01			